CLASSIC KOSHER COOKING

Classic Kosher Cooking

by
Sara Finkel

Targum-Feldheim

First published 1989

ISBN 0-944070-14-0

Phototypeset at Targum Press

Published by:
Targum Press Inc.
22700 W. Eleven Mile Rd.
Southfield, Mich. 48034

Distributed by:
Philipp Feldheim Inc.
200 Airport Executive Park
Spring Valley, N.Y. 10977

Distributed in Israel by:
Nof Books Ltd.
POB 23646
Jerusalem 91235

Printed in Israel

*To my devoted husband, for his encouragement and
support throughout the writing of this book.*

*To the memory of my parents,
Samuel and Kreindel Rosenblum (z"l),
who imbued me with the beauty and significance of our
heritage in our home, which was permeated with
hachnassat orchim and chesed.*

ACKNOWLEDGMENTS

I would like to express special thanks to a number of people for their invaluable help and encouragement in bringing this book to fruition.

- To Nechama Berg, who processed all of the recipes. Nechama's efficiency was exceeded only by her sparkling personality.

- To Hilary Cemel, who patiently edited and proofread the recipes.

- To Chaim Phillips and Naomi Ragen, for their many hours of work.

- To Sholom Katz, an expert chef, who carefully checked each recipe and added his own microwave tips.

- To Rabbi Zissel Ellinson, publisher of Jewish Woman's Outlook. It was the food column that I wrote for this popular magazine which gave me the inspiration to write this cookbook. Thanks also to Henny Walkin and Yocheved Engel, innovative editors of the magazine, who originally invited me to write their column on food, and to Denise Weitman, its art director, for her special work.

- To Miriam Litke, for the assistance she gave me in checking over the recipes and for her comments and marvelous recipes.

- To Ruth Zisken, who excels in the culinary arts, who so wholeheartedly shared with me some of her excellent recipes.

- To Shulamit Kowalsky, who eagerly offered her special recipes for my collection. I am grateful to Shulamit for the helpful interest she showed.

- To Evelyn Silver, whose friendship throughout the years has proved to be a catalyst to my writing endeavors. Her important comments in discussing some of the recipes were useful.

- To Miriam Shuman, for sharing with me some of her vegetarian recipes.

- To Edythe Samson (z"l), a gourmet cook, who in the early stages of this manuscript eagerly assisted me in various ways and shared with me her philosophy of cooking.

- To my devoted sons, for encouraging me to write this work.

- To my devoted daughters-in-law, Leah and Mimi, for giving of their own special talents, often filling me in with background material, testing and sharing with me their own tried and true recipes, as well as for the encouragement and support they gave me throughout the preparation of my manuscript.

- To Priscilla Fishman, for her excellent editorial help in the early years of my writing for Jewish Woman's Outlook.

•To Charlotte Finkel, for her fabulous Scandinavian Medley and other recipes.

•To Basia Rottenberg, for so graciously volunteering her assistance at a time when it was needed.

•To Zippora Schechter, one of the members of my cooking class, who volunteered to type recipes when the idea of a book was still in its embryonic stages.

•To Libby Sharfman, for bringing me material on nutrition, all the way from New York, from the classes she taught.

•To Margo Zacharias, for sharing with me some of her special recipes.

•To my beloved grandchildren, for allowing me to take away valuable time, which I felt belonged to them, in order to complete this time-consuming endeavor. This part was not easy for me.

•To my granddaughters, Zahava, Goldie and Tsippie, for coming into my kitchen to help while I tested recipes.

•Acharon acharon chaviv: My deep appreciation to my devoted husband, Rabbi E. Meyer Finkel, who was with me throughout the writing of this manuscript, patiently listening to parts of the text as they unfolded and developed.

•Many thanks to all of the relatives and friends who shared with me their own treasured recipes.

With a sense of deep humility, I feel profoundest gratitude to HaShem for His guidance, which I deeply and genuinely experienced throughout the writing of this book.

Sara Finkel
Jerusalem

Table of Contents

Shabbat and Festivals

Introduction

A taxi driver once asked the late Reb Arye Levin where he lived. "I would give you my address," the revered tzaddik of Jerusalem replied, "but since my beloved wife was taken from this world, I have no home." Indeed, a great sage was known to say, "I do not call my wife, 'my wife'; I call her, 'my home.'"

Women possess intuitive insights into the Jewish home, the foundation of Jewish life. One of our greatest opportunities to build this way of life lies in preparing meals for our families and friends, and for the destitute and downtrodden, who should always find a welcome at our table.

We Jewish women are privileged to nourish our families spiritually as well as physically. Indeed, our tables are likened to the altar of the holy Temple. When kosher food is served and the proper blessings recited, our homes become places of sanctity and celebration. The festive meals we prepare immeasurably enhance Shabbat and holidays, and enable others to partake of the goodness of this world.

I have always considered food and love intertwined. Graciousness in matters of food indicates sensitivity and affection. When I was young, my mother would tell me in Yiddish: "It is a mitzvah to give a child something to eat or drink." Sometimes I think this generosity benefits the giver more than the receiver, because it strengthens his capacity for loving kindness.

This book is not just about cooking—it's about giving. Our Sages teach that giving leads to love. It's like magic. Just think about all the work involved in feeding a baby. Spoonful by laborious spoonful, we deepen our love for the child.

When I think about giving, I automatically think of the wonderful women who have given me many of these recipes. Besides volunteering their culinary know-how, they have shared their derech, their way of life. These are women who are always thinking of others, reaching out, providing, listening, and sharing. To all of these women, my sincerest thanks.

Man's greatness lies partly in his ability to sense and fulfill the needs of his fellow man. The Torah, our guiding light, provides us with an obligation and an opportunity to develop food as a source of true sustenance for ourselves and others. This is the essence of Jewish cooking.

Shabbat

With a blessing on her lips and a prayer in her heart, the Jewish woman ushers Shabbat HaMalkah, the Sabbath Queen, into her home. Shabbat is one of the Jewish people's most time-honored and precious gifts, a loyal companion, healing all wounds and smoothing the most difficult paths. On Shabbat, the poorest man becomes rich and the rich become richer. The fallen are raised, the simple become wise, and the wise gain renewed appreciation for the source of their wisdom.

Upon completing His work, God blessed and hallowed the seventh day by prohibiting the 39 types of labor used in constructing the Sanctuary in the desert. By desisting from these labors, which symbolize man's mastery of nature, we affirm the supremacy of our Creator.

In the Jewish home, everything centers on Shabbat. We wear our loveliest clothes and serve the finest cuisine on our best china. We skimp on nothing: Our Sages teach that whatever we spend on Shabbat is returned to us throughout the year. Imbued with an additional soul, we bask in the warmth of family and friends as weekday pressures and tensions fade away.

We are obligated to partake of three festive meals on Shabbat: Friday night dinner, the Shabbat noonday meal, and seudah shlishit, the third meal, generally a light repast served before sundown. To sanctify the Shabbat, dinner and lunch begin with Kiddush, a testament to God's creation of the world. Kiddush is recited over wine because it "gladdens a man's heart" (Psalms 104:15) and signifies kindness and goodness. A blessing is then recited over two challot, symbolizing the double portion of manna that fell in the wilderness on Fridays, relieving the Israelites of the need to gather food on Shabbat.

The noonday meal is highlighted by cholent, a hearty dish of beans, barley, and meat. True to its etymological origins, the French words chaud (hot) and lent (slow), cholent simmers all night on a Shabbat hot plate and makes a hearty meal the next day. Our Sages considered it of great importance to eat meat on Shabbat. Another Shabbat favorite with a distinguished history is fish. The traditional gefilte fish does not require that bones be removed, a form of separation forbidden on Shabbat.

These delicacies are embellished by zemirot (Sabbath hymns) and words of Torah, followed by Grace after Meals.

We conclude Shabbat with Havdalah. Its fragrant spices cheer us as our additional soul departs, and its candle burns brightly with the promise and potential of the week ahead.

With the departure of Shabbat, many prepare and enjoy a melaveh malkah, a farewell banquet for a most important guest, the Sabbath Queen. This custom originated with King David, who knew he was destined to die on Shabbat. After every Shabbat, he celebrated his survival with an elaborate feast. Some people begin their melaveh malkah by lighting candles, in the hope that the spirit of Shabbat will linger in their homes all week.

Shabbat gives us a taste of paradise, which sustains us throughout the week. It is truly a heritage to be cherished and imparted from generation to generation.

Rosh Hashanah

Rosh Hashanah, the beginning of the Jewish year, is a time to reflect on the past, contemplate the future, and pray that we and our families be inscribed in the Book of Life. On Rosh Hashanah, we proclaim God's sovereignty and strive to be His worthy subjects. The piercing, powerful blasts of the shofar act as an evocative "call to arms," moving us to acknowledge and regret our shortcomings and misdeeds and to resolve to correct them. We ask forgiveness not just from God but from each other, and we readily pardon those who have wronged us. On the anniversary of the creation of the world, we begin to recreate ourselves, setting the tone for the rest of the year.

Although Rosh Hashanah is the start of the Days of Awe, the mood is celebratory as well as solemn. We dress festively and enjoy elaborate holiday meals. Rosh Hashanah is an especially auspicious time to bake challah. Traditional challot are round, symbolizing the continuity of life and God's blessings. From Rosh Hashanah to Simchat Torah we dip our challah in honey, expressing our desire for a sweet year. Similarly, honey figures prominently in the holiday menu, flavoring tzimmes, kugels, strudel, honey cakes, and taiglach.

Honey is just one of many symbolic foods served on the first night of Rosh Hashanah. Dipping an apple in honey, we ask for a good, sweet year. Over pomegranates, we pray that our merits be as numerous as the fruit's seeds, which are said to total 613, corresponding to the 613 mitzvot. A similar message underlies the eating of ruvia (black-eyed peas), whose Hebrew root means "many." The gastronomically adventurous among us partake of a lamb or fish head, reflecting the hope that we be "heads and not tails." Fish in particular symbolize fruitfulness. We pray that we multiply like the fish in the sea, which have no yetzer hara (evil impulse) because their eyes are always open and ever-watchful. Some eat dates and beets, whose Hebrew and Aramaic roots mean "to remove," as we seek to "remove" our enemies, including the yetzer hara. Some serve squash, which comes from the Aramaic word "to tear," praying for the tearing up of any evil decrees issued against us. Carrots, whose Yiddish root, "mehren," also means "to increase," are often combined with honey in a tsimmes, alluding to our hope that our merit increase. On the second night of Rosh Hashanah a new fruit is served, over which we recite the Shehecheyanu blessing, thanking God for bringing us once again to this season of renewal.

Another Rosh Hashanah custom is Tashlich. Standing over a body of water, we symbolically cast our sins into the sea, as depicted by the prophet Micah.

In compiling your shopping list for this hectic holiday season, make certain you keep a separate record of all the traits you wish to correct or acquire and the good deeds you hope to perform for others!

Yom Kippur

The period between Rosh Hashanah and Yom Kippur is called the Ten Days of Repentance, our last chance to secure a favorable decree through penitence, prayer, and charity. On Yom Kippur, prayer becomes the central medium as we confess our sins. We confess in the plural, shouldering the collective burden of our fellow Jews, for whom we are responsible.

Through fasting and prayer, we reach unparalleled heights of contrition and closeness to God. The day ends in joy, and we are ready to begin the new year with clean slates and pure hearts.

Because Yom Kippur is a fast day, its holiday meals are served beforehand and afterward. Despite the arduous day ahead, the pre-fast meal is festive, reflecting our confidence in God's mercy. The meal to break the fast celebrates the Divine compassion we have indeed been shown.

Sukkot

Sukkot recalls how the Israelites dwelled together in the desert. As a reward for leaving their homes in Egypt and dwelling together in the wilderness in harmony, God enveloped them in a sukkah of His own: the Clouds of Glory (embodying the Divine Presence). Consequently, we, too, eat and sleep in sukkot, frail structures reminding us that it is not our homes that shelter us but our trust and faith in God, our true shield and protector. These temporary dwellings—and the reading of the Book of Kohelet (Ecclesiastes) on Shabbat—teach us that everything material is ephemeral and only our spiritual accomplishments endure. The sturdy walls and flimsy roof of the Sukkah symbolize the nature of man, firm in his beliefs and practices, yet humble and ever-mindful of the Higher Power overhead.

We begin building sukkot immediately after Yom Kippur. When I was growing up it was a family affair, with Papa hammering away furiously and my youngest brother Victor handing him nails and making sure the thatched roof allowed more shade than sun. Today, my husband does the building, assisted by our children and grandchildren. When I think about what this frenzied activity represents, the din of construction sounds almost musical.

Decorations further enhance the sukkah. In my parents' sukkah, big, sweet red apples, golden bananas, and bountiful bunches of red and green grapes hung from the ceiling, along with colorful paper chains. Pictures adorned the walls. One should bring only attractive serving pieces into the sukkah, like the elegant tureen I save for special occasions.

Nowhere are aesthetics more paramount than in the selection of a lulav (palm frond) and etrog (citron). People spend hours scrutinizing etrogim with a magnifying glass, making sure theirs is blemish-free and just the right shade of yellow-green. Then they carefully turn the lulav from side to side, holding it at arm's length to ensure that its spine is perfectly straight.

A famous midrash relates that the lulav, etrog, hadasim (myrtle branches), and aravot (willows) represent four types of Jews: just as the lulav has flavor but no fragrance, some Jews are learned but remiss in performing good deeds; the hadasim have fragrance but no flavor, symbolizing Jews who perform many fine acts but neglect to study; the etrog has both flavor and fragrance, representing Jews who excel in both areas; and the aravot have neither, representing those who are deficient in both. On Sukkot, these four species are brought together to complement one another, just as it takes all kinds to form a strong, united Jewish people.

Each night of Sukkot we symbolically welcome one of our forefathers into the sukkah. I remember how our family sukkah would glow as Papa described our "guests," the ushpizin. History came alive and we felt privileged to have them in our midst. Mama always invited the needy and neglected, too, and our sukkah seemed to expand to accommodate them.

As a harvest holiday, Sukkot is also known as the Festival of the Ingathering. To symbolize our bounty it is customary to serve stuffed cabbage, kreplach, strudel, and other filled fare. The Shabbat of chol hamoed (the intermediate days of Sukkot), is particularly festive. Some families prepare two kugels, one each in honor of Shabbat and chol hamoed. Indeed, our Sages tell us that those who disregard chol hamoed will have no portion in the World to Come.

With all the holiday entertaining, some families even have a separate sukkah just for sleeping. In Jerusalem, Sukkot is truly a pilgrimage festival, with crowds of people flocking to the Western Wall.

Three times the Torah enjoins us to rejoice on Sukkot, the only holiday so honored, for the rejoicing of man personifies the spirit of holiness (Jerusalem Talmud, Sukkah, Chapter 5). The water drawing and libation in the Temple and the attendant torchlit procession were so joyous, says the Mishnah, that he who has never beheld them doesn't know what joy is. Today we commemorate this ritual with our own Simchat Beit Hashoevah, enlivened by music and dancing.

The week of celebration culminates in Simchat Torah, which coincides with Shemini Atzeret in Israel. Cradling Torah scrolls, we encircle the bimah seven times as children parade about waving miniature flags. The dancing goes on for hours. We finish the yearly cycle of Torah readings and immediately start again, for the Torah has no beginning and no end, and neither does our love for it.

Simchat Torah follows Hoshanah Rabbah (literally, "great supplication"), the last day of Sukkot, which marks the sealing of the Divine decrees issued on Yom Kippur. It is customary to immerse oneself in study and prayer all night. In the morning, some congregations circle the bimah. Aravot are bound together and their lip-shaped leaves are beaten on the floor as we shake ourselves free of sin. When we enjoy our last meal in the sukkah, we pray that next Sukkot will be spent in "King David's sukkah," the Temple. May it be rebuilt speedily in our days!

Chanukah

Chanukah commemorates the miraculous Jewish victory over the Hellenists in 165 B.C.E. and the subsequent rededication of the Temple, which had been defiled by Greek idolatry. Only one day's worth of pure olive oil was found to rekindle the menorah, but it miraculously lasted eight days, until more oil was prepared. Appropriately enough, Chanukah (literally, "dedication") is also the anniversary of the Israelites' completion and dedication of the Sanctuary in the desert.

To proclaim the miracle of the menorah, we kindle our own menorahs outside our doors or in our windows, adding a light every night to mark each additional day the oil unexpectedly burned. It is preferable to use an authentic oil menorah, filling it with olive oil. The lighting is followed by a spirited rendition of "Maoz Tzur," a 13th-century poem chronicling the triumphant history of the Jewish people.

The Chanukah candles symbolize the eternal, inextinguishable light of the Torah and its power to dispel the dark forces of oppression and assimilation. The story of Chanukah has inspired generations of courageous Jews to withstand persecution and remain true to their luminous ideals and heritage.

To recall the miracle of the oil, it is customary to enjoy deep-fried latkes (potato pancakes) and sufganiyot (donuts), a Chanukah favorite in Israel. Dairy dishes are also served in honor of Yehudit, the daughter of the high priest, who assassinated an Assyrian general after lulling him to sleep with cheese and wine. And since it is celebrated in mid-winter, Chanukah is a great occasion for making your fanciest piping-hot stews, chowders, and goulashes.

Another holiday tradition is spinning the "dreidel," a top emblazoned with the Hebrew letters nun, gimel, heh, and shin (or peh in Israel), which stand for Nes Gadol Hayah Sham (or Po)—a great miracle happened there (or here).

Tu BeShvat

Tu BeShvat is the new year for trees, marking a new tithing season. We rejoice on the day, confident that God will show compassion for humanity and for the trees it depends on, sources of sustenance and beauty and symbols of nobility and goodness. King David depicted the righteous as perennials that blossom in their appointed season (Psalms 1:3). Just as a tree grows gradually, our personal growth should be slow and steady, rather than fitful and overambitious. In Ecclesiastes, King Solomon writes that there is a time for planting and a time for harvesting. We must savor each stage of life before embarking on the next.

In Israel it is traditional to plant trees on Tu BeShvat, amid the winter rains, when the soil is most fertile. Since the holiday falls on the fifteenth of the Hebrew month of Shvat, some have the custom of reading the fifteen Psalms of Ascent and eating fifteen fruits, especially grapes, figs, pomegranates, olives, and dates, for which the land of Israel is praised in the Torah. I also try to serve a new, seasonal fruit, over which my family can recite the Shehecheyanu blessing, as well as fruity noodle kugel, apple strudel, or dates filled with fruit or marzipan.

Purim

Mishloach manot commemorates the friendship, gratitude, and brotherly love engendered by Queen Esther and Mordechai among the Jews of Shushan after they were saved from evil Haman's wicked scheme to destroy them. To fulfill the mitzvah, one must send two kinds of ready-to-eat foods to a friend, although it is meritorious to send to as many friends as possible. In contrast, the Purim mitzvah of matanot la'evyonim, gifts for the poor, may be fulfilled through money or other objects, to be sent to at last two needy people.

It is never too early to start saving containers for mishloach manot. Jars can be filled with homemade peanut butter, jam, mayonnaise, dressing, sauce, soup, pickles, snack mix, or dip, and eggnog can be poured into bottles. You can even enclose the recipe. Cover coffee cans with wrapping paper and fill them with cookies. Wrap an aluminum foil pan of brownies in cellophane. Decorate a shoe box and stuff it with goodies. Or send blintzes or kreplach on that odd platter you haven't used in years.

With the festive Purim meal in mind, bake challot—miniature or seudah-size. If you feel adventurous, cook up some stuffed cabbage for your Hungarian friends, or egg rolls for the local Chinese-food lovers. Health-food enthusiasts will appreciate whole-wheat haman-taschen, granola, tofu goulash, or vegetable cutlets.

If you're not up to cooking or baking, everyone loves assortments of nuts, dried or tropical fruit, an elegant basket of large, fresh strawberries or even a whole pineapple adorned with a ribbon. The main thing is to experience the joy of giving—and the joy of Purim.

Pesach

Pesach, the festival of freedom, begins on the fifteenth day of the Hebrew month of Nissan. During the eight days of Pesach (seven in Israel), we are forbidden to eat, possess, or bene-fit from chametz (leaven), since our forefathers left Egypt so quickly that their dough didn't have time to rise.

The Talmud likens chametz to the yetzer hara, the evil impulse that ferments and foments in our hearts and distances us from God. As we remove the chametz from our homes, we symbolically purge ourselves of this impulse and prepare to partake of the spiritual nourish-ment provided by matzo, an emblem of purity and humility. The Ari, the famous sixteenth-century kabbalist, taught that whoever rids his dwelling of every trace of chametz will not be tempted to sin for a year. Thus Pesach celebrates freedom not only from bondage but from temptation.

As an extra Pesach precaution, many people do not eat "gebruchts" ("dipping" in Yiddish), i.e., anything made with matzo or matzo meal and liquid, lest any unbaked matzo flour come in contact with liquid and ferment, forming chametz. My mother always made her fluffy gefilte fish without matzo meal in case any of our guests did not eat gebruchts. This custom is generally not observed on the eighth day of Pesach, which is rabbinic in origin.

In the old days, preparing for Pesach was a formidable undertaking. My Cousin Esther, who lived in Jerusalem over half a century ago, recalled that a block of ice in a sack served as the refrigerator. Fish was a luxury, and even the lowly potato—a Pesach staple—was expensive. The only other available vegetables were eggplant, squash, and maybe some tomatoes prepared in various ways to add variety to the meal. There was hardly any fruit other than citrus. Around Sukkot time, everyone joined in making Pesach wine from newly ripened grapes, honey, and raisins. Oranges ripened around Chanukah and were promptly used for orange marmalade and candied peels. Schmaltz was prepared on Chanukah, when geese were fattest. Some housewives even pressed their own olive oil. Many families baked their own shmurah matzo, made from wheat that had been kept away from water since the time of its harvest.

Nowadays, making Pesach is a lot easier, though still a lot of work. Weeks in advance, housewives are busy cleaning the chametz out of every nook and cranny of their homes and stocking up on matzo, wine, and other Pesach products. The entire household bustles with activity.

The cleanup effort culminates in bedikat chametz, a candlelight search for chametz the night before Pesach. Small pieces of bread are customarily planted throughout the house. This bread and any other chametz found during the search are traditionally swept onto a wooden spoon with a feather and burned the next morning, when we declare any overlooked leaven ownerless.

By Pesach night, the house is sparkling as the family gathers around an extended dining-room table for the seder, a symbolic reenactment of our ancestors' miraculous emancipation from slavery in Egypt and the spectacular parting of the Red Sea seven days later. We are commanded to remember the exodus from Egypt every day (Deuteronomy 16:30), but on Pesach we actually relive it by reading the Haggadah and eating symbolic foods like matzo, the celestial bread that resists the corruption and decadence of Egypt (Zohar).

Arrayed on the ornate seder plate are other symbols. Karpas, a small piece of potato, celery, or parsley, is dipped in salt water at the start of the seder to remind us of the tears shed by our ancestors in Egypt. The maror (bitter herbs), usually horseradish or romaine lettuce, recalls our forefathers' bitter plight in Egypt. The charoset, a mixture of chopped apples and walnuts, wine, and cinnamon, resembles the mortar used by the slaves to make bricks. The Talmud relates that the charoset should be eaten to mute the maror's potentially hazardous side effects without overpowering its bitter taste.

The roasted shank bone symbolizes the Korban Pesach, the lamb sacrificed on Pesach eve, whose blood marked the Israelite homes in Egypt, safeguarding them against the dreaded plague of the first-born. Some consider the shank bone a symbol of national unity because a roasted lamb stays whole while a boiled lamb falls apart. Moreover, in the days of the Temple, people ate the Pesach sacrifice in large groups, not individually. Known as the zeroa (arm) in Hebrew, the shank bone also alludes to God's outstretched arm, which delivered us out of Egypt. And a roasted egg represents the holiday offering brought to the Temple on the three pilgrimage festivals: Sukkot, Pesach, and Shavuot.

Despite this lofty symbolism, Pesach is very much a children's holiday. The Torah states that our children are bound to ask us about the exodus (Exodus 12:25), and we are commanded to tell them the story in full (Exodus 13:8). Indeed, the dipping of the karpas is designed to pique their curiosity and prompt them to ask the third of the Four Questions: "On other nights we don't dip at all; why do we dip twice tonight?" Similarly, the search for the coveted afikomen maintains their interest until the end of the meal.

But the significance of the evening is most appreciated by adults. Reveling in our newly acquired freedom, we recline, rejoice, and linger over a sumptuous festive meal. By the time the seder ends, usually long past midnight, we have drunk four cups of wine, commemorating the four stages of God's salvation: "I brought, I delivered, I redeemed, and I took you out of Egypt" (Exodus 6:6-7). We have poured a fifth cup for Elijah the Prophet, who is invited into every home to herald the coming of the Messiah. In our eagerness to hasten his arrival and the dawn of our redemption, we even open the door for him.

We conclude by expressing this our most fervent hope and dream in song: "Leshana Haba'ah BeYerushalayim Habenuya, Next Year in Rebuilt Jerusalem."

Shavuot

Shavuot, literally "weeks," occurs seven weeks after Pesach—the festival of freedom—and commemorates the giving of the Torah, the source of our spiritual freedom. The Talmud relates that God went from nation to nation, offering His greatest gift—the Torah. All the other nations spurned the Torah, intimidated by its sterling moral code, but the Jews zealously declared, "We will do and we will understand," embracing the mitzvot even before they understood them. Alluding to this remarkable intuition and dedication, the Song of Songs compares the Jewish people to an apple tree, which bears fruit before sprouting leaves.

Shavuot is also known as the Festival of the First Fruits. Just as the first fruits were brought to the Temple not by messenger but by the people themselves, we must reap the fruit of our own spiritual labors, rather than leaving Torah study and observance to others.

On Shavuot we relive revelation by staying up all night learning Torah. We adorn our homes with greenery to recall the blooming of Mount Sinai when the Torah was given.

And we serve dairy dishes, such as blintzes and cheesecake, because the Jews ate dairy until they had mastered their newly acquired laws of kashrut.

We also read the Book of Ruth, in which one woman's personal acceptance of Torah and acts of loving kindness triumphed over a spiritual famine and culminated in the birth of King David, from whom the Messiah will be descended, and who himself was born and died on Shavuot.

Menus

SHABBAT

Friday Night Meal

Traditional Challah (page 193)
My Favorite Gefilte Fish (page 33) with Homemade Horseradish (page 40)
Good Old-Fashioned Chicken Soup (page 63)
Roast Chicken with Tangy Apricot Sauce (page 79)
Carrot Kugel or Kugelettes (page 158)
Scandinavian Medley (page 132)
Frozen Chocolate Mousse Pie (page 263)

Shabbat Noonday Meal

Fish Salad (page 36)
Chopped Liver (page 43)
Traditional Cholent (page 106), served with Fluffy Kishke (page 108)
Traditional Jerusalem Kugel (page 159)
Chicken Salad Supreme in Orange Shells (page 44)
Cucumber Salad (page 49)
Fantastic Burnt Almond Ice Cream (page 185)
Best Mandelbrot (page 247)

Seudah Shlishit

Sliced Vegetable Relish (page 54)
Chopped Herring (page 37)
Tangy Eggplant and Mushrooms (page 52)
Pineapple Coleslaw (page 51)
Zucchini Cake (page 219)

ROSH HASHANAH

Round Honey Challah (page 195)
Gefilte Fish Loaf (page 35), served with Homemade Mayonnaise (page 40)
Chicken Livers with Mushrooms (page 43)
Chicken with Almonds and Prunes (page 80)
Carrot Tsimmes (page 129)
Sweet Potatoes in Orange Cups (page 133)
Beet Salad with Shredded Apples (page 130)
Crumb-Coated Baked Apples (page 183)
Honey Chiffon Cake (page 212)

EREV YOM KIPPUR (PRE-FAST)

Good Old-Fashioned Chicken Soup (page 63)
Boiled Chicken (from the soup)
Broccoli and Rice Bake (page 136)
Carrot Salad (page 56)
Surprise Lemon Torte (page 220)

SUKKOT

Sweetbreads and Mushrooms (page 42)
Tongue Gourmet (page 101)
Carrot Pineapple Tsimmes (page 129)
Kasha with String Beans (page 140)
Apple Cranberry Cobbler (page 187)

CHANUKAH

French Onion Soup (page 73)
Traditional Potato Latkes (page 164)
Israeli Cheese Salad (page 55)
Blintz Soufflé (page 173)
Sufganiot (page 252)

TU BESHVAT

Summertime Fruit Soup (page 72)
Potted Beef with Dried Fruit (page 95)
Broccoli and Rice Bake (page 136)
Fruit Crystal Ice Dessert (page 186)
Date Diamonds (page 239)

PURIM

Chicken Soup (page 63) with Kreplach (page 68)
Roast Turkey (page 87)
Cranberry Noodle Kugel (page 163)
String Bean Salad Supreme (page 49)
Elegant Cake Roll with Mocha Filling (page 221)
Hamantaschen (page 246)

PESACH

Seder Meal

Traditional Charoset (page 277)
My Favorite Gefilte Fish (page 33)
Good Old-Fashioned Chicken Soup (page 63) with Feather-Light Matzo Balls (page 279)
Boiled Chicken (from the soup)
Apple Kugel (page 284)
Carrot Salad (page 56)
Frozen Lemon Pie (page 298)
Pesach Mocha Bars (page 296)

Holiday Meal

Liver Kugelettes (page 282)
Roast Duck à L'Orange (page 88) with Pesach Stuffing (page 281)
Vegetable Matzo Kugel (page 283)
Shredded Tart Salad (page 57)
Gan Eden Layer Cake (page 294)

SHAVUOT

Dairy Meal

Shavuot Strawberry Soup (page 71)
Trout Amandine (page 121)
Cheese Kugel (page 160)
Cauliflower and Mushroom Soufflé (page 146)
Luscious Chiffon Cheesecake (page 269)

Meat Meal

Fish Fillets Florentine (page 118)
Sweet and Sour Hot Cabbage Borscht (page 67)
Special Ingredient Shoulder Roast (page 96)
Zucchini Kugel (page 160)
Ratatouille (page 131)
Apple Strudel (page 227)

Appetizers

Appetizers

My Favorite Gefilte Fish

I've been using this gefilte fish recipe for Shabbat for forty years. The combination of seasonings makes the difference in taste. This dish was innovated in order to serve fish without bones on Shabbat, when removing the bones is prohibited. Our Sages say that one who eats fish on Shabbat merits many blessings. If you have your fish dealer grind the fish for you, be sure to get the head and bones for the stock.

Stock
head and bones of fish
1 large onion, sliced
1 carrot, sliced
1 tablespoon sugar
1 teaspoon salt
1/4 teaspoon pepper
1 1/2 quarts water

Fish
2 pounds ground fish (carp, whitefish, pike, Israel casif, or a combination)
1 large Spanish onion, diced (about 1 1/2 cups)
1 level tablespoon salt
4-5 tablespoons sugar
1/2 teaspoon pepper
3 eggs
2 tablespoons matzo meal or bread crumbs, optional
1 carrot, thinly sliced, for garnish

P lace ingredients for fish stock into a large pot. Bring to a boil, and let simmer while preparing gefilte fish mixture. Combine ingredients for fish. With wet hands, form mixture into oval balls. Drop into boiling stock. Cover and simmer over low heat for 1 1/2 hours. Let cool slightly. Remove from pot and refrigerate, separately from the fish stock. Serve cold, topped with a slice of cooked carrot and jellied fish stock. Serves 8-10.

Serve Homemade Horseradish or Homemade Mayonnaise (see page 40) separately.

Variations

For a delicate sweet taste, add 2-3 tablespoons of ground almonds or 2 drops of almond extract to mixture.

Gefilte fish can be used for stuffing a whole, raw fish and baked; or stuff slices of whitefish, carp, trout, or pike with gefilte fish mixture, and cook as for gefilte fish.

Fry gefilte fish patties in oil on each side for 15-20 minutes. Cover, and lower heat for last 10 minutes.

Fishy smell can be avoided by adding 1 teaspoon of lemon juice or vinegar to fish mixture.

Baked Gefilte Fish Patties
in Tomato Sauce

A colorful gefilte fish variation—something different for Friday night.

Fish
Gefilte Fish (see page 33)

Sauce
1 large onion, diced
2 stalks celery, sliced
1 green pepper, diced
4 tablespoons oil
1 cup (8 ounces) tomato sauce
2 teaspoons lemon juice
2-3 teaspoons sugar
$^2/_3$ cup water
pinch of thyme, optional
$^1/_2$ teaspoon salt
$^1/_4$ teaspoon pepper

Combine all ingredients for fish. With wet hands, form patties and fry in hot oil on both sides. Place in a greased 2-quart casserole. Make the sauce by sautéing onion, celery, and green pepper in oil until tender. Add remaining ingredients. Cook over low heat for an additional 5 minutes. Pour over fish patties. Bake uncovered in a preheated 325° oven for 1 hour. (If necessary, add a little water after 30 minutes of baking.) Serves 6-8.

Variation

Without sauce: Place gefilte fish patties in a well-greased baking pan and bake in a preheated 350° oven for 50-60 minutes.

Menirte Herring and Apples
in Tomato Sauce

A richly flavored Continental recipe. Make it early in the week to allow time for marinating, and serve for Kiddush on Shabbat.

3 large schmaltz (salt) herrings, or 6 herring fillets
2 small apples, peeled and thinly sliced
1 large onion, sliced

Sauce
$^1/_2$ cup sugar
$^1/_3$ cup oil
$^1/_2$ cup vinegar
$^1/_2$ cup tomato paste
1 teaspoon prepared mustard

Soak herring overnight in water to cover. Remove skin and bones. Cut into 1-inch slices. Combine ingredients for sauce. Place fish in a bowl or jar, and add sauce and apple and onion slices. Refrigerate to marinate for 1-2 days. Serves 12-14.

Gefilte Fish Loaf

A decorative fish loaf. When the loaf is inverted, colorful rings of green pepper, carrot, and onion rings appear on top.

Fish
Gefilte Fish (see page 33)

For Garnish in Pan
1 green pepper, cut into rings
1 small onion, cut into rings
1 carrot, thinly sliced

Place wax paper on bottom and sides of a greased 12x4-inch loaf pan and spread with 2 tablespoons of oil. Make a decorative pattern by placing rings of green pepper on wax paper, rings of onion inside the pepper, and a thin slice of carrot in the center. Spoon gefilte fish mixture on top, packing down well. Cover with aluminum foil or greased waxed paper. Bake in a preheated 350° oven for 1 hour. To serve, invert pan on platter. The design will be on top. May be frozen. Serve Homemade Horseradish or Homemade Mayonnaise (see page 40) separately. Serves 6-8.

Mock Gefilte Fish

Tastes close to the real thing, and saves a trip to the fish market!

Fish Mixture
2 7$^1/_2$-ounce cans tuna fish (preferably white tuna), drained; or 1 16-ounce can salmon, drained
4 eggs, beaten
1 large onion, finely chopped
1 medium carrot, finely chopped
1 teaspoon sugar
1 teaspoon salt, or to taste
$^1/_2$ teaspoon pepper
$^1/_3$ cup matzo meal

Stock
1 large onion, thinly sliced
1 medium carrot, sliced
1 teaspoon salt
$^1/_4$ teaspoon pepper
1 teaspoon sugar
2$^1/_2$ cups water

Thoroughly mix together all ingredients for fish mixture. If using a food processor, be careful not to over-process. Refrigerate for $^1/_2$ hour. Place stock ingredients in a medium-sized pot, bring to a boil, and simmer for 2 minutes. Wet hands in cold water, and form fish mixture into balls or patties. Drop them gently into simmering stock. Cover and simmer for 40 minutes.

Fish Salad

This fish salad is served in the form of a fish. A black olive, a pimento, and green pepper slivers serve for the eye, mouth, and fins. For a delightful variation, the fish mixture can be used to fill avocado halves—a festive appetizer.

Salad

2 pounds fish fillets (flounder, haddock, hake, or cod)
1 large onion, sliced
1 large carrot, sliced
$^1/_2$ cup celery, chopped
$^1/_2$ cup green pepper, diced
$^1/_2$ cup onion, diced
2 tablespoons lemon juice
2-3 hard-boiled eggs, diced
salt and pepper, to taste
$^1/_2$ cup mayonnaise (approximately)

Garnish

1 tomato, cut into wedges
1 unpeeled cucumber, scored and thinly sliced
1 black olive
1 slice pimento
$^1/_4$ green pepper

Cover fish fillets half way in water, and cook with sliced onion and carrot until the fish flakes easily—about 20 minutes. Remove fish and flake with a fork. Combine with remaining ingredients, stirring in mayonnaise last. Pack mixture into a greased fish mold or shape with hands into form of a fish and refrigerate until firm.

If packed into a mold, invert onto a large platter and garnish with wedges of tomato and scored cucumber slices. (To score a cucumber, run tines of a fork down its length.)

To simulate a fish, use a black olive for the eye, a thin slice of pimento for the mouth, and thin slices of green peppers for the fins and tail. Press top of teaspoon gently over back at $^1/_2$-inch intervals, for the scales. Serves 8.

Variation

Fish-filled avocados: Add 2-3 tablespoons of ketchup to mayonnaise and combine with fish. Pile fish salad high in 8 ripe avocado halves—a delightful appetizer.

To absorb odors in refrigerator, place a little vanilla extract on a piece of cotton or charcoal in refrigerator.

Chopped Herring

Herring, a Jewish delicacy, is particularly popular for Saturday morning Kiddush. Schmaltz (salt) herrings need to be skinned and boned. Matjes herring fillets can also be used in this excellent old recipe, as well as jarred pickled herring fillets.

2 whole schmaltz or matjes herrings, or
    4 herring fillets, or 1 16-ounce jar
    herring fillets
2 slices white bread
2 tablespoons vinegar
1/2 onion
2 tart apples
2 teaspoons sugar
pinch of pepper
2 hard-boiled eggs, for garnish

Skin and bone herrings (if using the schmaltz variety). Soak overnight in cold water to cover, changing water once. Soak bread in vinegar. Grind—or finely chop—herring, onion, apples, and bread. Stir in sugar and pepper. Arrange on a serving platter. To garnish, chop yolks and whites of hard-boiled eggs separately and sprinkle half the herring with chopped egg whites, the other half with chopped yolks. Serves 6-8 as an appetizer.

Variation

For a quick version of chopped herring, begin with 1 16-ounce jar of herring fillets in wine sauce. Prepare as directed above. This keeps in the refrigerator for 1-2 weeks.

Pink German Herring Salad

An old German recipe. Bite-size pieces of herring, apples, and beets in a tantalizing combination. The beets give it a festive color and flavor. Herring is very high in calcium.

1 12-ounce jar pickled herring fillets,
    drained
1 medium potato, boiled, cooled, and
    diced
2 medium beets, cooked and diced
2 hard-boiled eggs, chopped
2 large apples, diced
2 medium pickles, diced, optional
1 medium onion, diced
2 teaspoons sugar
1/3 cup (or more) mayonnaise, or 1 cup
    sour cream

Cut herring into bite-size pieces. Combine with remaining ingredients. Serves 12-14 as an appetizer.

To give store-bought mayonnaise a home-made taste, stir in 1-2 tablespoons of pure virgin olive oil. Mix well until all trace of oil has disappeared.

Mock Chopped Herring

Quick, easy, and economical. A popular dish in mid-Eastern Europe a century ago. Enjoyed for its piquant flavor even today.

2 4-ounce cans boneless sardines
³/₄ cup finely chopped onion
1 large apple, finely chopped
3 hard-boiled eggs, chopped
2 tablespoons vinegar
2 teaspoons sugar
3 tablespoons bread crumbs
1 can anchovies, optional

Drain sardines, squeezing out oil. Mash them well with tines of a fork. Mix in remaining ingredients. Consistency should be slightly crunchy. Serves 6-8 as an appetizer.

Homemade Pickled Mackerel

Make this early in the week. It is nice to have on hand for Kiddush. Marvelous flavor.

3 large fresh or frozen mackerels
water to cover
¹/₃ cup salt

Sauce

4 medium onions, thinly sliced
2 teaspoons whole mixed pickling spice, or 6 bay leaves and 5 English peppers
1 cup vinegar
3 tablespoons sugar
water to cover

If using frozen mackerels, remove from freezer 20 minutes before slicing them into ¹/₂-inch slices. Place slices in a large container, and cover with cold water and salt. Refrigerate for 24-36 hours. (Fish may turn white.) Drain, discarding water. In a 2-quart jar, alternate layers of mackerel slices with onion slices. Add pickling spice (or bay leaves and English peppers). Then add vinegar, sugar, and cold water to cover. Refrigerate to marinate for 2 days. Yields 28-30 slices.

Sweet and Sour Fish

This piquant pickled fish is good to have on hand as a festive first course or as a main luncheon dish during the week. It keeps in the refrigerator for up to 2 weeks.

3 pounds fish (whitefish, trout, pike, pickerel, carp, or salmon), cut into 1-1½ inch slices
salt, for sprinkling
2 onions, sliced
1 large carrot, sliced
1 teaspoon salt
¼ teaspoon pepper
1½ teaspoons pickling spice
2 bay leaves
⅓ cup sugar
3 cups water
½ cup wine vinegar

Sprinkle fish lightly with salt. Refrigerate for 1 hour. Place all ingredients in a medium-sized pot. Cover and bring to a boil. Reduce heat and simmer for 1 hour. Let cool and refrigerate. Sauce will jell. Serves 9 as an appetizer.

Tarama—Greek Caviar

Have you ever purchased a fresh carp, only to find a large quantity of roe in it, which you just don't know what to do with? Tarama is a Greek caviar made from the roe of the carp, one of the most popular fish in Israel. Fresh carp comes from Lake Kinneret in Tiberias, and from fish ponds. It should be used as soon as it is purchased to keep the fish from becoming muddy. Tarama can be served as an accompaniment or garnish to a salad, or alone as an appetizer.

To prepare roe, first prick with a needle in several places to prevent the membrane from bursting and spattering. Do not cook it for too long— to prevent it from becoming hard and dry. Place roe in a small saucepan and cover with boiling water. Add 2 tablespoons of lemon juice and simmer over low heat for 6-12 minutes (depending on size). Drain off water, let cool, and remove the membrane. Add salt to taste.

4 tablespoons cooked carp roe
3 tablespoons lemon juice
3½ slices white bread, crustless
¾ cup olive oil or salad oil (or half of each)
salt and pepper, to taste

Place cooked roe and lemon juice in a bowl. Mix in an electric mixer on low speed, until thoroughly combined. Soak bread in cool water, squeeze out, and add to mixture. Continue mixing until well blended. Slowly add oil, while continuing to mix on medium-high speed, until mixture is consistency of thick mayonnaise. Add seasonings, to taste. Cover and refrigerate. Serve cold on a platter.

Homemade Mayonnaise

Why make your own mayonnaise when it's so readily available? Because there's nothing like the special taste of homemade mayonnaise without preservatives or additives. It transforms a simple salad into a delicacy. Refer to "Variation" of Homemade Horseradish (see following recipe) for a delicious sauce.

2 eggs, room temperature
1 tablespoon Dijon mustard
1 teaspoon sugar
1 teaspoon salt
2 cups pure virgin olive oil or vegetable
  oil
2 tablespoons vinegar

Mix eggs, mustard, sugar, and salt in a blender or food processor for about 4 seconds. Then, while motor is running, pour in oil in a slow, steady stream until mixture thickens. Stop motor and stir in vinegar by hand. Cover and refrigerate. Yields 2³/₄ cups.

Variation

Tartar sauce: Add 3-4 small, chopped, sweet or sour pickles to 1 cup of mayonnaise.

Homemade Horseradish

Horseradish and gefilte fish are almost inseparable companions. The combination originated in Russia, but today it is savored by Jews of many countries. Gefilte fish is served without horseradish on Rosh Hashanah, when many people avoid sharp or bitter foods and only eat sweet foods to symbolize a sweet year to come. The beets not only add color, but they make the wild root milder.

1 8-ounce horseradish root
4 medium beets, peeled and cooked
2 tablespoons sugar
1 teaspoon salt
4 tablespoons vinegar or lemon juice

Peel horseradish root. Grind horseradish and beets in a food processor or blender until fine. Stir in remaining ingredients. Pour into jars, cover, and refrigerate. Can be frozen (leave 1-inch space at top of jar for mixture to expand).
Yields approximately 2¹/₂ jars of 8 ounces each.

Variation

Horseradish sauce: Combine ²/₃ part mayonnaise and ¹/₃ part horseradish.

Ground Beef Wellington
with Mushroom Sauce

An attractive way to dress up ground beef and an elegant first course for a special occasion. It can also be served as a luncheon dish.

Easy Flaky Dough (see page 226), or 1 package puff pastry

Meat Filling
2 pounds ground beef
2 eggs
$^1/_4$ cup ketchup
1 medium onion, finely diced
$^1/_3$ cup matzo meal or bread crumbs
$^1/_8$ teaspoon pepper
$^1/_4$ teaspoon garlic powder
salt, to taste

Glaze
1 egg yolk, beaten with 1 teaspoon
   water

Combine all ingredients for meat filling. Roll out dough thinly into a rectangle. Place a $2^1/_2$-inch row of meat filling on inside edge of dough. Roll. Place on a large greased cookie sheet. Brush with glaze. Bake in a preheated 475° oven for 20 minutes. Reduce heat to 375°, and continue baking for an additional 35-40 minutes, until golden brown. Slice 1 inch thick. Serve hot with Mushroom Sauce. Serves 10 as an appetizer.

Mushroom Sauce
1 onion, diced
1 cup fresh mushrooms, sliced, or 1
   4-ounce can mushrooms
3 tablespoons oil
3 tablespoons flour
salt, to taste
$1^1/_2$ cups water

Sauté onion and mushrooms in oil until tender. Push aside and stir in flour until smooth. Slowly stir in salt and water until smooth and cook for 3 minutes until thickened. If desired, add a little water.

Variation

Meat loaf: Form into 2 loaves without the dough. Bake, topped with mushroom sauce or tomato sauce, in a 350° oven for 1 hour.

To clean mushrooms, place them in a bag with some flour. Shake the bag to coat mushrooms, then add water and reshake. Drain and dry.

Sweetbreads and Mushrooms

This delicacy makes an elegant appetizer. Sweetbreads are perishable and should be cooked as soon as possible after buying. Brains can be substituted if you're on a budget—it's hard to tell the difference.

3 pairs of veal sweetbreads
1 tablespoon vinegar
2 large onions, diced
1 small sweet red pepper, cut into thin strips
2 ribs celery, diced
1 cup fresh mushrooms, sliced, or 1 8-ounce can sliced mushrooms (reserve liquid)
4 tablespoons oil
4 tablespoons flour, sifted
2 cups chicken soup or water
1 teaspoon salt
¹/₈ teaspoon pepper
6 prepared patty shells, optional

Cook sweetbreads in vinegar and water to cover for 20 minutes. Plunge into cold water. Remove membranes and tubes. Cut into 1¹/₂-inch pieces. Sauté onions, red pepper, celery, and mushrooms in oil until tender. Push vegetables aside and stir in flour until smooth. Slowly stir in chicken soup or water, salt, and pepper. (If using canned mushrooms, reserved liquid can be used as part of soup.) Cook for 3 minutes until thickened. Add sweetbreads and cook for 2 more minutes. Serve in pastry shells or on toast. Serves 6.

Variations

Calf, lamb, or beef brains can be prepared in the same way. Make sure they are very fresh and properly koshered.

Add a cup of fresh or frozen green peas in addition to sweetbreads and cook for about 5 minutes until tender.

Chicken Livers with Mushrooms

A hot, creamy, mushroom sauce with pieces of chicken livers and sliced mushrooms. Serve in pastry shells, or spoon over fluffy rice for a light luncheon dish, or serve over triangles of toast as an appetizer. A popular dish enjoyed by everyone.

2 large onions, diced
3-4 tablespoons oil
1 small green pepper, diced
$^2/_3$ cup sliced mushrooms
$^1/_2$ sweet red pepper, diced
3 tablespoons flour, sifted
1$^1/_2$ cups chicken soup or water
1 pound chicken livers, koshered and
    cut into quarters or sixths
3 slices toast, cut into triangles

Sauté onions in oil until soft. Add green pepper, mushrooms, and red pepper. Continue cooking for an additional 5 minutes. Stir in flour until smooth, then gradually stir in chicken soup or water until smooth. Simmer over low heat for about 3 minutes. Add chicken livers and heat well. Spoon the mixture onto triangles of toast and serve as an appetizer. Serves 6.

Chopped Liver

An all-time favorite that never loses its appeal. Koshering livers is, in effect, broiling them after they have been sprinkled with coarse salt, so they usually need no further cooking. A pinch of sugar enhances the flavor of the chopped liver.

2 large onions, diced
4 tablespoons oil
generous pinch of sugar
1 pound beef, calf, or chicken livers,
    koshered
3 hard-boiled eggs
salt and pepper, to taste

Garnish
8 lettuce leaves
2 tomatoes, cut into wedges

Sauté onions in oil until golden and add sugar. Remove from heat. Combine with liver, eggs, and seasonings. Grind in a food grinder or processor, or chop finely in a wooden bowl. Scoop onto lettuce leaves and garnish with tomatoes. Serves 8.

Calf's-Foot Jelly (Petcha)

If you're looking for a high-calcium dish, this is it. An old-time favorite that was much more popular a generation ago, yet is still enjoyed today.

1 calf's foot, cut into thirds or quarters
2 teaspoons salt
$^1/_2$ teaspoon pepper
1 bay leaf
1 medium onion
4-5 cloves garlic, diced
juice of 1 lemon
2 eggs, hard-boiled and sliced
lettuce leaves, for garnish

Cook all ingredients, except hard-boiled eggs and lemon juice, in water to cover plus 3 inches. Cook for 3-4 hours until meat is soft and falls off bone easily, or cook in a pressure cooker with water to cover for 30 minutes. Add lemon juice. Remove meat from bone and cut into small pieces. Place in a 9x13-inch pan. Strain liquid over top. Scatter slices of eggs throughout. Refrigerate until jelled. Cut into 2-inch squares and serve cold on lettuce leaves as an appetizer. Yields about 20 squares.

Variation

Add cubes of broiled liver before refrigerating.

Chicken Salad Supreme in Orange Shells

This attractive salad is a great way to use leftover chicken. Ideal as an appetizer. An especially big hit with children if you turn the orange shells into "baskets," making handles from strips of orange peel or colored pipe cleaners.

4 oranges
2$^1/_2$ cups cooked diced chicken
$^1/_4$ cup slivered almonds
2 stalks celery, diced
$^1/_3$ cup mayonnaise
$^1/_4$ teaspoon salt
whole blanched almonds, for garnish

Cut the oranges into halves. With a grapefruit knife, hollow out fruit from peels. Chop fruit coarsely. Combine with remaining ingredients. Pile high in orange shells and garnish with almonds. Makes 8 orange "baskets."

Variation

Combine chicken or turkey cubes with small green grapes (instead of oranges), thinly sliced celery, diced green pepper, coarsely chopped nuts, and mayonnaise. Pile high on a platter and garnish with small bunches of green and red grapes, and curly parsley.

Barbecued Chicken Wings

Marvelous tangy flavor.

2 pounds chicken wings
$^1/_4$ cup sesame seeds, optional

Sauce
1 cup ketchup
$^2/_3$ cup brown sugar
1/4 teaspoon salt
pinch of pepper
$^1/_4$ cup water

Combine sauce ingredients and pour over chicken wings. Spread out in a 9x12-inch pan. Sprinkle wings with sesame seeds, if desired. Bake uncovered in a 350° oven for 45 minutes, basting once or twice.

Mushroom Turnovers

A delightful way of preparing mushrooms.

Easy Flaky Dough (see page 226) or phyllo dough (prepared as directed on package)

Filling
1 large onion, diced
3 tablespoons margarine
$^1/_2$ pound mushrooms, sliced
$^1/_2$ teaspoon salt
pinch of pepper
2 tablespoons flour, sifted
1 cup water
$^1/_4$ teaspoon thyme, optional

Sauté onion in margarine until tender. Add mushrooms and cook for 5-7 minutes while stirring. Add salt and pepper. Push onion and mushrooms aside and stir in flour until smooth. Gradually stir in water and cook over low heat, stirring until thickened. Let cool. Roll out dough $^1/_8$ inch thick. Cut into 3-inch squares or rounds. Place a teaspoonful of mushroom filling in center of each. Fold dough over filling and press edges together tightly with tines of a fork. Place on a baking sheet. Prick tops with fork. Bake in a preheated 450° oven for 30-35 minutes until golden. Yields 26-28 turnovers.

Chicken, Turkey, or Fish Egg Rolls

*A delightful variation on the classic
Chinese egg roll.*

Classic Blintz Leaves (see page 171)

Filling
1 cup sliced mushrooms
3 cups coarsely chopped cabbage or
  bean sprouts
2 stalks celery, diced
2 green onions, diced
1 cup cooked chicken, turkey, or fish,
  diced
1 tablespoon soy sauce or tamari sauce
$^2/_3$ teaspoon salt
$^1/_4$ teaspoon pepper
oil, for deep-frying

Mix all ingredients together. Place
1 tablespoon of mixture on each
blintz leaf. Fasten with a toothpick.
Deep fry in oil for about 5 minutes
until golden. Remove toothpicks.

Chinese Egg Rolls

*Not classically Jewish, perhaps, but
definitely delicious!*

Classic Blintz Leaves (see page 171)

Filling
2 medium onions, chopped
4 tablespoons oil
2 stalks celery, diced
8 ounces (1 cup) mushrooms, drained
  and sliced
$1^1/_2$ cups bean sprouts, or 1 cup
  shredded cabbage
1 cup bamboo shoots, chopped
1 tablespoon soy sauce
salt and pepper, to taste
oil, for deep-frying

Sauté onions in oil until soft. Add
celery and mushrooms and cook
for an additional 5 minutes. Combine
with remaining vegetables. Season
with soy sauce, salt, and pepper. Place
1-2 tablespoons of mixture on each
blintz leaf and roll tightly, tucking
sides in. Fasten with a toothpick or
seal with beaten egg white. Deep-fry
in oil until golden. Remove
toothpicks. Can be frozen and
reheated in a preheated 350° oven.
Serve with a hot sauce or sweet and
sour sauce. Yields 18 egg rolls.

Vegetarian Chopped Liver

Tastes and looks exactly like chopped liver, yet far easier to digest.

3 large onions, diced or thinly sliced
¹/₄ cup vegetable oil
1 1-pound, 4-ounce can peas, drained
¹/₂ - ²/₃ cup walnuts
¹/₂ teaspoon salt, or to taste
¹/₈ teaspoon pepper
3 hard-boiled eggs
tomatoes and cucumbers, sliced, for
   garnish

Sauté onions in oil until deep brown. (It is important for the onions to become a deep brown—without burning—in order for color to be the same as chopped liver.) Drain peas, thoroughly squeezing out liquid. Grind walnuts in a food processor or grinder. Add onions and process for an additional half-minute. Add peas and remaining ingredients and process with only a few on-off bursts until combined and smooth. Do not over-process. Serve on lettuce leaves. Yields 8 appetizers.

Three-Bean Salad

A mixture of three kinds of canned beans, with sliced onions, marinated in a tart dressing.

¹/₄ cup vegetable oil
²/₃ cup vinegar
¹/₂ teaspoon salt
3 cloves garlic, crushed
¹/₃-¹/₂ cup sugar, or to taste
1 1-pound, 4-ounce can green beans
1 1-pound, 4-ounce can yellow beans
1 1-pound, 4-ounce can kidney beans
1 medium onion, thinly sliced
1 small red pimento or sweet red
   pepper, diced
1 small green pepper, cut into thin
   strips

In a saucepan, bring to boil oil, vinegar, salt, garlic, and sugar. Cook for 2 minutes, cool, and combine with drained beans and remaining ingredients. Chill.

Variation

Fill scooped-out tomatoes with bean salad and serve on a bed of lettuce.

Caesar Salad

A highly seasoned, fresh lettuce salad. You make the dressing right in the bowl, adding the lettuce last.

1 large head romaine lettuce, or 2
   heads bibb lettuce
3 large cloves garlic, crushed
1 flat can of anchovy fillets in oil
salt, to taste, optional
generous pinch of pepper
1 teaspoon Worcestershire sauce
¹/₄ cup safflower oil
1 egg yolk, beaten
dash of Tabasco sauce
1 cup Sautéed Toasted Croutons
¹/₃ cup grated Parmesan cheese,
   optional

Carefully wash and check lettuce leaves and tear them into large bite-size pieces. Place garlic and anchovies, with their oil, into a large salad bowl. Mash thoroughly with a fork until mixture forms a paste. Stir in salt, pepper, Worcestershire sauce, safflower oil, egg yolk, and Tabasco sauce, mixing well. Add croutons, allowing them to soak for several minutes. Then add cheese, if desired. Finally, add lettuce and toss. Serves 6-8.

Sautéed Toasted Croutons
¹/₄ cup olive oil
5 slices dry white bread or challah,
   crusts removed, cut into small cubes
3 cloves of garlic, crushed
2 teaspoons dill, optional

Heat oil and add bread cubes and garlic, stirring until bread is lightly toasted. Sprinkle with dill, if desired. Remove from heat.

Variation

Reserve anchovies until the end. Cut them into small pieces and toss with the lettuce, using only anchovy oil, but omitting safflower oil.

To reconstitute wilted lettuce, place in ice water with lemon juice and salt.

String Bean Salad Supreme

Easy to prepare, and delicious to the taste.

**1 10-ounce package frozen string
    beans, or 1 pound fresh string beans
1 4-ounce can mushrooms
1/2 cup cooked corn kernels
1 small red pepper, cut into strips
1/3 cup vinegar
1/2 teaspoon salt
2 tablespoons oil
2 tablespoons sugar
pinch of oregano**

Cook string beans until tender but crisp. Add to remaining ingredients. Toss, mix, and chill.

Cucumber Salad

Always a good accompaniment to a chicken or meat meal. Piquant and refreshing.

**6 unpeeled cucumbers
salt, to taste
1 medium onion, sliced
5 tablespoons sugar
1/4 cup vinegar
1/2 cup diced sweet red or green
    pepper, optional
pinch of pepper
chopped dill**

Wash cucumbers. Slice thinly. Sprinkle lightly with salt. Let stand for 20 minutes. Drain. Combine with remaining ingredients. Correct seasonings to taste, if desired. Refrigerate and serve chilled. Serves 10.

Variation

Creamy cucumber salad: Add 3-4 tablespoons of mayonnaise or 1 cup of sour cream to mixture.

Eggplant Salad or Spread

There are reputedly 1,001 ways to prepare an eggplant. Below are a few of my favorites. Baking an eggplant on top of the stove gives it a delicious smoked taste. Marvelous.

1 large unpeeled eggplant
3 cloves garlic, minced
juice of 1 lemon
4 tablespoons mayonnaise
salt and pepper, to taste

Prick skin of eggplant with a fork in several places, and place on a grate. Bake eggplant over low heat, turning on all sides, until soft (about 20 minutes); alternatively, bake in a 350° oven for 1 hour. Scoop out eggplant, mash, and combine with remaining ingredients, or give all ingredients a twirl in a food processor for a few seconds. Do not over-process.

Variations

Bake as above. Combine scooped-out eggplant with 3-4 tablespoons of oil, ¹/₂ teaspoon of pepper, salt to taste, and 2-3 chopped green scallions (or 1 small finely chopped green pepper). Serve as a salad—spread or piled into scooped-out tomatoes. Sprinkle with chopped scallions or green pepper.

To mashed eggplant, add 1 diced pimento, 1-2 diced pickles, 3-4 tablespoons of mayonnaise, 1 teaspoon of mustard, and 2 chopped hard-boiled eggs.

To mashed eggplant, add about ¹/₃ cup of thin short shreds or coarsely chopped red or green cabbage, 1 or 2 diced pickles (or thin half-slices of cucumber), juice of half a lemon, 3-4 tablespoons of mayonnaise, salt and pepper to taste, and, if desired, 1 diced tomato.

Instead of baking eggplant on top of the stove, it can be sliced and steamed in water to nearly cover for about 15-20 minutes, until tender. Drain well.

Coleslaw

A dish as tasty as it is easy to prepare.

1 small head green cabbage, shredded
2 large carrots, shredded
1 green pepper, shredded or diced
6 tablespoons lemon juice or vinegar
$^1/_2$ teaspoon salt
3-4 tablespoons honey or sugar, or to
    taste
$^1/_4$ - $^1/_2$ cup mayonnaise

Combine all ingredients. Chill for several hours or overnight. Serves 6.

Pineapple Coleslaw

This recipe is about 40 years old. I still recall my mother making it regularly for Shabbat. Mayonnaise is not used in this delicious coleslaw combination.

1 medium green cabbage, shredded
2-3 medium carrots, shredded
1 medium green pepper, cut into thin
    strips
$^1/_4$ cup sugar
$^1/_3$ cup vinegar
1 teaspoon salt
$^1/_4$ teaspoon pepper
2 7$^1/_2$-ounce cans crushed pineapple

Place all ingredients in a large bowl and toss well. Add more sugar and vinegar, to taste. Refrigerate overnight. Serves 8.

Variations

Use red cabbage instead of green for a lovely color. Substitute pineapple tidbits for crushed pineapple.

Use 3 large, shredded kohlrabi instead of cabbage.

Tangy Eggplant and Mushrooms

Cubes of eggplant, sautéed with mushrooms and sweet red pepper strips, and marinated in a piquant sauce. You'll love it.

2 medium unpeeled eggplants, cut into 1-inch cubes
salt, for sprinkling
2 large sweet red peppers, cut into thin strips
5 tablespoons (or more) oil, for frying
$^1/_4$ pound sliced fresh mushrooms, or 1 4-ounce can mushrooms
6 cloves garlic, minced
$^2/_3$ cup vinegar
1 teaspoon salt
2 teaspoons sugar

Sprinkle eggplant with salt and let stand for 30 minutes. Rinse with cold water and blot dry. Sauté eggplant and red pepper in 4 tablespoons of oil until soft, but retaining shape (about 25-30 minutes, covering during last 5-10 minutes). Transfer to a bowl. Sauté mushrooms and garlic in remaining oil, stirring over low heat for 5 minutes. Add to remaining ingredients. Marinate for at least 2 hours or overnight. Serve cold or hot. Serves 8-10.

Tangy Rice Salad

An unusual salad and a good way to use up leftover rice.

$1^1/_2$ cups cooked rice (or $^3/_4$ cup raw rice, cooked)
2 tablespoons oil
2 tablespoons vinegar or lemon juice
$^1/_4$ teaspoon mustard powder
1 large tomato, diced
1 green pepper, diced
1 medium onion, chopped
1 teaspoon sugar
salt and pepper, to taste

Combine all ingredients and chill well. Correct seasoning, if desired. Serves 6 as a side dish.

Greek Salad

A marvelous, light, crisp salad, with shredded cabbage, small slices of herring, and salty feta cheese.

1 small head of cabbage, shredded
2 stalks celery, thinly sliced
4 scallions, sliced
2-3 medium tomatoes, cubed (bite-size pieces)
1 cucumber, thinly sliced
1-1^1/$_2$ cups feta cheese
2 herring fillets, cut into ^{3}/$_4$-inch pieces
6-8 black olives

Dressing
^{1}/$_3$ cup sugar
^{1}/$_2$ cup vinegar
3 tablespoons oil
pepper, to taste

In a large bowl, combine all ingredients except olives. Toss. Combine ingredients for dressing and pour over vegetables in bowl. Toss well. Scatter olives on top.

Edith's Saucy Carrots

A neighbor who shared this recipe with me entered it in an Israeli food contest. It won.

8-10 medium carrots, thinly sliced
1 medium onion, finely chopped
1 large green pepper, finely chopped
2 tablespoons tomato paste
2 tablespoons water
3 tablespoons honey
^{1}/$_2$ teaspoon thyme
^{1}/$_2$ cup oil
^{1}/$_2$ cup vinegar
1 teaspoon salt
^{1}/$_2$ teaspoon mustard powder
1-2 cloves garlic

Cook carrots in water to almost cover for exactly 8 minutes. Drain well and combine with onion and green pepper. Blend remaining sauce ingredients in a blender or food processor and combine with carrots, onion, and green pepper. Marinate in refrigerator overnight. Serves 6-8 as a side dish.

Victor's Pickles

These pickles are easy to prepare. The hot pepper and garlic give them a wonderful taste.

1 rounded teaspoon pickling spice
1 rounded tablespoon coarse salt
10-12 small cucumbers
1 hot pepper
1 stalk celery, cut up
2 whole cloves garlic

Place all ingredients into a freshly rinsed quart jar. Add water to cover and seal. Let stand at room temperature for 5 days. Refrigerate.

For a simple, delicious, low-calorie side dish, place cabbage wedges in pickle brine for several days.

Sliced Vegetable Relish

You can never have too much of this delicious, tart, pickle relish on hand. It makes a good accompaniment to a meal and adds a flair to even the simplest sandwich lunch. Serve it as a side dish or as a relish.

3 carrots
3 sweet red peppers
3 medium onions
12 cucumbers
5 cups water
2¹/₂ cups vinegar
2-3 teaspoons salt
¹/₂ cup sugar
3 bay leaves

Slice vegetables thinly by hand or in a food processor. In a large pot, bring to a boil water, vinegar, salt, sugar, and bay leaves. Add sliced carrots and bring to a boil again. Add sweet peppers and onions and bring to a boil for a third time. Finally, add cucumbers and bring to a boil for the last time. Simmer for 5 minutes. Let cool, then pour into a freshly rinsed 2-quart jar. Store in refrigerator. Yields 2 quarts.

Zucchini Salad

Something new and different.

1 large onion, diced
2 cloves garlic, minced
4 tablespoons oil
6 medium unpeeled zucchini, thinly
    sliced
2 hard-boiled eggs, sliced
2-3 tablespoons mayonnaise
$^1/_2$ teaspoon garlic powder
salt and pepper, to taste

Sauté onion and garlic in oil until transparent. Remove from oil. Sauté half of the zucchini slices over medium heat until brown on both sides. If necessary, add a little oil. Remove from pan and combine with sautéed onion and garlic and remaining ingredients, including remaining raw slices of zucchini.

Variation

Chopped zucchini and hard-boiled eggs: Sauté onion in oil until golden. Remove from oil. Sauté all of the sliced zucchini over medium heat until golden brown. In a wooden chopping bowl, or in a food processor with several on-off pulses, coarsely chop sautéed onion, sautéed zucchini, and hard-boiled eggs. Combine with remaining ingredients. Chill. Serve on lettuce leaves. Serves 6-8.

Israeli Cheese Salad

Try this salad for Chanukah or Shavuot, when dairy foods are popular. For diet-watchers try it with fat-free cottage cheese.

12 ounces cream cheese
3 tablespoons sour cream or plain
    yogurt
1 medium carrot, shredded
1 medium radish, shredded
$^1/_2$ green pepper, finely diced
6 green olives, finely diced
$1^1/_2$ teaspoons prepared mustard
$^1/_2$ teaspoon paprika
salt and pepper, to taste

Mix together all ingredients. Spoon onto a platter, smoothing top to make a dome shape. Use as a spread or a dip, surrounded by crackers.

To slice cheese thinly and easily, heat knife first.

Carrot Salad

A colorful salad to enhance your Shabbat table. Carrots are very high in vitamin A and good for eyesight. The combination of ingredients is very nutritious.

1/2 cup raisins
6 medium carrots, shredded
1/2 cup walnuts, coarsely chopped
4 rounded tablespoons orange juice
   concentrate, or juice of 2 oranges (if
   using fresh oranges add 1-2
   tablespoons sugar)
1/2 cup shredded coconut, optional
6 whole lettuce leaves, for garnish,
   optional

Plump raisins by soaking in boiling water for 10-15 minutes. Combine all ingredients except lettuce and chill. Serve in a glass bowl or in individual lettuce cups (made by soaking whole leaves of iceberg lettuce in ice water for 10 minutes). Serves 6.

Variations

Add 3 large, shredded apples and 1 medium, diced onion.

Add 1 cup of crushed pineapple or drained pineapple pieces to mixture.

Green Salad Dressing

A unique Purim present. Bottle it and send it for Mishloach Manot!

2 tablespoons parsley
3 scallions (green part only)
1/2 cup oil
1 teaspoon Dijon mustard
2 teaspoons sugar
1 tablespoon mayonnaise
1/2 teaspoon salt
1/8 teaspoon pepper
4 tablespoons lemon juice

Combine all ingredients in a blender or food processor and blend until smooth. Alternatively, mince parsley and scallions, add to remaining ingredients, and combine by shaking up in a tightly sealed jar. Yields approximately 1 cup.

Shredded Raw Beet Salad

A favorite of mine. Beets are high in important minerals.

1 pound raw beets, peeled and shredded
3 cloves garlic, minced
$^1/_3$ cup vinegar
$^1/_3$ cup oil
1 teaspoon oregano
1 teaspoon salt
$^1/_3$ teaspoon black pepper
2 tablespoons soy sauce or tamari sauce

Combine all ingredients. Mix well. Chill. Serves 12-14.

Shredded Tart Salad

A delightful salad combining zucchini, apples, celery, and red and green peppers.

3 medium zucchini, shredded
3 red apples, shredded
3 stalks celery, shredded
1 red pepper, diced
1 green pepper, diced
1 small onion, grated
3 ounces frozen apple juice concentrate
3-4 tablespoons vinegar
$^1/_3$ cup water
salt and pepper, to taste
juice of 1 lemon, sprinkled on
    shredded apple to retain color

Combine all ingredients. Chill.

Soups

Soups

Good Old-Fashioned Chicken Soup

Doctors today are discovering what Jewish mothers and grandmothers have known for centuries: Chicken soup helps cure some illnesses, to say nothing of the tender loving care it shows. That is why chicken soup is referred to as "Jewish penicillin."

1 4-pound chicken, cut into eighths or quarters
3 quarts cold water
2 medium onions, quartered
2 carrots, cut into chunks
2 stalks celery, cut into large pieces
1 parsley root, cut in half
1 parsnip, cut into thirds
1-2 medium zucchini, cut into thirds
pinch of white pepper
salt, to taste (not too much, since chicken is salted in koshering)
2 sprigs fresh parsley, and 2 sprigs fresh dill, wrapped in cheesecloth and tied with white thread to inside handle of pot, optional

Place chicken in a large soup pot. Add cold water and bring close to boiling point. Skim froth from top before soup actually boils. Add remaining ingredients. Cover and simmer for 1¹/₂ hours or until chicken is tender. Remove from heat. Remove chicken and allow soup to cool. When cool, refrigerate and remove the fat. Yields about 2¹/₂ quarts. Serves 10.

Variation

Creamed chicken soup: Dilute 2 teaspoons of cornstarch in ¹/₈ cup of cold water per cup of soup. Pour into simmering broth. Add some diced chicken.

Beefy Stew Soup

A delicious meal in itself.

1 large onion, quartered
2 stalks celery, sliced
¹/₂ green pepper, seeded and cubed
2 tablespoons oil
1¹/₂ pounds goulash meat, cut into 1¹/₂-inch chunks
salt and pepper, to taste
1 bay leaf, crumbled
7 cups water
2 potatoes, cubed
2 carrots, thickly sliced
2 heaped tablespoons flour

Sauté onion, celery, and green pepper in oil until soft. Add goulash meat and sear on all sides. Cover and cook over low heat for about 30 minutes. Add remaining ingredients except flour. Cover and simmer for 1¹/₂ hours. Dissolve flour in ¹/₄ cup of cold water, and stir into simmering mixture. Cook for 2 more minutes.

Variation

Tofu stew soup: In place of 1 onion, sauté 3 large diced onions in 3-4 tablespoons of oil. In place of goulash meat, add 1 pound of cubed tofu.

Soups, pot roasts and even stews can be prepared early in the day, refrigerated, or frozen for half an hour before removing the fat.

Leah's Vegetable Soup

This rich, pareve soup is made with a variety of shredded vegetables. Good for diet-watchers.

2 large onions, diced
2 cloves garlic
3-4 tablespoons butter or oil
3 carrots, shredded
2 zucchini, shredded
1 bay leaf
2 stalks celery, thinly sliced or diced
7 cups water
1 medium potato, shredded
2 teaspoons salt
$1/8$ - $1/4$ teaspoon pepper, to taste
dash of onion powder
$1/4$ cup uncooked rice, optional
$1/2$ cup raw peas

In a stainless steel pot, sauté onions and garlic in butter or oil until soft. Stir in carrots, zucchini, bay leaf, and celery. Sauté for an additional 10 minutes until vegetables are nearly tender. Add water and remaining ingredients except peas and bring to a boil. Lower heat, cover, and simmer for 30 minutes. Add peas during last 5 minutes of cooking to retain their color. Serves 8.

Variation

This soup can be varied in a multitude of ways. Omit rice and add $1/2$ cup of fine noodles during last 10 minutes of cooking. For a richer flavor, add 1-2 teaspoons of pareve chicken soup powder, reducing the amount of salt accordingly. Or use other vegetables, such as $2/3$ cup of cut string beans, $1/3$ cup of fresh corn kernels, 1 cup of fresh or canned tomatoes, 1 diced parsnip, or $1/3$ cup shredded cabbage. To thicken, make *einbren* (roux):

Heat 2 tablespoons of oil in a small pan. Stir in 2 tablespoons of flour. Slowly stir in $1/2$ cup of the vegetable soup until smooth. Cook for 1 minute and return mixture to pot of soup.

Whole Grain Vegetable Soup

I use this recipe often. Simple to prepare and healthy to eat. The peas, beans, and barley complement one another to make a complete protein dish. A large quantity can be divided into containers and some of it frozen.

1 large onion, diced
1 bay leaf
3 tablespoons oil
1 cup split peas
$^1/_2$ cup lima beans, soaked overnight in
    water to cover
$^1/_4$ cup barley
10 cups water
3 stalks celery, diced
2 carrots, sliced
1 potato, cubed
2 teaspoons salt
$^1/_2$ teaspoon celery salt
$^1/_4$ teaspoon pepper
$^1/_2$ teaspoon thyme
$^1/_2$ teaspoon basil

Sauté onion and bay leaf in oil until golden. Add split peas, lima beans, barley, and water. Bring to a boil, cover, and simmer for 1 hour. Add remaining ingredients, cover, and cook for 1 more hour. Serves 8.

Barley Mushroom Soup

In the Eastern European shtetl, this recipe was made with dried mushrooms and relished by everyone. A warming and tasty soup for a winter evening.

1 large onion, diced
1 bay leaf, crumbled
3 tablespoons margarine
$^1/_2$ pound fresh mushrooms, sliced
2 tablespoons flour, sifted
8 cups water
$^2/_3$ cup pearl barley, cleaned and rinsed
    in a colander
1 stalk celery, diced
1 carrot, diced
2 teaspoons salt, or to taste
$^1/_4$ teaspoon pepper

Sauté onion and bay leaf in margarine until tender. Add mushrooms and sauté until onions are golden. Push vegetables aside and stir in flour until smooth. Gradually stir in water. Add remaining ingredients. Bring to a boil and simmer for $1^1/_2$-2 hours. Serves 8.

Variation

For a hearty meat soup, add $1^1/_2$ portions of flanken with water, and cook as above.

Potato Soup

A good old-fashioned recipe.

2 large onions, diced
1 clove garlic, minced
4 tablespoons butter or margarine
3 tablespoons flour
6 cups water
3 medium potatoes, cubed
2 teaspoons salt
$1/4$ teaspoon pepper, or to taste

Sauté onions and garlic in butter or margarine until golden. Stir in flour until smooth. Slowly stir in water, while cooking, until smooth. Add remaining ingredients, cover, and simmer for 25 minutes. If desired, serve with grated cheese sprinkled onto each portion. Serves 8.

Variations

Vichyssoise: Sauté 3 medium-sized cleaned and chopped leeks and use only one onion. Blend all ingredients in a blender or food processor after cooking.

Potato carrot soup: Add 2 sliced medium-sized carrots.

Potato spinach soup: Stir in 1 10-ounce package of frozen spinach during last 10 minutes of cooking.

Potato mushroom soup: Add 1 cup of sliced mushrooms after onions and garlic are tender and sauté for 10-15 minutes.

Spinach soup: Omit potatoes. After cooking for 5 minutes, add 1 10-ounce package of frozen spinach. Cook for another 10 minutes. For a lighter, cream-colored soup, sauté onions until just tender instead of golden brown.

Mint Pea Soup with Pareve "Buttered" Croutons

Try this unusual pea soup with mint flavor for a cold winter night.

2 large onions, diced
2 tablespoons margarine
6 cups water
1 pound fresh or frozen green peas, shelled
$1^{1}/_{2}$ teaspoons salt, or to taste
generous pinch of white pepper
$1/8$ teaspoon sugar
1 teaspoon dried mint, crushed
1 tablespoon cornstarch, diluted in $1/4$ cup cold water

In a large soup pot, sauté onions in margarine over medium heat until tender. Add water, peas, and remaining ingredients. Cover and simmer for 15-20 minutes or until peas are tender. Let cool and purée mixture in a blender or food processor. Heat and serve with Pareve "Buttered" Croutons.

Pareve "Buttered" Croutons
3-4 slices dry challah or white bread, cut into $1/2$-inch cubes
2-3 tablespoons margarine
$1/2$ teaspoon garlic powder, optional

Sauté bread cubes in melted margarine until golden and crisp on all sides. If desired, sprinkle with garlic powder before frying.

Instant Pea Soup

Excellent flavor!

1 can green peas
2^1/$_2$ cups water
salt and pepper, to taste
1 clove garlic, minced

Combine all ingredients in a blender or food processor. Blend until smooth, and transfer to a pot, bringing mixture to a boil. Gradually, in a steady stream, pour Egg Drops (see page 70) into simmering soup. Cook for 2-3 minutes. Serves 6.

Salvage a salty soup by adding a large, cut-up potato or a teaspoon sugar.

Sweet and Sour Hot Cabbage Borscht

Cabbage is praised in the Talmud for its medicinal and nutritive values. Today, we recognize that it is full of vitamin C. This is a tangy and hearty soup.

1^1/$_2$ pounds flank steak (flanken)
8 cups water
1 medium head cabbage, shredded
1 15-ounce can stewed tomatoes
^{1}/$_3$ - ^{1}/$_2$ cup brown or white sugar, to taste
4 ounces tomato sauce
1 teaspoon salt
juice of 1 lemon

Place meat and water in a large soup pot. Cover and simmer for 1 hour. Add remaining ingredients and simmer for an additional 1^1/$_2$ hours. Flavor improves when soup is refrigerated overnight and fat is skimmed off the top. Serves 10-12.

Variation

For a heartier version, add ^{1}/$_3$ cup of uncooked rice during last ^{1}/$_2$ hour of cooking; or add ^{1}/$_2$ cup of raisins with remaining ingredients.

Fish Chowder

This chowder is like a kosher bouillabaisse.

1 pound fish fillets (cod, halibut,
    flounder, mackerel, or whitefish) cut
    into 1¹/₂-inch cubes
2 large onions, diced
2 stalks celery, diced
¹/₂ green pepper, seeded and cubed
2 tablespoons oil
5 cups water
2 medium potatoes, cut into 1-inch
    cubes
1 medium carrot, sliced
2 medium zucchini, sliced into ¹/₂-inch
    pieces
1 teaspoon salt
¹/₈ teaspoon pepper
¹/₄ teaspoon thyme, optional

Check the fish carefully for bones.
Set aside. In a large pot, sauté
onions, celery, and green pepper in
oil for 15 minutes. Add water,
potatoes, carrots, zucchini, and
seasonings. Bring to a boil, then
reduce heat, cover, and simmer for 10
minutes. Add pieces of fish and cook
for another 20 minutes. Serves 6.

Kreplach

*Kreplach are like Jewish ravioli. These
delectable filled dumplings are usually
added to soups (especially chicken soup).
They can also be eaten as a side dish,
boiled, sautéed in margarine, or fried and
served with Onion Sauce. Fruit kreplach,
such as cherry varnikas, make a good side
dish. Meat kreplach are often served on
Purim, Erev Yom Kippur, or Hoshanah
Rabbah, while the cheese variety is popular
on Shavuot or Chanukah.*

Classic Kreplach Dough

2 eggs
3-4 tablespoons water
¹/₂ teaspoon salt
pinch of white pepper
2 tablespoons oil
2 cups flour, sifted

Beat eggs, adding water, salt,
pepper and oil. Stir in flour. Mix
until smooth and soft. Add a little
flour if too sticky. Knead for 5
minutes. Cover and let rest for at
least 20 minutes. Divide into 3 parts.
Roll out each part into a rectangle ¹/₈
inch thick. Cut into 3-inch squares or
circles and place a teaspoonful of
filling in center. Fold diagonally to
make a triangle. Wet edges with cold
water or egg white and pinch to seal.
To cook, drop gently into a large pot
of boiling salted water or soup and
simmer for 15-20 minutes. Serve in
soup, or fry in oil and serve as a side
dish with Onion Sauce. Yields 30
kreplach.

Spinach Kreplach Dough or Noodles:
To make spinach kreplach dough,
omit water and oil and add ¼ cup of
chopped, cooked spinach, drained
and squeezed out. Knead for 3
minutes. Let rest for 10 minutes. Roll
out into rectangles ⅛ inch thick.
Proceed as directed. For green
spinach noodles, roll very thinly. Let
dry and cut into thin strips with a
sharp knife.

Kreplach Fillings and Accompaniments

Meat Kreplach Filling
1 medium onion, diced
1 clove garlic, minced
2 tablespoons oil
2½ cups cooked chicken, beef, or
   liver, diced or ground
⅛ teaspoon pepper
pinch of cinnamon

In a large skillet, sauté onion and
garlic in oil over medium heat until
tender. Add meat and seasonings and
cook for 10 minutes while stirring.

Savory Cheese Kreplach Filling
1½ pounds farmer cheese
½ cup grated cheddar cheese
2 tablespoons melted margarine
2 eggs, beaten
2 tablespoons chopped onion

Mix all ingredients together
thoroughly. Fill dough and seal.
Boil for 15-20 minutes, then fry in oil.

Sweet Cheese Kreplach Filling
1½ pounds farmer cheese
4 tablespoons sugar
2 tablespoons melted margarine
½ teaspoon cinnamon
⅛ teaspoon salt
2 eggs, beaten
1 teaspoon grated lemon rind

Mix all ingredients together
thoroughly. Fill dough and seal.

Cherry Kreplach (Varnikas)
¾ cup cherry juice
2 tablespoons cornstarch
1½ cups pitted cherries (or blueberries)
oil, for frying

Combine juice and cornstarch in a
saucepan. Cook while stirring
until thickened. Stir in cherries (or
blueberries) and cook for another
minute. Fill dough and seal. Boil for
15 minutes, then fry in oil.

Onion Sauce
2 large onions, diced
4 tablespoons oil
2 tablespoons flour, sifted
1 cup water
½ teaspoon salt
¼ teaspoon white pepper
pinch of cinnamon, optional
⅓ cup grated cheddar cheese, optional

Sauté onions in oil until golden,
stirring occasionally. Stir in flour
until smooth. Continue stirring and
pour in water. Cook until thickened.
Stir in remaining ingredients, adding
cheese, if desired, to serve with dairy
kreplach. Yields 1¼ cups.

Egg Drops for Soup

A quick and easy-to-prepare accompaniment to chicken, vegetable, or creamed soups.

1 large egg
$^1/_8$ teaspoon salt
pinch of pepper
4 tablespoons flour, sifted
2 tablespoons cold water

With a fork, beat egg, salt, and pepper. Stir in flour until smooth. Gradually stir in cold water. Pour mixture into soup gradually from a tablespoon. Cook for 5 minutes. Enough for 3-4 quarts of soup.

To absorb soup fat, place a piece of tissue paper or lettuce on the surface of soup, then remove and discard it.

Cold Beet Borscht

Years ago, housewives kept on hand a barrel of Russel borscht—large quantities of beets left to ferment in water for three or four weeks. Skimming off the white froth on top, they took out what was needed for that day. It was heated up with an onion or sugar—the sourness slightly diluted by the water—or used as a pot liquid for brisket. This version is much simpler, but just as colorful and tasty.

2 pounds young beets
$2^1/_2$ quarts water
$^1/_2$ teaspoon salt
$^1/_8$ teaspoon pepper
juice of 1 large lemon (or $1^1/_2$ medium lemons)
$^1/_4$ cup sugar, or to taste
2 egg yolks
sour cream, for garnish, optional

Wash, peel, and cut beets into quarters. Add water, salt, and pepper. Bring to a boil. Cover and simmer for 30 minutes (or more if the beets are not young). Remove cover during last 5 minutes of cooking to retain red color. Add lemon juice and sugar and cook for 2 more minutes. Remove beets. Beat egg yolks, blending in a few tablespoons of beet liquid. Stir egg mixture into pot. Shred $^1/_4$ or $^1/_2$ of the beets and return to the pot, if desired. Chill. Serve cold with a heaped tablespoon of sour cream. Serves 8.

Shavuot Strawberry Soup

Shavuot is the season when luscious strawberries ripen, and the time for dairy meals. This fresh soup is different and delightful for the holiday. A gourmet recipe.

1 quart fresh strawberries, checked and hulled, or 1 10-ounce package frozen strawberries
2 cups water
1 cup orange juice
1/2 6-ounce can frozen apple juice or cherry juice, or 1/4 cup sugar
1/4 teaspoon cinnamon
1/2 cup sweet red wine
2 tablespoons cornstarch, dissolved in 1/8 cup water
1 cup plain yogurt or sour cream

Set aside 6 whole strawberries for garnish. In a pot, combine remaining strawberries with remaining ingredients except cornstarch and yogurt. Cover and bring to a boil. Reduce heat and simmer for 5 minutes. Stir dissolved cornstarch into simmering mixture until thickened. If desired, pureée in a food processor or blender. Chill thoroughly. When ready to serve, stir in yogurt or sour cream. Serves 6.

Variations

Without cooking: Place all ingredients, except cornstarch and yogurt or sour cream, in a food processor or blender. Blend until smooth. Stir in yogurt or sour cream, and blend thoroughly. Chill.

Cherry soup: Instead of strawberries, use 2-3 cups of fresh pitted cherries (or a 16-ounce can of sweet red cherries) and a 3 1/2-ounce can of mandarin oranges, with juice. Proceed as for cooked or uncooked strawberry soup. (If a food processor or blender is used, remember to use pitted cherries.)

Refreshing Summer Gazpacho

A chilled soup made with blended raw vegetables, with a tomato base.

2 large tomatoes, cubed
4 cups tomato juice
1 medium cucumber
1 medium onion, cubed
2 cloves garlic
1 small green pepper, seeded and cubed
$^1/_4$ teaspoon salt, or to taste
$^1/_8$ teaspoon pepper
$^1/_2$ teaspoon oregano
2 tablespoons lemon juice
2 tablespoons olive oil
$^1/_2$ cup water
green onions or green peppers, for garnish, optional

Blend all ingredients in a food processor or blender. Chill. Stir well and serve with chopped green onions or green peppers, or pour over ice cubes. Serves 6.

Summertime Fruit Soup

A delightful cold soup with a sweet taste, which can be made without sugar.

3 cups fresh fruits, diced (apricots, apples, peaches, plums, cantaloupes, or strawberries)
6 cups water
$^1/_2$ can (or more) frozen apple juice concentrate, or $^1/_4$ cup sugar or honey, or to taste
$^1/_3$ cup raisins
$^1/_4$ teaspoon cinnamon, optional
2 tablespoons cornstarch, mixed into $^1/_4$ cup cold water

Combine all ingredients except cornstarch in a large pot. Bring to a boil, cover, and simmer over low heat for 1 hour. Stir cornstarch and water into simmering mixture. Cook for an additional 5 minutes. Let cool and refrigerate. Serve cold and garnish with a tablespoon of sour cream or whipped cream.

French Onion Soup

Both cooked and raw onions have been found to help dissolve blood clots, and to alleviate certain heart disorders.

4-5 large onions, thinly sliced
4 tablespoons butter or vegetable oil
1 teaspoon sugar
4 tablespoons flour
6 cups water
1$^1/_2$-2 teaspoons salt, to taste
$^1/_4$ teaspoon pepper
2 teaspoons soup powder, or 2 soup cubes
3 slices cheddar or Swiss cheese, cut into halves, or $^1/_2$ cup grated Parmesan cheese

Sauté onions in butter or oil until golden brown. Add sugar. Push onions aside and stir in flour until smooth. Gradually stir in 1 cup of water until smooth. Add remaining water and seasonings, cover, and simmer for 20 minutes. Place a half slice of cheese in each bowl—or sprinkle the Parmesan cheese into each bowl—and ladle hot soup over cheese. If ovenproof bowls are used, put them in the oven or under the broiler for a few minutes to partly melt the cheese. Serves 6.

Poultry

Poultry

Winning Ways with Roast Chicken

This is my favorite way of preparing roast chicken. Marvelous at the Shabbat table!

pinch of salt
1/2 teaspoon pepper
2-3 cloves garlic, minced, or 1 teaspoon
   garlic powder
2/3 teaspoon cinnamon
1 3 1/2-pound chicken
paprika, for sprinkling
1 onion, thinly sliced

Combine salt, pepper, garlic, and cinnamon. Clean chicken well. Leave whole, or cut into quarters. Rub mixture well into all parts of the chicken. Refrigerate for at least an hour or overnight. Place in a small roasting pan. Sprinkle with paprika. Scatter onion slices around chicken, and roast uncovered in a preheated 400° oven for 35 minutes. Reduce heat to 350°, stir onion slices, add a cup of water, and continue roasting for an additional 50 minutes until tender. Baste occasionally.

Exotic Sauces

Tangy Apricot Sauce
2 tablespoons apricot jam
2 tablespoons ketchup
2 tablespoons lemon juice
2 tablespoons mayonnaise
2 tablespoons powdered onion soup mix

Bring ingredients to a boil. Cook for 1 minute. Let cool and pour over chicken quarters. Bake uncovered in a 350° oven for 1 1/2 hours.

Sweet and Sour Sauce
1/2 cup ketchup
1/3 cup brown sugar

Sprinkle chicken with garlic powder. Combine sauce ingredients and pour over chicken. Cover and roast in a 350° oven for 35 minutes. Remove cover and roast for an additional 40- 50 minutes until tender.

Honey-Mustard Sauce
4 tablespoons honey
2 tablespoons prepared mustard
3-4 apples, peeled and cubed

Combine honey and mustard. Rub over inside and outside of chicken. Add apples to roasting pan. Cover and roast in a 350° oven for 40 minutes; then uncover and bake for an additional 35 minutes or until tender.

Italian Marinade
1 cup Italian dressing
1 cup seasoned bread crumbs

Marinate quartered chicken in Italian dressing for 2 hours or overnight, turning chicken 2 or 3 times. Dip in bread crumbs. Bake uncovered in a 350° oven for 1 1/2 hours.

Cranberry-Onion Sauce

Combine 1 can of whole cranberries with 1 envelope of onion soup mix and pour over chicken in pan.

Southern Fried Chicken

Serve it with a fresh salad—a refreshing summer meal.

1 cup flour
1 teaspoon baking powder
salt, to taste
¼ teaspoon pepper
½ teaspoon garlic powder
1 teaspoon paprika
1 3½-pound chicken
oil for frying

Mix together flour, baking powder, salt, pepper, garlic powder, and paprika. Dredge pieces of chicken in flour mixture. Fry in hot oil, about 1½ inches deep, on both sides until golden brown. Reduce heat and continue cooking on both sides for about 35-40 minutes until tender.

Spring chickens and fryers have less fat than large soup chickens.

Chicken with Almonds and Prunes

I enjoyed this dish, which was served boneless, at a buffet dinner at the Jerusalem Plaza Hotel honoring the former U.S. ambassador to Israel, Samuel Lewis. A top-of-the-stove dish with a Mediterranean flavor. The bite-size pieces of chicken make this ideal for buffets.

½ teaspoon cinnamon
¼ teaspoon ground ginger
⅛ teaspoon salt, optional
¼ teaspoon pepper
2 pounds boneless chicken breasts, or a
   3½-pound chicken, cut into 2-inch
   pieces
3 tablespoons oil
1 large onion, diced
1 cup pitted prunes
¼ cup honey or apricot jam
juice of 1 lemon
1 cup orange juice
½ cup roasted blanched almonds,
   halved or whole

Combine cinnamon, ginger, salt, and pepper. Sprinkle on chicken pieces, coating well. Heat oil in a large skillet and sauté onion until golden. Add the seasoned chicken pieces and cook on all sides. Add remaining ingredients except almonds. Cover and cook over low heat for 40 minutes or until chicken is tender, stirring occasionally. Stir in almonds, reserving some for top. Serve hot as a main course with fluffy rice, or as an appetizer. Serves 6 as a main course, 8 as an appetizer.

Boneless Breast of Chicken with Mock Chestnut Dressing

An elegant dish. Serve it on that special occasion. One of the popular items on our bill of fare when we were in the catering business in Chicago. Whole bran gives this recipe a chestnut flavor. It can be made in the oven or on top of the stove.

6 chicken breasts
2 cloves garlic, crushed
$1/4$ teaspoon pepper
pinch of salt
6 green or red pepper rings, for garnish
6 mushroom caps, for garnish

Top-of-the-Stove Method
1 large onion, diced
1 bay leaf
1 small green pepper, diced
4 tablespoons oil
$2/3$ cup water
2 teaspoons chicken soup powder, or 2
    bouillon cubes
2 tablespoons flour, for thickening

Stuffing
$1^3/4$ cups bread crumbs
1 cup diced onions
1 carrot, grated
2 stalks celery, diced
$1/8$ teaspoon pepper
$1/8$ teaspoon salt
2 tablespoons margarine
$1/4$ cup whole bran
$1/2$ cup fresh or frozen peas

Flatten chicken breasts with a mallet or your palm. Rub with garlic, pepper, and salt. Let stand to absorb flavors while preparing stuffing. Combine all stuffing ingredients. Place 2 heaped tablespoons of stuffing in center of each chicken breast. Wrap chicken around stuffing and shape into an oval.

Top-of-the-Stove Method: In a Dutch oven, or a skillet with a cover, sauté onion, bay leaf, and green pepper in oil until onion is tender. Add stuffed breasts, seam side down, and cook uncovered over medium heat for 15 minutes. Add water and soup powder or bouillon cubes. Cover and simmer for about 15 more minutes. Thicken gravy by dissolving flour in cold water and stirring into pan until thickened and smooth. Baste breasts 2-3 times. Place a pepper ring and a mushroom cap on top of each breast. Cover and cook over low heat for an additional 15 minutes.

Oven Method: Roast stuffed breasts, seam side down, uncovered in a preheated 375° oven for 20 minutes. Top each breast with a pepper ring and a mushroom cap, and continue roasting for 20-30 more minutes. Baste occasionally. Serves 6.

Shake and Bake Chicken

A delicious and quick recipe. The chicken is just as good eaten cold the next day. Make it with or without sesame seeds.

$1/2$ **cup bread crumbs**
$1/3$ **cup flour**
$1/2$ **teaspoon garlic powder**
$1/2$ **teaspoon onion powder**
$3/4$ **teaspoon paprika**
$1/4$ **teaspoon pepper**
$1/2$ **teaspoon sugar**
$1/4$ **teaspoon salt**
$1/4$ **cup sesame seeds, optional**
1 3-pound chicken, cut into quarters or eighths

Place all ingredients except chicken into a plastic bag. Place chicken pieces, a few at a time, into bag and shake until well coated. Place chicken pieces in a large greased baking pan, skin side up. Bake uncovered in a preheated 400° oven for 45-50 minutes. Serves 4.

For better tasting fowl, cook within 10 to 24 hours after slaughtering.

Fresh poultry should not be kept in a refrigerator for more than a day or two before cooking.

Chicken Kiev

Chicken Kiev was brought by the Russians to America and Israel. A festive way to prepare chicken breasts and easy to eat because the chicken is boneless. In planning this dish, allow at least 1 hour for the seasoned margarine to firm in the freezer.

$2/3$ **cup margarine, softened**
3 tablespoons chopped scallions
2 tablespoons chopped parsley
2 cloves garlic, minced
$1/4$ **teaspoon pepper**
$1/2$ **teaspoon salt**
8 chicken breasts, skinned and boned
8 toothpicks
1 cup matzo meal
1 egg, beaten together with 2 tablespoons water
oil, for deep-frying

Combine margarine with scallions, parsley, garlic, pepper, and salt. Freeze for 1 hour until firm, then divide into 8 cubes. Place each chicken breast between 2 pieces of waxed paper and pound to $1/4$-inch thickness. Place a seasoned margarine cube in center of each chicken breast. Wrap breast around cube to completely cover it. Fasten with a toothpick. Dip in matzo meal, then in egg-water mixture, then again in matzo meal. Deep-fry in oil until golden brown. Remove toothpicks before serving. Serves 8.

Broiled Chicken with Wine and Mushrooms

Elegant, and easy!

1 3-pound spring chicken, cut into
  quarters or eighths
2 tablespoons lemon juice
$^1/_2$ teaspoon garlic powder
$^1/_2$ teaspoon cinnamon, optional
salt and pepper, to taste

Sauce
1 medium onion, diced
2 tablespoons oil
$^1/_4$ pound fresh mushrooms, sliced
$^1/_4$ cup dry white wine

Rub chicken with lemon juice. Sprinkle with garlic powder, cinnamon, salt, and pepper. Broil chicken under the broiler for about 15 minutes per side. Meanwhile, sauté onion in oil until soft. Add mushrooms and sauté for an additional 5 minutes. Add wine and chicken pieces. Cover and simmer over low heat for about 15-20 minutes. Serves 4.

Variations

Flambé chicken: Place chicken on a platter. Before serving, pour 1 ounce of warmed brandy, combined with 1 teaspoon of sugar, over chicken. Light brandy with a match.

Sliced zucchini, carrots, or other vegetables can be added in addition to the mushrooms, wine, and chicken pieces. Prepare as directed above.

Barbecued Chickenburgers

Economical and relatively low in cholesterol, these tasty patties make a good dish for chol hamoed Sukkot. They're juicy and delicious.

1 pound ground chicken
1 medium onion, chopped
1 medium zucchini, shredded
1 medium carrot, shredded
2 cloves garlic, crushed
2 tablespoons ketchup
2 eggs, beaten
$^1/_2$ cup matzo meal
salt and pepper, to taste

Combine all ingredients. Let stand for 10 minutes. Form into patties, top with Barbecue Sauce, and broil or fry on both sides until golden brown, basting often. Serves 4-5.

Barbecue Sauce
3 tomatoes, chopped
2 tablespoons vinegar
2 tablespoons brown sugar
2 tablespoons prepared chili sauce, or
  $^1/_3$ cup ketchup
1-2 teaspoons prepared mustard
salt and pepper, to taste
3-4 tablespoons water

Simmer all ingredients in a saucepan for 5 minutes. Let cool before pouring over chickenburgers.

Schnitzel

A long-time favorite for holidays and other special occasions like weddings or bar mitzvahs. Any leftovers make great sandwiches. The sugar in the batter keeps the breading from falling off and enhances the flavor of the meat.

1 cup matzo meal
salt, to taste
$^1/_4$ teaspoon pepper
2 cloves garlic, minced
2 eggs
$^1/_2$ teaspoon sugar
$^1/_4$ cup water
1$^1/_2$ pounds boneless chicken or turkey breasts, cut into 6 slices and pounded to $^1/_4$-inch thickness
$^1/_4$ cup oil

Combine matzo meal with salt, pepper, and garlic. Beat eggs together with sugar and water. Dip each chicken or turkey slice in seasoned matzo meal, then in egg mixture, then again in matzo meal. Fry in hot oil over medium-high heat for 5-10 minutes per side until golden brown. Drain on absorbent paper. Serve hot. If desired, top with Mushroom Sauce. Serves 6.

Mushroom Sauce
1 medium onion, diced
3 tablespoons oil
$^1/_2$ cup canned mushrooms, or 1 cup fresh mushrooms, sliced
2$^1/_2$ tablespoons flour
1$^1/_2$ cups chicken soup, or 1 bouillon cube dissolved in a cup of boiling water
salt and pepper, to taste

Sauté onion in oil until tender. Stir in mushrooms and sauté for 5 more minutes. Stir in flour until smooth. Slowly add chicken soup, salt, and pepper, and cook until thickened while stirring. Place fried, breaded schnitzel in a 7x11-inch baking dish. Pour sauce on top, cover, and bake in a preheated 350° oven for 20 minutes, or cover and simmer on top of stove for 15-20 minutes.

Baked Schnitzel

The combination of mayonnaise and ketchup adds a delicious flavor to these thin slices of chicken or turkey, dipped in bread crumbs and baked.

**2 pounds chicken or turkey schnitzel
    slices**
$1/2$ cup mayonnaise
$1/2$ cup ketchup
$2/3$ cup bread crumbs

Flatten schnitzel by pounding on both sides with a mallet. Combine mayonnaise and ketchup. Dip schnitzel in mixture, then in bread crumbs. Place on a greased, 10x17 inch cookie sheet. Bake in a 375° oven for 20-30 minutes. Serves 6-8.

A 3-pound chicken, cooked, will make 2$1/2$ cups diced chicken for chicken salad or creamed chicken, etc. A 5-pound chicken will make 4$1/2$ cups diced or cubed chicken.

Chicken Chow Mein

A delightful and versatile recipe.

2 medium onions, sliced
3 stalks celery, sliced diagonally
4 tablespoons oil
1 can bean sprouts
**$1/2$ cup canned button mushrooms, or
    $1/3$ pound fresh mushrooms, sliced**
$1/2$ cup water chestnuts
$2/3$ cup chicken soup
$1/4$ cup soy sauce
**$1^1/2$-2 cups cooked chicken, cut into
    bite-size pieces**
2 tablespoons cornstarch
$2/3$ cup toasted almonds, optional
3 cups hot cooked rice

Sauté onions and celery in oil until onions are tender. Rinse bean sprouts in cold water, drain well, and add to sautéed onions and celery. Add mushrooms and water chestnuts and stir-fry for about 2 minutes. Add chicken soup and soy sauce and mix well. Stir in chicken pieces. Cover and cook for 20 minutes. Combine cornstarch with a little cold water and stir into simmering mixture. Cook for 5 more minutes. Serve with almonds and hot rice. Serves 6-8.

Variation

Veal or beef can be used instead of chicken.

Rock Cornish Hens

Cornish hens are small enough to serve a whole one per person. Garnish with a cherry in the middle of a pineapple slice, attached with a fancy toothpick, or as directed below. Cover the ends of the legs with paper frills to dress up this novelty dish. (Pigeons, the counterparts of these tiny hens, are often served to the bride and groom at Jewish weddings.)

6 Rock Cornish hens (about 1 pound each)
2-3 cloves garlic, crushed
$^1/_3$ teaspoon pepper
$^1/_2$ teaspoon salt, or to taste
1 teaspoon paprika
Chicken Liver Stuffing (see page 88)
3 tablespoons honey
juice of 1 lemon
1 cup orange juice
cranberry sauce, for garnish
lemon slices, for garnish
parsley, for garnish

Tie legs of each hen together, close to the body. Combine garlic, pepper, salt, and paprika. Rub mixture on inside and outside of hens. Refrigerate for at least 1 hour. Add stuffing. Place hens in a roasting pan. Brush with honey combined with lemon juice. Roast uncovered in a preheated 350° oven for about 1 hour, basting occasionally. Add orange juice to pan midway through roasting. To serve, arrange on a platter and garnish with cranberry sauce, lemon slices, and parsley. Serves 6.

Turkey Goulash

If you want to avoid red meat, make this goulash instead. Just like an old-fashioned stew—with turkey instead of beef.

1 large onion, sliced
2 cloves garlic, crushed
4 tablespoons oil
2 pounds boneless dark turkey, cut into 1$^1/_2$-inch cubes
salt and pepper, to taste
1 teaspoon paprika
$^1/_4$ pound mushrooms, sliced
2 medium carrots, cut into chunks
2 stalks celery, sliced
3 medium potatoes, cubed
1$^1/_2$ cups water
4 tablespoons ketchup
2 tablespoons cornstarch

Sauté onion and garlic in oil over medium heat until transparent. Add turkey cubes, salt, pepper, and paprika, and sear on all sides. Cover and cook over low heat for 30 minutes. Add remaining ingredients. Cover and simmer for about 1 hour until turkey is tender. If stew is too thick, add a little water; if too thin, stir in 1-2 tablespoons of cornstarch dissolved in an additional $^1/_4$ cup of water, and cook for 10 more minutes. Serves 6-8.

Variation

Add 1 can of whole, jelled cranberries and juice of 1-2 lemons. Cover and cook for 10 more minutes.

Roast Turkey

Roast turkey is a popular dish when entertaining a large group for a special dinner. Roasting time is 25 minutes per pound for a stuffed turkey, or 20 minutes per pound for an unstuffed turkey.

1 12-pound turkey
3 cloves garlic, minced, or 1-1$^1/_2$
    teaspoons garlic powder
salt, to taste
$^1/_2$ teaspoon pepper
1 teaspoon paprika
$^1/_2$ teaspoon cinnamon
oil, for brushing turkey
triple portion stuffing (see pages 88-89)
2 cups water

Glaze (optional)
$^1/_3$ cup orange marmalade
4 tablespoons lemon juice
1 tablespoon tamari sauce

Garnish
orange slices
clusters of grapes, or kumquats

Combine seasonings and rub on inside and outside of turkey. Refrigerate for at least 2 hours or overnight for seasonings to penetrate. Tie turkey legs together and fasten wings to sides. Brush turkey with oil. Stuff loosely with a triple portion of stuffing. Roast turkey, breast side up, uncovered in a preheated 325° oven for 1$^1/_2$ hours. Combine ingredients for glaze and brush over turkey. Add 2 cups of water to pan (with part orange juice, if desired). Roast for an additional 2$^1/_2$-3 hours, basting 3-4 times. When the drumstick pulls away easily from body, turkey is done. If turkey becomes too brown, cover with a tent of aluminum foil during last $^1/_2$ hour. Remove turkey from oven and let stand for 20 minutes before slicing. Serve with garnish. Serves 14-15.

Variation

Add 1 can of whole-cranberry sauce to your favorite stuffing recipe.

A young, small turkey has half the calories per pound of a mature, fat one.

Turkey is the most perishable fowl and also the leanest. When serving a large crowd it is the most economical.

Roast Duck à l'Orange

This makes an attractive dish. Garnish with thin, string-like orange strips strewn over the duck with the gravy.

1 4¹/₂-5-pound duckling
¹/₂ teaspoon each: garlic powder, salt, pepper, and cinnamon
stuffing (see following recipes)
¹/₂ can frozen orange juice concentrate, or juice of 2 oranges
3 tablespoons honey or orange marmalade
orange rind, cut into thin string-like strips, or 1 tablespoon grated orange rind

Combine seasonings and rub on inside and outside of duckling. Refrigerate for 2 hours or overnight. Stuff duck loosely. Prick skin all over. Place duckling on a rack in a roasting pan. Roast uncovered in a preheated 375° oven for 1¹/₂ hours. Pour off fat. Brush with orange juice and honey or orange marmalade, and continue roasting in a 350° oven for 1 more hour until tender, basting a few times. Pour off gravy, and remove fat. Add orange rind to gravy and heat. Place duck on a serving platter and pour heated gravy on top.

To absorb fat from a chicken or duck, place a peeled apple inside it. Discard apple after roasting.

Stuffings

A tasty basic stuffing recipe, with several variations to make your roast chicken a special dish. Poultry should be stuffed just before putting in oven. Never refrigerate or freeze raw poultry with stuffing inside. Bread crumbs should be dry. Stuff chicken loosely.

1 medium onion, diced
¹/₄ cup oil
1 carrot, grated
1 teaspoon salt
¹/₄ - ¹/₂ teaspoon pepper
1¹/₂ cups bread crumbs
1 large egg, beaten, optional
1 teaspoon oregano, or ¹/₂ teaspoon sage or thyme

Sauté onion in oil until tender. (If desired, onions can be used raw instead of sautéed.) Remove from heat and combine with remaining ingredients. Let cool and stuff chicken loosely. Yields enough stuffing for a 4-pound chicken.

Chicken Liver Stuffing

Add ¹/₂ pound (or more) of broiled (koshered) chicken livers, cut into quarters, to above mixture. Reduce bread crumbs to 1 cup.

Rice and Almond Stuffing

Substitute 2 cups of cooked rice for bread crumbs and stir in ¹/₃ - ¹/₂ cup of toasted slivered almonds or water chestnuts.

Wild Rice and Mushroom Stuffing

In place of bread crumbs, use 2 cups of cooked wild rice combined with 1 cup of sliced fresh mushrooms, sautéed with onion until tender. Add to remaining ingredients.

Prune and Apple Stuffing

Add 1 cup of soaked, pitted prunes, 2 large diced apples, 1/3 cup of raisins, 3 tablespoons of brown sugar, and juice of half a lemon. Reduce bread crumbs to 1 cup. Omit oregano (or sage or thyme).

Carrot Stuffing

Omit oregano. Add 4-5 medium shredded carrots, 2-3 tablespoons of brown sugar, grated rind and juice of half an orange, and 1/2 cup of raisins. Reduce bread crumbs to 1 cup.

Florentine (Spinach) Stuffing

Use 1 10-ounce package of frozen spinach and 1 1/2 cups of rice instead of bread crumbs. Add 1 beaten egg.

Chestnut Stuffing

Add 1 1/2-2 cups of cooked, peeled, and chopped chestnuts. Reduce bread crumbs to about half a cup. To cook chestnuts, cover and simmer in boiling water to cover for 20 minutes. Drain and rinse in cold water. Remove shell, chop coarsely, and add to remaining ingredients.

Cranberry Stuffing

Add 1 can of whole, jelled cranberries. Omit oregano (or sage or thyme).

Ground Meat Stuffing

Reduce bread crumbs to 2/3 cup. Add 1/2 pound of ground raw meat or chicken. Omit carrots and oregano (or sage or thyme).

Salami Stuffing

Dice 1/4 pound of salami—or other sausage—and add to basic stuffing mixture.

Kasha Stuffing

Use 3 cups of cooked kasha instead of bread crumbs. Add 1/2 cup of sliced water chestnuts.

Fruit and Nut Stuffing

1 cup pitted prunes, soaked in hot water for 20 minutes
1 cup dried apricots, soaked in hot water for 20 minutes
1 cup bread crumbs
2 tart apples, cubed
1/2 teaspoon cinnamon
3 tablespoons oil
1/2 cup raisins
2 stalks celery, diced
1 cup broken or coarsely chopped walnuts
salt and pepper, to taste
3 tablespoons brown sugar
1/4 cup water

Combine all ingredients and stuff loosely.

Meat

Meat

MEAT

Pot Roast Supreme

A delicious pot roast with a tantalizing flavor. The secret is in cooking it very slowly on top of the stove.

3 tablespoons onion soup mix
1 4-pound chuck roast
$^1/_4$ cup apricot jam
1 large onion, thickly sliced
2 tablespoons oil
1-2 bay leaves
1 cup water
3 carrots, cut into 2-inch pieces
3 medium potatoes, cut into sixths

Rub onion soup mix into roast. Spread with jam. Sauté onion in oil in a Dutch oven or large pot. Add bay leaves. Sear and roast meat on both sides over medium heat. Cover and cook over very low heat for 45 minutes. Add water, turn the meat, cover, and cook for 1 more hour. Add carrots and potatoes, cover, and continue cooking over low heat for an additional hour until tender. If desired, stir 2-3 tablespoons of matzo meal into gravy and cook for 10 minutes to thicken. Serves 8-10.

Variation

Good old-fashioned pot roast: Omit soup mix and jam. Instead, sprinkle roast generously with garlic powder (or 3 minced garlic cloves) and $^1/_2$ teaspoon of pepper. Refrigerate overnight. Cook as directed.

Potted Beef with Dried Fruit

Dried apricots or prunes, in addition to ginger and cinnamon, enhance the flavor of this easy-to-prepare potted chuck roast. Also try it with shoulder roast.

2 cloves garlic, minced
$^1/_4$ teaspoon pepper
$^1/_4$ teaspoon cinnamon
3 tablespoons flour
$3^1/_2$ pounds boneless chuck roast
1 large onion, sliced
2 tablespoons oil
$1^1/_2$ cups water
1 pound dried prunes or apricots
2 tablespoons honey
$^1/_8$ teaspoon ginger, optional
4 medium potatoes, cut into quarters, optional

Combine garlic, pepper, cinnamon, and flour, and rub into chuck roast. Sauté onion in oil until soft. Add meat and sear over medium-high heat on all sides. Cover and cook over low heat for 30 minutes. Add water and cook over low heat for 1 more hour. Then add apricots or prunes and remaining ingredients. Cover and simmer over low heat for 1 hour or until meat is tender. Serve meat with the dried fruit and gravy. For a thicker gravy, stir in 2-3 tablespoons of matzo meal and cook for 10-15 more minutes. Serves 8-10.

Special Ingredient Shoulder Roast

The special ingredient is Coca Cola, which lends a light caramel taste to the roast.

1 5-pound shoulder roast
4 tablespoons (1 envelope) onion soup mix
²/₃ cup ketchup
1 can Coca Cola

Rub roast well with onion soup mix. Place in a roasting pan. Roast in a preheated 325° oven for 1¹/₂ hours. Turn roast, pour ketchup and Coca Cola over it, and continue roasting uncovered for another 1-1¹/₂ hours until tender, turning once midway.

Variations

Hawaiian roast: Remove roast from oven half an hour before end of cooking time and place 6 half-slices of pineapple on top, with cherries in the center. Fasten with toothpicks. Return to oven and continue cooking (basting a few times) for half an hour. Remove gravy, chill, then remove fat from top of gravy. Heat gravy and thicken, if desired, with 2 tablespoons of matzo meal, and cook over low heat for 10 minutes. Spoon gravy over slices of roast before serving.

With cranberry sauce: Combine 1 16-ounce can of cranberry sauce, 2 tablespoons of onion soup mix, and 1 cup of water. Pour over meat, cover, and roast in a 325° oven for about 3 hours until tender.

Chopped Meat Roulade

A meat roulade is shaped like a jelly roll, with meat on the outside and a layer of mashed potatoes on the inside. An unusual way of preparing chopped meat and a big hit with children. Serve it as an appetizer or as a main dish, with or without sauce.

Meat Layer
1¹/₂ pounds ground beef
2 eggs, beaten
1 medium onion, finely diced
6 tablespoons matzo meal
¹/₈ teaspoon pepper
¹/₄ teaspoon garlic powder

Potato Layer
1 large onion, diced
¹/₂ cup chopped mushrooms
2 tablespoons oil
5 medium potatoes, boiled and mashed
2 eggs, beaten
¹/₂ cup matzo meal
salt, to taste
pepper, to taste

Make the potato filling by sautéing onion and mushrooms in oil until tender. Remove from heat and combine with remaining potato-layer ingredients. Set aside. Combine all ingredients for meat layer and spread evenly on a 9x13-inch sheet of waxed paper. Spread potato filling on top of meat layer. Lifting edge of the paper as a guide, roll as for jelly roll. Place on a greased baking sheet and bake in a preheated 350° oven for 1 hour. Slice and serve hot. For an extra touch, serve with Sweet and Sour Sauce (see page 101) or Mushroom Sauce (see page 84). Serves 6.

Old-Fashioned Beef Stew

Nothing is quite as welcome and satisfying on a wintry night as a bowl of good, old-fashioned beef stew. The meat and vegetables together constitute almost a complete meal. Serve with just a green salad and dessert.

1 large onion, diced
2 stalks celery, sliced into ¹/₂-inch
   pieces
3 tablespoons oil
2 pounds boneless beef, cut into 2-inch
   chunks
salt and pepper, to taste
1¹/₂ cups water
4 tablespoons ketchup
3 large carrots, sliced into ¹/₂-inch
   pieces
2 large potatoes, cut into large cubes
1 bay leaf
1 teaspoon honey
2 medium zucchini, sliced into 1-inch
   pieces
³/₄ cup fresh green peas, optional
2 tablespoons flour, dissolved in ¹/₄ cup
   cold water

In a large, heavy pot, sauté onions and celery in oil over medium heat until onions are tender. Add meat seasoned with salt and pepper. Sear on all sides over medium-high heat. Cook over low heat for 30 minutes, stirring occasionally. Add water and remaining ingredients except zucchini, peas, and flour. Cover and simmer for 1¹/₂-2 hours or until meat is tender. Add zucchini, cover, and cook for an additional 15 minutes. Add peas during last 5 minutes of cooking. Mix flour in water and stir into simmering liquid to thicken gravy. Cook for 10 more minutes. Serves 6.

Variations

Pineapple stew: Add a 10-ounce can of pineapple chunks in addition to zucchini.

Tofu stew: Add 2-3 more sautéed diced onions. Use 1¹/₂ pounds of tofu, cut into 1¹/₂-inch cubes, and proceed as above.

Tougher, leaner cuts of meat can be tenderized or marinated in wine, orange juice or lemon juice before roasting or broiling.

Barbecued Beef "Spareribs"

Bake with sauce, or pre-cook beef spareribs in water to remove some of the fat and make them more palatable.

3 pounds beef spareribs, cut into
    2½-inch pieces
2 tablespoons vinegar
4 tablespoons brown sugar
2 cloves garlic, minced
1 tablespoon prepared mustard
1 cup ketchup
⅓ cup water
1 medium onion, finely chopped
1 tablespoon Worcestershire sauce
salt and pepper, to taste
parsley, for garnish

Preheat oven to 350°. Place beef spareribs in a roasting pan. Combine remaining ingredients for sauce and pour over spareribs. Cover and bake for 1½ hours, stirring occasionally. Remove cover and bake for an additional 30 minutes. Skim off fat. Serve on a platter, garnished with parsley.

Variations

Barbecued lamb riblets: Use 3 pounds of lamb riblets cut into 2½-inch pieces. Proceed as above. Cover and bake for 1 hour. Remove cover and bake for an additional 20 minutes.

Ribs can be simmered in water for 30 minutes, then baked with sauce ingredients for 1 hour.

Meat Balls with Shredded Cabbage

Tastes like stuffed cabbage—without the work of stuffing cabbage! The cranberries add a marvelous flavor.

1 medium cabbage, shredded thickly
⅓ cup uncooked rice

Meat Balls
2½ pounds ground beef or veal
2 large eggs
1 medium onion, chopped
⅔ cup bread crumbs
2 cloves garlic, crushed
pepper, to taste

Sauce
1 cup ketchup
1 8-ounce can tomato sauce
1 16-ounce can whole, jelled
    cranberries
juice of ½ lemon
¼ teaspoon salt
3-4 cups water

Place cabbage, rice, and sauce ingredients in a large pot. Bring to a simmer over low heat. Meanwhile combine meat, eggs, onion, bread crumbs, garlic, and pepper. Form into 1½-inch balls and gently add to simmering sauce. Cover and cook over low heat for 1½ hours. If necessary, add more water. Serves 8-10.

Variation

½ cup of brown sugar or apricot jam can be substituted for cranberries.

Sweet and Sour Meat Balls Gourmet

Great for buffet-style entertaining. This delicious, exotic, sweet and sour sauce can also be used to cook chunks of beef. A gourmet stew.

Meat Balls
1 pound lean ground beef
1 small-medium onion, chopped
1/4 cup ketchup
2 eggs
2 cloves garlic, minced
1/3 cup bread crumbs or matzo meal
1/4 cup water

Sweet and Sour Sauce
1/2 cup ketchup
1/4 teaspoon salt
1/8 teaspoon pepper
1 can Coca Cola
3/4 cup water
1/4 cup apricot jam

Combine all ingredients for meat balls. Form into 1 1/2-inch balls. Combine sauce ingredients and bring to a boil. Gently drop meat balls into simmering pot of sweet and sour sauce and cook for 45 minutes. If necessary, add more water.

Variation

Meat loaf: The ground beef mixture can be shaped into a loaf and baked in a 350° oven for 1 hour. If desired, pour sauce on top before baking. Omit water.

Brisket of Beef

Old-fashioned brisket of beef—with a variation for beer brisket. Tantalizing flavors.

1 5-pound brisket of beef
4 cloves garlic, minced, or 1 teaspoon garlic powder
salt, to taste
1/2 teaspoon pepper
2 bay leaves
1 onion, sliced

Combine garlic, salt, and pepper, and rub into brisket of beef. Refrigerate overnight. Place in a roasting pan. Add bay leaves and onion slices around it. Roast uncovered at 350° for 1 hour. Turn once. Add 1 1/2 cups of water and roast at 325°. Cover and continue roasting for 2 hours or until tender.

Variations

Beer brisket: Bake at 325° for 2 1/2 hours. Add 1 can of beer and 1 cup of chili sauce and roast for 1 more hour.

Barbecue brisket: Combine 1 1/2 cups of ketchup, 1 cup of brown sugar, and 1 tablespoon of soy sauce. Pour over brisket, basting occasionally. After 1 hour of roasting, add 1/2 cup of water, cover and roast at 325° for 2 hours or until tender.

Stuffed Cabbage

Stuffed cabbage can be served as an appetizer or as a main dish. Prepare with either of these sauces.

1 large head of cabbage
1 pound ground meat
1 large egg
$1/4$ cup uncooked rice
salt and pepper, to taste
1 large onion, sliced
brown sugar, to taste

Sauce 1

1 16-ounce can tomato sauce
1 20-ounce can tomatoes
juice of 1 lemon
$1/3$ cup brown sugar, or to taste
$1^1/2$ cups water

Sauce 2

2 cups chili sauce
1 cup grape jelly
juice of 1 lemon
$1^1/2$ cups water

Remove core from cabbage. Separate leaves, check, and cook in water to cover for about 3 minutes to soften leaves. (Alternatively, cabbage leaves can be made pliable by placing in freezer for 24-48 hours.) Drain. Combine meat, egg, rice, and seasonings. Place 2 tablespoons of meat mixture on each cabbage leaf. Roll, tucking in sides. Place onion slices, leftover pieces of cabbage, and sugar in roasting pan. Cover and cook for about 10 minutes. Place stuffed cabbage rolls in roasting pan, close together. Combine sauce ingredients and add to pan. Cover and cook in a preheated 400° oven for 1 hour, or cover and simmer on top of stove in a Dutch oven or large pot for $1^1/2$-2 hours.

Variation

Add a cup of prunes 1 hour before end of cooking time.

For low-cholesterol diets, use ground veal instead of beef.

Tongue Gourmet

This is an old recipe my mother used for holidays and special occasions, especially Simchat Torah and Sukkot. She used the same sauce for meat balls as well as chicken fricasee. Everyone loved it. I've since used it to roast cut-up chicken.

1 4-pound beef tongue
slivered almonds
orange slices, for garnish
parsley, for garnish

Sweet and Sour Sauce
1 medium onion, diced
2 tablespoons vegetable oil
1 cup ketchup
²/₃ cup brown (packed) or white sugar
¹/₃ cup raisins
³/₄ cup water

Cook tongue in a medium-sized covered pot with slightly salted water to cover for about 3 hours until fork tender. Remove from water and let stand for 5-10 minutes. While tongue is still quite hot, peel off skin (cold tongue is difficult to peel). Let cool and slice. To prepare sauce, sauté onion in oil until tender. Add remaining ingredients. Simmer for 2 minutes. Add more sugar, to taste. Add sliced tongue, cover, and cook over low heat for about 20-30 minutes. If sauce is too thin, cook without cover for 10 minutes. To serve, sprinkle with slivered almonds and garnish platter with orange slices and parsley. Serves 8-10.

Roast Beef

Delicious any time.

1 5-pound rib roast
3 cloves garlic, minced, or 1 teaspoon garlic powder
¹/₂ teaspoon pepper
¹/₂ teaspoon salt
¹/₂ teaspoon onion powder
2 rounded tablespoons flour, optional

Combine all seasonings and flour and rub well into roast. Refrigerate for at least 2 hours or overnight for seasonings to penetrate. Place roast—rounded side up—on a rack in an uncovered roasting pan. Roast in a preheated 300° oven, basting occasionally with drippings—2¹/₂ hours for well-done, or according to instructions below. Let stand for about 20 minutes before slicing.

Time needed for roasting:

Rare: 18-20 minutes per pound
Medium: 22-25 minutes per pound
Well-done: 30 minutes per pound

Cranberry Orange Relish
1 pound fresh cranberries
2 oranges, cut into chunks
²/₃ cup walnuts
1¹/₄ cups sugar

Mix first three ingredients in a food processor. Stir in sugar. Refrigerate overnight. Excellent with chicken or cold cuts as well.

Sukiyaki

Small thin slices of beef stir-fried with a variety of Far Eastern vegetables.

$1/4$ cup oil
$1^1/2$ pounds beef, sliced into 2-inch pieces, $1/4$ inch thick
1 large onion, sliced
2 cups celery, sliced diagonally
1 cup scallions, cut into $1^1/2$-inch pieces
2 tablespoons brown sugar
1 cup sliced mushrooms
1 cup bamboo shoots
1 large tomato, thinly sliced
1 cup chicken soup
1 cup broccoli or spinach
2 tablespoons soy sauce
2 tablespoons cornstarch

Heat oil in a wok or skillet, and brown pieces of meat lightly on both sides. Add onion, celery, and scallions, and stir-fry for 5 minutes. Add remaining ingredients except cornstarch, and stir-fry for 5 more minutes. Dilute cornstarch in a little cold water, and stir into mixture. Cook until thickened. Serve with Chinese Fried Rice or plain boiled rice. Serves 4.

Chinese Fried Rice

In a skillet sauté 1 large diced onion and 2 scallions (cut into small pieces) in 4 tablespoons of oil until tender. Add 2 beaten eggs. Cook for about 2 minutes. Add salt, to taste, and $1/4$ teaspoon of pepper, stir in 3 cups of cooked rice and heat through.

Chinese Pepper Steak

A tasty way of preparing steak. The pineapple or kumquats add a special flavor.

2 pounds round or tenderloin steak, cut into $1x2^1/2$-inch pieces
salt and pepper, to taste
$1/4$ cup oil
2 cloves garlic, minced
5 green peppers, cut into strips
2 scallions, sliced
2 cups chicken soup
2 tablespoons soy sauce
$1/3$ cup flour
$1/4$ cup cold water
3-4 cups hot cooked rice

Sprinkle meat with salt and pepper and brown in oil on both sides. Add garlic, green peppers, scallions, and chicken soup. Cover and cook over low heat for about 30-45 minutes until tender. Add soy sauce. Combine flour with cold water and slowly stir into simmering mixture. Cook for a few minutes until thickened. Serve with hot cooked rice.

Variation

Add a cup of pineapple chunks or kumquats and heat before serving.

For less salty meat, soak it in water with 1 cup vinegar. To tenderize meat, soak it in a vinegar-water solution.

MEAT

Roast Shoulder of Lamb with Grape Jelly and Mustard

Your family and guests will have a hard time guessing this unusual combination of ingredients which imparts a delicious taste. If kosher grape jelly is unavailable, cranberry sauce can be substituted, but omit the mustard.

2 cloves garlic, diced
1/2 teaspoon paprika
salt, to taste
1/8 teaspoon black pepper
1/8 teaspoon onion powder
1 5-pound shoulder of lamb
1 large onion, thickly sliced
1 cup water
1/2 cup grape jelly or 1 can cranberry sauce
3 tablespoons Dijon mustard (if using grape jelly)

Combine garlic, paprika, salt, pepper, and onion powder. Rub lamb shoulder with mixture. Place lamb in a roasting pan and scatter onion slices around it. Roast uncovered in a preheated 400° oven for 30 minutes. Lower heat to 325°, add water, and continue cooking for an additional 1 1/2 hours or until tender, turning once. Spread grape jelly and mustard on top. Cover during last 1/2 hour. Pour off drippings, refrigerate them, remove layer of fat, and thicken into a gravy. Serves 10-12.

Stuffed Veal "Birds"

Slices of veal rolled around stuffing and shaped to resemble little birds. The salami in the stuffing gives the veal just the right flavor.

2 medium onions, diced
1 stalk celery, diced
3 tablespoons oil
3-4 slices salami, chopped
1 cup bread crumbs
salt and pepper, to taste
6 slices of raw veal, thinly pounded
toothpicks
1 tablespoon flour
1 cup water
1/4 cup wine

Garnish
6 mushroom caps
6 green pepper rings

Sauté 1 onion and celery in oil until tender. Mix with salami, bread crumbs, salt and pepper. Spread mixture on slices of veal. Roll and fasten with toothpicks. In a skillet, sauté other onion until soft. Place stuffed veal slices—seam side down—in skillet. Brown over medium heat for about 8 minutes. Stir in flour. Add water and wine. Cover and simmer for 35-45 minutes until tender. Place a mushroom cap and a ring of pepper on top of each veal "bird." Serve with thickened gravy spooned on top. Serves 6.

Simply Delicious Veal Roast

Simple to prepare, yet delicious.

2¹/₂-3 pounds veal roast (shoulder or
    round)
¹/₃ teaspoon paprika
¹/₃ teaspoon garlic powder
¹/₄ teaspoon pepper

Sauce
¹/₂ cup pineapple juice
1 rounded tablespoon onion soup
    powder
1 tablespoon soy sauce
2 tablespoons ketchup
1 medium onion, grated

Place roast on a piece of aluminum
foil large enough to wrap over the
meat. Sprinkle with combined
paprika, garlic powder, and pepper.
Combine ingredients for sauce and
pour over roast. Wrap roast tightly in
foil. Place in a small oval roasting
pan. Cook in a preheated 375° oven
for about 2 hours until tender. Serves
6-8.

*To improve flavor of veal or lamb roast, rub
it with a little ginger, cinnamon or nutmeg.*

Potted Veal Roast

A succulent, top-of-the-stove pot roast.

pinch of salt
¹/₄ teaspoon pepper
2 cloves garlic, minced
¹/₄ teaspoon nutmeg
1 3¹/₂-pound boneless veal shoulder (or
    other veal roast)
1 medium onion, diced
1¹/₂ tablespoons oil
¹/₂ cup water or dry wine
1 bay leaf
4 carrots, cut into 1¹/₂-inch pieces
1 green pepper, cut into 1-inch pieces
2 stalks celery, cut into large pieces
3 medium potatoes, quartered

Combine salt, pepper, garlic, and
nutmeg, and rub into veal roast.
Sauté onion in oil until soft. Add
meat and brown quickly on all sides
over medium-high heat. Lower heat,
cover, and simmer for about 20
minutes. Add water or wine, bay leaf,
carrots, green pepper, and celery.
Cover and cook over low heat for 2
hours or until tender. Add potatoes
(and, if necessary, a little water)
during last hour. Serves 8.

*For tastier lamb or veal chops or other
meats, marinate in French dressing or garlic
powder.*

Veal Roast with Honey-Mustard Sauce

The combination of honey and mustard enhances the flavor of this veal roast.

2 cloves garlic, minced
pinch of salt
$^1/_4$ teaspoon pepper
2 tablespoons flour
1 4-pound veal shoulder
2 tablespoons honey
2 tablespoons prepared mustard or
   lemon juice
1 large onion, thickly sliced
1 bay leaf
1 cup water

Combine garlic, salt, pepper, and flour. Rub veal shoulder well with mixture. Refrigerate for several hours or overnight if possible. When ready to roast, rub veal with combined honey and mustard. Scatter onion slices in bottom of a roasting pan. Add meat and bay leaf. Place in a preheated 350° oven and roast uncovered for 45 minutes. Reduce heat to 325°, turn meat over, and add 1 cup of water. Cover and roast for an additional 1$^1/_2$ hours or until tender. Slice veal on a platter, serving gravy separately. To thicken gravy, dissolve 1 tablespoon of cornstarch (per cup of gravy) in a little cold water and add to simmering gravy. Cook for 2 minutes until thickened. Serves 8.

Veal has less fat than beef, and is excellent for the weight-conscious.

Stuffed Veal Breast

Scrumptious.

$^1/_2$ teaspoon garlic powder, or 3 cloves
   garlic, minced
$^1/_2$ teaspoon salt
$^1/_4$ teaspoon pepper
$^1/_2$ teaspoon paprika
1 5-pound veal breast with pocket

Stuffing

1 medium onion, diced
3 tablespoons oil
$^1/_4$ pound mushrooms, sliced
1$^1/_2$ cups cooked rice
1 pound spinach, cooked 5 minutes, or
   2 10-ounce packages frozen chopped
   spinach, thawed and drained
$^1/_2$ teaspoon salt, or to taste
$^1/_4$ teaspoon pepper
1 egg, beaten
$^1/_3$ teaspoon thyme
1 medium onion, sliced
1 cup water

Combine seasonings and rub into veal. Refrigerate for 2 hours, if possible. Prepare stuffing: sauté onion in oil until tender; add mushrooms and sauté while stirring for 3 minutes; let cool. Combine with remaining ingredients, except onion and water, and stuff the veal breast. Place in a roasting pan. Scatter with onion slices. Roast uncovered in a 350° oven for 35 minutes. Add 1 cup of water, cover and roast for an additional 2 hours until tender. Uncover during last 30 minutes. Baste occasionally. Thicken gravy with a little flour combined with cold water.

Traditional Cholent

Since cooking is forbidden on Shabbat, cholent was innovated by Jews in many countries: a Shabbat noon hot-meal tradition, prepared the day before, then left to cook overnight, over covered low heat, in a 225° oven, or in a crockpot. In Eastern Europe, cholent was taken to the town baker before Shabbat to be kept warm in his oven through the night. A large dumpling, called kugel or kishke, was included on top of the cholent. This delicious stew-type dish, which includes meat or chicken, potatoes, barley, and beans, cooks slowly while its flavors blend, spreading a delightful aroma throughout the house. In Israel chicken, which is more economical, lower in cholesterol, and more readily available, is used instead of meat. A whole chicken placed on top of the other ingredients will remain intact throughout the night.

1 cup barley, washed, checked, and
   soaked overnight
salt and pepper, to taste
²/₃ cup lima beans, washed, checked,
   and soaked overnight
6-8 medium potatoes, peeled and
   quartered
2-2¹/₂ pounds flanken or chuck meat,
   or 1 whole chicken

Place all ingredients in a pot, with potatoes and meat or chicken on top. Add water to cover, plus 1 inch. Bring to a boil, cover, and simmer over low heat for 1 hour. Do not stir (so that chicken will remain whole). Place pot on a covered stove-top (*blech*) over low heat to cook overnight; or place in a 225° oven until lunchtime the next day; or put cholent ingredients into a slow-cooking crockpot, cook on high heat for nearly an hour, then cook overnight over low heat. To add a richer brown color and more flavor, start by caramelizing some sugar: In a pot, add 2 tablespoons of sugar to 2 tablespoons of oil. Cook slowly over medium-low heat until mixture turns a deep brown, then immediately add a cup of water to stop browning. Place Fluffy Kishke (see page 108) on top of cholent. Serves 8-10.

Variation

Instead of caramelizing sugar, add 6 pitted prunes or 2 tablespoons of honey to cholent.

If cholent has too much liquid, remove cover or leave cover ajar during last 1-2 hours before serving.

Pareve Cholent

A meatless cholent.

3 large onions, thinly sliced
4 tablespoons oil
$^2/_3$ cup lima or navy beans
$^2/_3$ cup barley
2 teaspoons salt, or to taste
$^1/_4$ teaspoon pepper
$^1/_2$ teaspoon onion powder
1 bay leaf
3 tablespoons ketchup
2 tablespoons honey, optional
2-3 tablespoons onion soup powder, optional
6-8 medium potatoes, cut into eighths, or 1 pound tofu
Kasha Kishke (see following recipe)

In a large pot, sauté onions in oil until golden brown. Add remaining ingredients, except Kasha Kishke, in order listed. (Potatoes should be on top.) Add water to cover, plus 1 inch. Cover, bring to a boil, reduce heat, and simmer for about half an hour. Place Kasha Kishke on top. Cover and place in a 200-225° oven, or cook in a slow-cooking crockpot or over a covered stove-top over very low heat to cook slowly overnight. Do not stir. Taste cholent after half an hour of cooking. If necessary, add salt or soup powder. For a deeper caramel color, begin with 2 tablespoons of oil in pot, sprinkled with 3 tablespoons of sugar. Cook over medium heat until mixture turns a deep brown color, then add a cup of water immediately to stop browning action. Add remaining ingredients, except honey, which is omitted.

Pareve Kasha Kishke for Pareve Cholent

Traditionally, kishke is stuffed derma with a mixture of flour, fat, onions, salt, and pepper, but in today's cholesterol-conscious society, a variety of vegetables may be used in place of the fat.

$^1/_3$ cup margarine, cut into small pieces
1 medium onion, diced
$^1/_4$ cup raw kasha
$^1/_3$ cup flour
1 teaspoon salt
$^1/_4$ teaspoon pepper
1 egg, beaten, optional
$^2/_3$ cup water

Mix ingredients together in above order. Wrap securely in aluminum foil or cheesecloth and place on top of cholent just before leaving it to cook overnight.

Low-Calorie Vegetarian Cholent

Cholent used to be considered a "no-no" for people on a diet: it included meat, usually high in fat. This modern vegetarian variation is healthful, has a tangy flavor, and is a pleasant change.

3 cloves garlic, diced
2-3 onions, sliced
4 tablespoons oil
$1/2$ eggplant, cut into 1-inch cubes
1 medium cabbage, shredded (2-3 cups)
8 whole plum tomatoes, or a 16-ounce can whole tomatoes
1 pound tofu, cut into $1^1/2$-inch cubes; or 3 medium potatoes, cubed
$1/2$ cup barley or rice, checked
$1^1/2$ teaspoons oregano
1 tablespoon basil
2 bay leaves
2 teaspoons salt
$1/4$ teaspoon cayenne pepper, optional
8-10 cups water
3 zucchini, cut into 3-inch pieces

In a large stainless steel pot, sauté garlic and onions in oil until tender. Add remaining ingredients except zucchini. Cover and bring to a boil. Reduce heat and simmer for $1/2$ hour. Add zucchini and cook over very low heat for 10 minutes. Place pot on a covered stove-top (*blech*) over very low heat or in a 200-225° oven and cook overnight. A crockpot may also be used. Serves 8.

Fluffy Kishke for Cholent

Try adding this kugel-like kishke, wrapped in aluminum foil or cheesecloth and placed on top of the cholent. All the flavors seep in and it's delicious.

3 tablespoons water
1 slice challah or white bread
1 small potato, grated
1 medium onion, diced
2 tablespoons matzo meal
$3/4$ cup flour
$1/3$ cup oil
1 teaspoon salt
$1/2$ teaspoon pepper

Pour water over challah and squeeze out. Combine with remaining ingredients and form into a ball or loaf. Wrap in aluminum foil or cheesecloth. Place on top of cholent ingredients. Unwrap when ready to serve.

Variation

Use 1 cup of oatmeal instead of challah and potato.

Kurdistan Hamin

Hamin, which means "hot," is the Sephardi name for cholent. This Kurdish version exemplifies the Sephardi custom of including whole stuffed vegetables surrounded by meat or chicken, in the cholent. A meal in a pot.

8 whole vegetables (green peppers, red peppers, tomatoes, eggplant halves, zucchini, etc.)
6-8 medium potatoes, cut into quarters
1¹/₂ cups chickpeas (garbanzo beans), soaked overnight
1-1¹/₂ pounds beef, or 8 chicken legs
salt and pepper, to taste

Stuffing
³/₄ pound ground beef
¹/₄ cup uncooked rice
¹/₂ onion, diced
1 egg, beaten
salt and pepper, to taste
2 cloves garlic, diced

With a sharp knife, cut out inside flesh of vegetables, leaving a ¹/₄-inch shell. Combine all stuffing ingredients and fill the vegetables. Place potatoes and chickpeas in a roasting pan. Place stuffed vegetables and meat or chicken legs on top. Add water to cover vegetables halfway. Add salt and pepper. Cover and simmer for 30 minutes. Place in a 225° oven to cook slowly overnight. Serves 8.

Vegetarian Kishke

Bake it in the oven or wrap it in foil, and let it cook on top of cholent.

2 medium carrots
2 stalks celery
1 small zucchini
1 large onion
1 teaspoon salt
¹/₄ teaspoon pepper
²/₃ cup oil
1¹/₂ cups flour (half bread crumbs can be used)

Chop or shred all vegetables by hand or in a food processor. Combine with remaining ingredients. Wrap securely in aluminum foil and bake in a preheated 350° oven for 1¹/₂ hours, turning over after 45 minutes; or bake in a 1¹/₂-quart casserole pan for 1 hour. Serves 8-10.

Dafeena (Middle Eastern Cholent)

The eggs in this Oriental version of this Shabbat dish take on a marvelous taste, creamy texture, and rich brown color.

2-2¹/₂ pounds beef, cut into large
    chunks; or 1 whole chicken
2 cups chickpeas (garbanzo beans),
    soaked overnight
1 large onion, sliced
6 raw eggs, with carefully washed shells
6 medium potatoes, cut into quarters
    or eighths
2-3 cloves garlic, diced
¹/₂ teaspoon cinnamon
¹/₂ teaspoon allspice
¹/₄ teaspoon ginger
1¹/₂ teaspoons salt
¹/₄ teaspoon pepper
water to cover (about 8-10 cups)
1 cup uncooked rice, checked, washed,
    and wrapped in cheesecloth

Place all ingredients, except rice, in a large pot with meat or chicken, potatoes, and eggs on top. Add water to cover, plus 1 inch. Place rice in cheesecloth—loose enough for rice to double in volume—and tie securely. Place cheesecloth in pot, mostly below surface of water. Cover and bring to a boil. Lower heat and simmer for 1 hour. Place in a 225° oven, or cover and cook on a covered stove-top over very low heat overnight, or cook slowly in a crockpot over high heat for almost an hour, then over low heat until ready to be eaten. Serves 8.

Variation

The Sephardi Jews, especially the Persians, often stuff the whole chicken before placing it on top of ingredients in pot. Combine 1 cup of raw rice with 1 medium diced onion, cut-up gizzards if desired, 1 teaspoon of salt, ¹/₄ teaspoon of pepper, and ¹/₂ teaspoon of cumin. Stuff chicken and sew or skewer opening together. Place on top of other ingredients with the potatoes and eggs, cover, and cook slowly overnight until lunch the next day.

If you want to use less meat in the cholent itself, add chilled and skimmed gravy from roast chicken or roast beef. Beef bones also add flavor.

Fish

Fish

Whole Baked Fish with Vegetable Stuffing

An elegant way of serving fish. Although the fish is served whole, the slices are marked and the stuffing can be seen between the slices. Stuffed whole fish requires a longer baking time than unstuffed fish.

1 3-pound whitefish or carp, whole
1 teaspoon salt
1/2 teaspoon pepper
1/2 teaspoon garlic powder
1 teaspoon sugar
1/2 teaspoon paprika
2 tablespoons lemon juice
2 tablespoons oil
1/4 cup slivered almonds, for garnish, optional

Stuffing

1 medium onion, diced
3-4 tablespoons oil
1 stalk celery, diced
1 medium carrot, shredded or ground
1 zucchini, shredded or ground
1/2 green pepper, diced
1 teaspoon salt
1/4 teaspoon pepper
1/2 teaspoon oregano, optional
2 eggs, beaten
1/2 cup bread crumbs
paprika, to taste

Stuff fish whole, or have your fish man slice fish—only 2/3 way down— at 1 1/2-inch intervals, leaving some meat and skin intact on bottom layer. Combine seasonings, lemon juice, and oil, and rub on inside and outside of fish. Meanwhile, make the stuffing by sautéing onion in oil for about 7 minutes until soft. Add remaining ingredients except eggs, bread crumbs, and paprika. Sauté for an additional 5 minutes. Remove from heat. Stir in eggs and bread crumbs. Let cool. Place stuffing inside the fish, packing tightly enough for it to be seen between slices. Sprinkle with paprika. Cover and bake in a preheated 375° oven for 30 minutes. Remove cover and bake for an additional 20 minutes. Garnish with almonds, if desired. Serves 6.

Variations

Top-of-the-Stove Method: Use a smaller fish and half the amount of stuffing. In a large skillet, sauté 1 medium onion in 3 tablespoons of oil until tender. Place stuffed fish on top. Cover and simmer over medium heat for 10 minutes. Add 1/4 cup of water, cover, and cook for another 20 minutes. Sprinkle with slivered almonds.

With spinach stuffing: Use 1 10-ounce package of frozen spinach, thawed and drained, in place of carrots, zucchini, green pepper, and celery. Combine with remaining ingredients.

With mushroom stuffing: Sauté 1 medium onion in 1/4 cup of oil until soft. Add 2 cups of sliced fresh mushrooms and sauté for an additional 5 minutes. Remove from heat. Stir in 1/2 cup of bread crumbs, 3 tablespoons of dry wine, 1 teaspoon of salt, and 1/4 teaspoon of pepper.

Steamed Fish with Vegetables

My favorite way of preparing sliced fish on top of the stove. The fish steams in its own juice, enhanced and complemented by the added vegetables. Serve it as an appetizer or as a luncheon main dish.

2 pounds carp, whitefish, salmon, or
  pike, sliced 1¹/₂ inches thick
salt, to taste
¹/₄ teaspoon pepper
2 cloves garlic, minced
1 large onion, diced
¹/₂ green pepper, diced
2 tablespoons oil
2-3 unpeeled zucchini, sliced
3 carrots, thinly sliced
paprika, to taste

Sprinkle fish lightly on both sides with salt and pepper, then rub with garlic. Refrigerate for 30 minutes. In a large skillet, sauté onion and green pepper in oil over medium heat until tender. Add zucchini and carrots, and cook for 5 minutes, stirring occasionally. Cover and steam over low heat (without water) for 10 minutes. Push vegetables aside and add fish slices to bottom of skillet. Cook on each side for 3-4 minutes. Sprinkle with paprika. Cover and continue cooking over low heat for 20 minutes. If necessary, add 2-3 tablespoons of water. Serve immediately, basting with pan juices. Surround with vegetables. Serves 6.

Variations

String beans, mushrooms, cauliflower, or peas can be used.

Fish slices can be steamed without vegetables. Prepare as above until onions are nearly golden. Add fish slices. Cook over medium heat for 3-4 minutes per side. Cover and steam over low heat for 20 minutes. If necessary, add 3 tablespoons of water midway through cooking.

Fish Loaf Wellington

Fish loaf rolled in flaky pastry dough to simulate a fish. Very eye-catching.

2 pounds fish fillets (halibut, cod,
    whitefish, carp, hake, or flounder)
$^1/_4$ cup water
2 eggs, beaten
$1^1/_2$ cups bread crumbs
$^1/_2$ cup mayonnaise
1 medium onion, chopped
1 tablespoon lemon juice
salt, to taste
$^1/_4$ teaspoon pepper
$^1/_4$ teaspoon oregano, optional
$1^1/_2$ portions Easy Flaky Dough (see
    page 226), or 1 package ($^1/_2$ pound)
    puff pastry
1 egg yolk, beaten, for brushing top

Cook fish in lightly salted water for about 15-20 minutes until tender. Drain well and flake fish. Combine flaked fish with remaining ingredients except dough and egg yolk. Roll out dough thinly into a 9x13-inch rectangle. Form fish mixture into a fish shape in center of dough. Carefully wrap dough around fish shape. Attach scraps of pastry to form a tail and fins. Press tail and fins with tines of a fork and snip top of pastry with a small scissors to simulate scales. Brush with egg yolk and place carefully on a greased cookie sheet. Bake in a preheated 475° oven for 20 minutes, then reduce heat to 375° and bake for 40 more minutes until golden brown. Slice and serve with a mushroom or tomato sauce or Creole Sauce (see page 119). Serves 8-10.

Crispy Fried Fish

Try this recipe with a variety of batters. They're all tasty.

$2^1/_2$ pounds fillets (halibut, cod,
    flounder, or mackerel)
salt and pepper, to taste
dry dill, to taste
oil, for deep-frying

Batter
**Classic Batter or Beer Batter (see
    page 134)**

In a blender or electric mixer, beat all ingredients for batter until smooth. Refrigerate for 1 hour. Meanwhile, season fish fillets lightly with salt, pepper, and dill. Pat dry, then dip in batter. Deep-fry in hot oil until golden brown. Serves 6-8.

To keep breading on food during frying, add $^1/_2$-1 teaspoon sugar to batter.

Fish Fillets Florentine

Rolled and stuffed fish fillets with a spinach, mushroom, or mashed potato filling. Can be baked with or without a sauce.

2 pounds fish fillets (flounder, sole, or hake)
pinch of salt, pepper, and garlic powder
toothpicks
1 tablespoon margarine

Stuffing
1 pound spinach, or 1 10-ounce package frozen chopped spinach, thawed and drained
1 large onion, diced
2 tablespoons oil
1 large egg, beaten
1 teaspoon salt
pepper, to taste
1/4 cup bread crumbs or matzo meal

Sprinkle fish lightly with salt, pepper, and garlic powder. Check spinach and wash thoroughly in cold water. Steam over low heat until limp, with only the moisture that clings to leaves. Do not overcook. Drain and chop. Sauté onion in oil. Let cool. Combine with chopped spinach and remaining stuffing ingredients. Spread spinach mixture thickly on fish fillets, roll, and fasten with toothpicks. Place, end side up, in a well-greased baking pan. Dot with margarine. Bake in a preheated 400° oven for 20 minutes until fish flakes easily with a fork. Serves 6.

Variations

With sweet and sour sauce: Serve sauce with spinach-stuffed fish. Bring to a boil 1/2 cup of ketchup, 1/4 cup of water, 1 tablespoon of lemon juice, 1/4 cup of sugar, and a pinch of oregano. Let cool and pour over fish. Bake as directed.

Mashed potato stuffing: Instead of spinach, combine 2 cups of mashed potatoes with 1 medium diced sautéed onion, 2 tablespoons of matzo meal, and 1 beaten egg.

Without stuffing: Roll and fasten fish fillets without stuffing. Combine 1/2 cup of ketchup with 1/2 cup of mayonnaise. Spread on top of fish and bake as directed.

Immediately after purchase, fish should be frozen in a double plastic bag filled with water and placed near the freezer wall. Fish should not be refrozen.

Fish is high in protein and polyunsaturate fat, which lowers the body's cholesterol level.

Baked Halibut Creole

This tangy Creole Sauce can be served hot over baked fish or, alternatively, fish can be baked topped with the sauce. Also delicious combined with tuna and served over hot spaghetti.

**6 slices halibut, ³/₄ inch thick
    (haddock, hake, or sliced salmon
    may also be used)
salt, to taste
garlic powder, to taste
3 tablespoons margarine**

Creole Sauce
**1 medium onion, diced
2 stalks celery, thinly sliced
1 green pepper, cut into thin strips
2 tablespoons oil
2 large tomatoes, cubed
4 ounces (1 small can) tomato sauce
²/₃ cup water
¹/₂ teaspoon salt
2 cloves garlic, minced
1 teaspoon sugar
pinch of oregano
¹/₂ teaspoon thyme, optional**

Sprinkle fish lightly with salt and garlic powder. Let stand for 20-30 minutes to absorb seasonings. Place fish in a well-greased 10x17-inch baking pan and dot each fillet with margarine. Bake in a preheated 350° oven for 30 minutes. Meanwhile, make the Creole Sauce: Sauté onion, celery, and green pepper in oil until soft; add tomatoes, tomato sauce, water, and seasonings; cover and simmer for 20 minutes, stirring occasionally. When ready to serve, place fish on a platter or on individual plates, and spoon hot sauce over it. Serves 6.

Variations

Pour Creole Sauce over sliced fish or fillets in baking pan and bake as directed.

Cut fish fillets into 1-inch cubes and simmer in Creole Sauce for 15-20 minutes.

Most fish contains less riboflavin and niacin than meat, but saltwater fish is rich in iodine and phosphorus and herring is full of calcium, as are the soluble bones in canned salmon and sardines. Bass, flounder, hake, halibut, St. Peter's fish, and sole contain up to 5% fat, while carp, herring, mackerel, red salmon, shad, sardines, smelt, and tuna contain as much as 20%.

Baked Fillet of Sole

Most other types of fish fillets can also be used for this recipe. Serve with the sauce of your choice. Remember that lemon juice or vinegar removes fishy odor and adds flavor to baked or broiled fish.

2½ pounds fillet of sole (about 7 pieces)
salt, for sprinkling
juice of 1 lemon
1 teaspoon garlic powder
⅔ teaspoon paprika
1 teaspoon chopped dill
¼ teaspoon pepper
¾ cup bread crumbs or cornflake
crumbs
5 tablespoons mayonnaise

Sprinkle fish lightly with salt, brush with lemon juice, and sprinkle with seasonings. Refrigerate for ½-1 hour, to allow seasonings to penetrate. Dip fillets in crumbs and place on a well-greased 10x17-inch baking sheet. Spread 2 teaspoons of mayonnaise on each fillet and bake in a preheated 375° oven for 20 minutes or until fish flakes easily with a fork. Serves 6-7.

Variations

Broiled with puffy sauce: Combine 2 stiffly beaten egg whites with ⅓ cup of mayonnaise, 1 tablespoon of chopped dill, and 2 tablespoons of lemon juice or 1 tablespoon of chopped pickles. Spread evenly over baked fish. Bake for an additional 15 minutes or broil for 4-5 minutes until sauce is puffy and golden. Serve immediately.

Baked sole with Creole Sauce: Prepare fish as directed—without mayonnaise—and bake with Creole Sauce (see page 119).

Amandine: Brown ⅔ cup of slivered almonds in 1 tablespoon of margarine and spoon over fish before serving.

Most people overcook fish. It's actually tastiest when cooked until opaque white and easily flaked. It should be served immediately after baking or broiling, lest it dry out.

Baked Fish with Mushroom Sauce

A really delicious and easy way of preparing baked fish. Some have the custom not to bake fish with milk.

2 pounds fillets or sliced fish (whitefish, salmon, halibut, or perch)
salt, to taste
1 can cream of mushroom soup, diluted with $1/2$ can milk or water

Sprinkle fish lightly with salt. Pour soup over fish fillets or slices. Bake in a preheated 375° oven: 20 minutes for fillets and 25-30 minutes for sliced fish.

Fresh fish is odorless and characterized by shiny scales and bright-red gills. Once caught, fish should be drawn (stripped of its intestines and gills) as quickly as possible, to prevent bacterial growth.

Trout Amandine

For a special dinner party, when you don't want to serve a meat meal, serve whole baby trout with almonds and dill.

6 rainbow trout
salt and pepper, to taste
juice of 1 large lemon
$1/4$ cup margarine, melted
$1/2$ cup slivered almonds, toasted
1 tablespoon chopped dill or parsley
lemon slices, for garnish

Sprinkle trout with salt and pepper. Let stand for 20 minutes. Place in a large but shallow greased baking dish. Sprinkle generously with lemon juice. Spoon margarine on top. Bake uncovered in a 400° oven for 25 minutes. Sprinkle with almonds and dill. Return to oven for 5 more minutes. Arrange trout on a serving platter and garnish with lemon slices. Serves 6.

To enhance the flavor of any baked or broiled fish, sprinkle lightly with onion soup mix before baking—about 2 tablespoons per 2 pounds of fish.

Baked Flounder Supreme

Halibut, perch, or sliced whitefish may be used instead of flounder.

2 pounds flounder fillets
salt and pepper, to taste
2/3 cup French dressing
2 tablespoons lemon juice
1 cup French-fried onion rings or
    potato chips, crushed
1/2 cup grated Parmesan cheese

Thaw fish if frozen. Place in a deep bowl and sprinkle lightly with salt and pepper. Combine French dressing and lemon juice and pour over fish. Refrigerate for about 1 hour, turning after half an hour. Remove fish from sauce and place in a large, well-greased baking pan. Combine onion rings or potato chips with cheese. Sprinkle over fish. Bake in a preheated 350° oven for about 25 minutes until fish flakes easily with a fork. Serves 7.

Variation

In place of French dressing, Parmesan cheese, and onion rings or potato chips, sprinkle fish lightly with two tablespoons of onion soup powder and bake as directed.

Fish can be cooked while partly frozen.

Cantonese Tuna Chow Mein

Your family will love this tasty tuna dish.

2 large onions, diced
1 green pepper, diced
2 stalks celery, thinly sliced
4 tablespoons oil
1 cup bean sprouts
1 4-ounce can mushrooms
1 small can bamboo shoots or water
    chestnuts
1 pimento, diced, optional
salt and pepper, to taste
1 cup vegetable soup stock
1/4 cup soy sauce
2 tablespoons cornstarch
2 cans tuna, drained
Chinese noodles (about 6 ounces)
1/2 cup slivered almonds

Stir-fry onions, green pepper, and celery in oil over medium-high heat for about 5 minutes until onions are tender. Add bean sprouts, mushrooms, and bamboo shoots or water chestnuts and stir-fry for 3 more minutes. Add pimento, salt, pepper, soup stock, and soy sauce and cook for 5 minutes. Combine cornstarch with a little cold water and stir into mixture while cooking until thickened. Add tuna and heat through. Serve hot over Chinese noodles. Sprinkle with almonds.

Tuna and Chopped Spinach Bake

Scrumptious!

4 tablespoons margarine
4 tablespoons flour
2 cups milk
$^1/_4$ teaspoon onion salt
1 teaspoon lemon juice
$^1/_2$ cup mayonnaise
$^1/_4$ teaspoon pepper
1 teaspoon salt
2 teaspoons mustard
2 10-ounce packages chopped frozen
   spinach
2 cans tuna fish, drained and flaked

In a skillet, melt margarine and stir in flour until dissolved. Gradually stir in milk until smooth. Remove from heat and combine sauce with remaining ingredients. Pour into a 2-quart casserole. Bake in a 350° oven for 35 minutes.

No-Bake Tuna with Almonds

A marvelous casserole-type dish. Made on top of the stove in a jiffy.

2 stalks celery, diced
1 small onion, chopped
$^1/_4$ cup oil
$1^1/_2$ teaspoons curry powder
1 teaspoon salt
$^1/_4$ teaspoon pepper
$^1/_4$ cup flour
$2^1/_4$ cups milk
2 teaspoons lemon juice
2 $7^3/_4$-ounce cans tuna, drained
$^1/_2$ cup chopped almonds
3 cups cooked pasta shells

Sauté celery and onion in oil until onions are tender. Add curry powder, salt, and pepper. Stir in flour until smooth. Gradually stir in milk until smooth. Combine with lemon juice, tuna, almonds, and pasta shells. Cook over low heat for about 5 minutes until heated through.

Super Tuna Bake

Easy to prepare, yet delicious.

1 can cream of celery soup
1/2 cup mayonnaise
1/2 cup milk or water
2 7-ounce cans tuna, drained
1 10-ounce package frozen mixed
   vegetables, cooked and drained
2 cups cooked macaroni
1 small onion, diced
1 cup slightly crushed potato chips

Mix together celery soup, mayonnaise, and milk or water until smooth. Add remaining ingredients except potato chips. Pour into a 1 1/2-quart casserole. Sprinkle with potato chips. Bake in a 350° oven for 30 minutes. Serves 6-8.

Salmon, Vegetable, and Cheese Bake

Perfect for lunch or for a melaveh malkah.

4 tablespoons margarine
4 tablespoons flour
2 cups milk or water
2 teaspoons prepared mustard
1 teaspoon salt
pinch of pepper
1/4 pound yellow cheese, grated
1 16-ounce can salmon, drained
3/4 pound fresh green beans, or 1
   10-ounce package frozen string
   beans, cooked and drained (reserve
   liquid for water in recipe)
1 10-ounce package frozen broccoli,
   cooked and drained

In a saucepan, melt margarine and stir in flour until smooth. Slowly stir in milk (or water or green bean liquid) until smooth and slightly thickened. Add mustard, seasonings, and cheese (reserving 3 tablespoons for sprinkling on top). Cook for 2 more minutes. Flake salmon and carefully combine with sauce and vegetables. Pour mixture into a greased 2-quart casserole. Sprinkle with remaining cheese. Bake in a preheated 400° oven for 25 minutes. Serve hot. Serves 6-8.

Vegetables

Vegetables

Carrot Tsimmes

The carrots in this recipe are steamed without water to retain their natural flavor, which is enhanced by a blend of honey, orange juice, cinnamon, and raisins.

2 pounds carrots, thinly sliced
5 tablespoons honey
3 tablespoons oil
1/2 teaspoon salt
dash of pepper
1/2 6-ounce can frozen orange juice
   concentrate, or juice of 2 oranges
1/2 cup raisins
1/4 teaspoon cinnamon

Place carrots in a medium-sized saucepan, cover, and cook without water for 5 minutes over medium heat. Stir once or twice. Add honey, oil, salt, and pepper. Cover and continue cooking over very low heat for 1 1/2 hours. Carrots may become slightly brown, which adds to flavor. Add orange juice, raisins, and cinnamon, and cook over low heat for an additional 10 minutes. Serves 6-8.

Variation

Soak 1/2 pound of prunes in boiling water to cover for 30 minutes. Add prunes—and their water—to carrot mixture after 1 1/2 hours of cooking. Cook over low heat for an additional 20 minutes.

Carrot Pineapple Tsimmes

The pineapple in this recipe adds that special touch to the tsimmes.

2 pounds carrots, sliced
1 cup water
1/3 cup apricot jam or honey
3 tablespoons oil
4 tablespoons frozen orange juice
   concentrate
1/2 teaspoon cinnamon
1/2 teaspoon salt
1 7 1/2-ounce can crushed pineapple
2-3 tablespoons matzo meal

Cook all ingredients except pineapple and matzo meal in a covered medium saucepan for 1 hour. Add pineapple and matzo meal, cover, and cook for 10-15 more minutes, stirring occasionally. Serves 6-8.

To preserve the color of cooked vegetables, uncover pot for the last few minutes of cooking.

Holiday Sweet Potato Tsimmes

Since tsimmes requires many ingredients and is time-consuming to prepare, the expression, "Don't make a tsimmes over it"—don't blow it out of proportion—became popular. This is a delicious side dish, popular on Rosh Hashanah or Sukkot, when sweet potatoes are plentiful.

2 pounds sweet potatoes, peeled
1 tablespoon cornstarch, diluted in 4
** tablespoons cold water**
3 large tart green apples, peeled and
** thickly sliced**
8 ounces prunes
$^1/_2$ cup brown sugar
$^1/_2$ cup water
$^1/_2$ cup sweet red wine or orange juice
juice of 1 lemon
1 teaspoon cinnamon

Cut sweet potatoes into 1$^1/_2$-inch chunks. Dissolve cornstarch in water. Set aside. Mix sweet potatoes together with remaining ingredients. Pour into a well-greased 9x12-inch baking pan or a 2$^1/_2$-quart casserole. Cover and bake in a preheated 375° oven for about 1 hour. Stir in diluted cornstarch with hot liquid and return to oven uncovered for 5 minutes. Serve hot. Serves 8-10.

To keep sweet potatoes from discoloring, place in salt water right after peeling (1$^1/_2$ tablespoons salt to 1 quart water).

Beet Salad with Shredded Apples

This salad, which originated in Eastern Europe, made its way to many parts of the world. Usually served hot, on Shabbat, as a side dish with meat or chicken, it can also be served cold as a salad.

1 pound beets, cut into quarters
2 large tart apples, peeled
$^1/_3$ cup brown sugar or orange
** marmalade**
juice of 1 lemon
$^1/_2$ teaspoon salt
2 tablespoons oil, optional
$^1/_3$ cup raisins
2 tablespoons matzo meal

Cook beets in water to cover until tender—about 30 minutes. Let cool. Shred beets and apples and return to pot with about 1$^1/_2$ cups of beet liquid from cooking. Add brown sugar or orange marmalade, lemon juice, salt, oil, and raisins. Cover and cook over low heat for 30 minutes. Stir in matzo meal to thicken slightly. Cook for 10 more minutes. Remove cover during last few minutes of cooking to retain bright color of beets. Serves 6.

To remove discoloration around fingernails after scouring pots or peeling vegetables, rub area with fresh lemon.

Zucchini-Carrot Squares

Zucchini do not require peeling. Most of the nutrition is just beneath the skin so choose fresh, clean zucchini. For best results, sprinkle with salt after shredding. The wheat germ adds extra nutrition to this vegetarian favorite.

4 medium unpeeled zucchini, shredded
1 teaspoon salt
2 large onions, diced
4 tablespoons oil
$^1/_2$ teaspoon pepper
3 large carrots, shredded
3 eggs, beaten
$^1/_2$ cup bread crumbs or matzo meal
$^1/_4$ cup wheat germ
6 tablespoons flour, sifted
$^1/_2$ teaspoon oregano and thyme, optional
2 tablespoons margarine, cut into small pieces

Sprinkle zucchini with salt. Let stand for 15 minutes. Squeeze out liquid. Sauté onions in oil until soft. Remove from heat and combine with remaining ingredients, except margarine. Pour into a well-greased 7x11-inch baking pan. Dot with margarine. Bake in a preheated 375° oven for 1 hour. Cover during last 15 minutes. Cut into squares. Serve hot. Yields 12-15 squares.

Ratatouille

A tasty blend of a variety of vegetables with a tomato base. Serve it on its own, hot or cold, or over brown rice.

1 large onion, diced
2 large green peppers, cut into strips
4 tablespoons safflower oil
1 medium eggplant, cubed
2 medium zucchini, sliced
4 medium tomatoes, cut into eighths
1 teaspoon oregano
$^1/_2$ teaspoon basil, optional
3 cloves garlic, diced
$^1/_2$ cup tomato sauce
$^1/_2$ cup water
$^1/_4$ teaspoon pepper
salt, to taste

Sauté onion and green pepper in oil until soft. Add eggplant and continue cooking over low heat for 5-10 minutes. Add remaining ingredients, cover, and cook over low heat for 45 minutes until vegetables are tender. If necessary, add a little water. Sauce should be fairly thick. If too thin, remove cover and cook for an additional 5-10 minutes. Serves 6-8.

Tender-Crisp Vegetables

An appetizing, low-calorie, vegetable dish. The purpose of successful stir-frying is to avoid over-cooking. Vegetables cooked until just tender-crisp retain their color and more nutritional value.

4 tablespoons vegetable or safflower oil
2 large onions, diced
2 medium carrots, cut into 2-inch sticks
3 stalks celery, sliced diagonally into
   1-inch slices
1 green pepper, cut into short strips
2 medium zucchini, cut into 2-inch
   sticks
1/4 pound fresh mushrooms, sliced or
   whole, optional
4-6 ounces fresh or frozen string beans
1 teaspoon salt, or to taste
1/4 teaspoon pepper
1 teaspoon pareve chicken soup
   powder, optional

Heat oil in a large skillet or wok and sauté onions until soft. Add carrots, celery, and green pepper and sauté for 5-7 minutes, stirring occasionally. Add remaining vegetables, seasonings, and 3-4 tablespoons of water. Cover and steam for about 10 minutes until vegetables are tender, but crisp. Stir in soup powder, cover, and cook for an additional 2-3 minutes. If necessary, add a few tablespoons of water. Serves 6.

Scandinavian Medley

A variety of vegetables baked with a thin layer of rice. This is a hearty dish that can be used as a vegetarian main dish or as a side dish. A real favorite!

1 medium eggplant
2 green peppers
2 zucchini
2 large onions
2 carrots
2 medium potatoes
2/3 cup uncooked rice
1/2 cup water
1/3 cup oil
3 teaspoons salt
1/2 teaspoon pepper
2 tablespoons wine vinegar
2 tablespoons parsley
1-2 teaspoons dill, optional
4 medium tomatoes, sliced

Cut all vegetables except tomatoes into 1-inch chunks and mix together. Put half of mixture in a 10x15-inch baking pan. Spread rice on top. Cover with remaining vegetables. Combine water, oil, salt, pepper, vinegar, parsley, and dill, and pour evenly over vegetables. Place sliced tomatoes on top. Cover pan securely with a lid or aluminum foil. Bake in a preheated 350° oven for 1 hour. Serve hot. Serves 10-12.

Sweet Potatoes in Orange Cups

Sweet potatoes—also known as yams—are far more perishable than regular white potatoes. They are high in vitamin A. To keep from darkening after peeling, sprinkle with lemon juice. This is a festive way of serving sweet potatoes. It can be made the day before and heated before serving. Use the scooped-out orange pulp for fruit salad or fresh orange juice.

6 medium sweet potatoes, cooked
3 tablespoons margarine
$^1/_2$ teaspoon cinnamon
$^1/_2$ teaspoon salt
$^1/_2$ cup brown sugar
$^1/_3$ cup raisins
1 $7^1/_2$-ounce can crushed pineapple, drained
6 oranges, cut into halves

Peel and mash sweet potatoes with margarine, cinnamon, salt, and brown sugar. Stir in raisins and pineapple. Prepare orange cups by scooping out orange pulp or pressing out with a juicer, being careful to leave the shells intact. Pile hot mixture high in the orange shells. Place on a greased cookie sheet and heat in a preheated 350° oven for 15 minutes. Serve immediately. Makes 12 orange cups.

Variation

Sweet potato balls: Roll mixture into balls. Tuck a pineapple chunk in center of each, then roll in crushed cornflake crumbs. Bake in a 375° oven for 25-30 minutes.

Potato Shells

This is an attractive way of serving vegetables. It can be made ahead of time, then filled with cooked or creamed vegetables and heated just before serving. Lends a professional touch to your table.

$2^1/_2$ pounds potatoes, cooked, drained, and mashed
2 tablespoons margarine
salt and pepper, to taste
2 eggs, beaten

Combine all ingredients. Fill a pastry bag with mixture and squeeze to form 8-10 flat solid circles on a well-greased baking sheet. Pipe an additional circle on the edge of each circle to form a shell. Bake in a 375° oven for 15-20 minutes. Fill baked shells with hot seasoned vegetables—cooked peas, string beans, carrots, or as desired. Yields 8-10 $2^1/_2$-inch shells.

Variation

To form shells without using a pastry bag, place a small mound of mashed potatoes on a well-greased baking sheet. Hollow out center and smooth edges to form a shell. Bake as directed above. Fill with steamed or creamed vegetables.

Deep-Fried Vegetables

For a puffier coating, deep-fry in the Beer Batter. Fruit can also be deep-fried.

2 medium zucchini, sliced diagonally into $^1/_2$-inch slices or 2-inch strips
$^1/_2$ pound whole fresh green beans, precooked in salted water for 5 minutes
$^1/_2$ pound large whole fresh mushrooms
1 small cauliflower and broccoli, separated into florets and blanched in boiling salted water for 2 minutes
oil, for deep frying

Classic Batter

1 egg
1 cup water or milk
1 cup flour, sifted
$^1/_2$ teaspoon salt
$^1/_2$ teaspoon baking soda

Beer Batter

1 egg
$^1/_2$ cup beer
$^1/_2$ cup flour, sifted
pinch of salt
1 tablespoon oil

Combine all ingredients—for either batter—in a blender or food processor and blend until smooth. Cover and refrigerate for 1-2 hours. Wash room-temperature vegetables and pat dry carefully. Fill a deep-fryer or medium-sized pot halfway with oil and heat until hot, but not smoking (360°). Dip vegetables into batter, using a dry fork. Drip off excess batter and lower vegetables carefully into hot oil. Fry several at a time until golden brown.

Drain on absorbent towels and keep warm in a paper-lined pan placed in a 250-300° oven. Yields 25 hors d'oeuvres.

Variations

Fry vegetables on both sides in a large skillet with $^1/_4$ inch of oil until golden.

For onion rings, cut 3 large onions into $^1/_4$-inch slices and separate into rings. Let soak in iced water for 1 hour. Dry thoroughly and dip in batter or simply dredge in flour. Fry in hot oil until golden brown.

To deep-fry fruit, add 1 tablespoon of sugar to batter. Use $^1/_2$-inch-thick apple slices, pineapple or orange wedges, or 1-inch-thick diagonally cut banana slices. Fruit can be marinated first in cherry liqueur or brandy, if desired. Serve sprinkled with powdered sugar—luscious!

Pashtida

Pashtida is a Sephardi kugel. It is like a knish, with a layer of flaky pastry on the bottom only.

³/4 **portion Easy Flaky Dough (see page 226) or Special Knish Dough (see page 149)**
2 **large onions, thinly sliced**
¹/3 **cup oil**
3 **large red peppers, diced**
2 **large green peppers, diced**
3 **stalks celery, thinly sliced**
8 **large potatoes, peeled, cooked, and mashed**
4 **eggs, beaten**
2 **teaspoons salt**
¹/4 **teaspoon pepper**

Roll out dough to fit an 11x17-inch cookie sheet or, for thicker portions, a 9x13-inch baking pan. Sauté onions in oil until soft. Add remaining vegetables, except potatoes, and sauté for an additional 10 minutes. Combine with potatoes, eggs, and seasonings. Spread over dough. Bake for 1 hour in a preheated 350° oven. Cut into 1-inch rectangles. Yields about 28 pieces.

Cheese Strudel

A delightful, sweet strudel for that special occasion.

2 **portions Easy Flaky Dough (see page 226)**
2 **pounds farmer cheese**
¹/2 **cup sugar**
3 **eggs, beaten**
1 **teaspoon vanilla extract**
2 **tablespoons melted margarine**
¹/2 **cup raisins**
juice and grated rind of 1 small lemon
pinch of cinnamon
1 **egg yolk, combined with 1 teaspoon water, for glaze**

Divide dough into 4 parts. Roll out each part into a ¹/8-inch-thick rectangle. Combine the filling ingredients thoroughly. Spread over dough, leaving a 2-inch margin on outer edges. Roll up carefully. Place, seam side down, on a greased 11x17-inch cookie sheet. Brush with glaze. Bake in a preheated 450° oven for 35-40 minutes. Yields approximately 36-40 pieces.

Variation

Add 1 package of instant vanilla pudding and omit sugar and vanilla extract.

Cabbage Strudel

This cabbage strudel—sweet or savory—makes a delicious side dish for a holiday dinner.

1½ portions **Easy Flaky Dough** (see page 226)
1 medium head of cabbage, shredded or chopped
⅓ cup oil
¾ cup raisins
½ cup honey or white or brown sugar
½ cup chopped pecans
1 teaspoon salt
juice of 1 lemon
1 teaspoon cinnamon
pinch of nutmeg
¼ cup bread crumbs
1 egg yolk, combined with 1 teaspoon water, for glaze

Fry cabbage in oil for about 10 minutes until tender, stirring occasionally. Remove from heat. Stir in remaining ingredients. Divide dough into 3 parts. Roll out each part into a thin 9x13-inch rectangle. Spread with cabbage mixture, leaving a 2-inch margin on outer edge. Roll up carefully as for jelly roll. Place on a greased 11x17-inch cookie sheet, brush with glaze, and bake in a preheated 450° oven for 40-50 minutes. Yields about 25 slices.

Variation

Savory cabbage strudel: Omit raisins, honey or sugar, and cinnamon. Instead, begin with 1 diced onion, sautéed until soft.

Broccoli and Rice Bake

Broccoli is best eaten when all green. Yellow parts are tougher. Rice, a long-time favorite in the Land of Israel, was introduced there around the time of the Second Temple.

1 large onion, diced
3 tablespoons margarine
2 tablespoons flour, sifted
1½ cups milk or water
1 teaspoon salt
pinch of pepper
2 eggs, well beaten
1 pound broccoli, steamed and chopped, or 1 10-ounce package frozen chopped broccoli
2 cups rice, cooked

Sauté onion in margarine until tender. Stir in flour until smooth. Slowly add milk, salt, and pepper, and stir until thickened. Remove from heat. Let cool slightly, then stir in eggs, broccoli, and rice. Pour into a greased 1½-quart casserole. Bake in a preheated 350° oven for 35-40 minutes. Serves 6 as a side dish.

Variation

Add 1 cup of grated cheddar cheese to mixture.

For fluffier rice, add a few drops of vinegar to water when cooking.

Stuffed Cabbage with Tuna and Rice

A pareve version of stuffed cabbage. To make cabbage leaves pliable for easier stuffing, cook them in water to cover for about 5 minutes or freeze them for 24-48 hours.

2 7¹/₂-ounce cans tuna
¹/₃ cup uncooked rice
1 large egg
1 teaspoon salt
¹/₄ teaspoon pepper
1 cup sliced mushrooms, optional
1 large head of cabbage

Sauce
3¹/₂ cups tomato juice
juice of 1 lemon
4 tablespoons brown or white sugar, or
    to taste
salt and pepper, to taste

Combine tuna, rice, egg, salt, pepper, and mushrooms. Separate and check cabbage leaves, and soften as directed above. Place 1-2 tablespoons of mixture on each cabbage leaf. Roll while tucking in sides. (Do not roll too tightly, to allow room for rice to swell.) Place closely together in a 10x12-inch casserole or roasting pan. Combine sauce ingredients and pour on top of cabbage rolls. Taste and correct sauce seasonings. Bake uncovered in a 375° oven for 1 hour.

Variations

Cheese-rice stuffed cabbage: In place of tuna mixture, combine 1 cup of uncooked rice with 1 cup of grated cheddar cheese and ²/₃ cup of sliced mushrooms.

Stuffed cabbage with rice: Combine 1¹/₂ cups of uncooked rice (or 3¹/₂ cups of cooked rice) with 1 cup of tomato sauce, juice of 1 lemon, 3-4 tablespoons of sugar, and, if desired, ²/₃ cup mushrooms.

Stuffed green peppers: Remove tops and insides of 10 medium-sized green peppers. Stuff with any of these mixtures. Place in a large pot. Pour sauce on top and cook for 1¹/₂ hours, or bake in oven as directed.

To peel tomatoes easily, dip them in boiling water for 30 seconds.

Pizza

Two kinds of pizzas: one dough made with yeast, the other with baking powder.

1 package dry yeast, or 1 cake
   compressed yeast
$1/4$ cup lukewarm water
1 cup hot water
2 tablespoons oil
salt, to taste
1 tablespoon sugar
$3 1/2$ cups all-purpose flour

Dissolve yeast in lukewarm water. In a mixing bowl, combine hot water, oil, salt, and sugar. Stir in flour and let cool. Stir in yeast mixture and beat at medium speed for about 10 minutes. Pat out and spread onto 2 greased 12-inch pizza pans. Add pizza sauce and toppings. Let rest for 10 minutes. Bake in a 400° oven for 25 minutes.

Quick Pizza

1 egg
$1/3$ cup oil
$2/3$ cup water
salt, to taste
2 cups flour
1 teaspoon baking powder

Mix together egg, oil, and water. Stir in remaining ingredients until smooth. Pat out into a greased 10x17-inch baking pan. Spread with sauce and bake in a 350° oven for 25 minutes.

Sauce

1 6-ounce can tomato paste
4 tablespoons oil
$1/2$ cup water
1 teaspoon oregano
1 teaspoon salt
$1/8$ teaspoon pepper
1 teaspoon sugar
$1 1/2$ cups grated sharp cheese, for
   sprinkling on top

Combine all ingredients except cheese and spread over pizza dough in pan before baking. Sprinkle with cheese. Top with sliced green or black olives, anchovies, thinly sliced tomatoes, or mushroom slices. Bake as directed.

Freeze leftover tomato sauce in ice-cube trays. Transfer frozen cubes to plastic bag and store in freezer.

Dairy Vegetable Lasagna

*Ideal for melaveh malkah. Both sauces
listed here are also perfect with spaghetti.*

2 10-ounce packages frozen spinach or
   broccoli, or 2 pounds fresh spinach
   or broccoli, cooked and chopped
2 tablespoons margarine
1 teaspoon salt
1/4 teaspoon pepper
2 eggs, beaten
1 pound cottage cheese
8 ounces cheddar cheese, shredded
1 8-ounce package lasagna noodles,
   cooked and drained
1/2 cup grated Parmesan cheese, for
   sprinkling on top

Steam spinach or broccoli in a small
amount of water for about 5
minutes until just tender. Remove
cover during last few minutes to
retain green color. Drain and stir in
margarine, salt, and pepper. Combine
spinach or broccoli, eggs, and cheeses
(except Parmesan) in a bowl. In
another bowl, prepare sauce. Pour 1/2
cup of sauce into a greased 9x13-inch
baking pan. Cover with a layer of
noodles, then a layer of filling. Repeat
layers of sauce, noodles, and filling,
ending with sauce. Top with
Parmesan cheese. Bake in a preheated
350° oven for 40 minutes. Let stand
for 5-10 minutes before cutting.
Serves 10-12.

Sauce 1

1 cup tomato sauce, or 1 6-ounce can
   tomato paste
1/2 cup (or more) water
2 cloves garlic, crushed
1 teaspoon salt, or to taste
1/2 teaspoon pepper, or to taste
1 tablespoon sugar
1 teaspoon oregano

Combine all ingredients and
simmer for 2 minutes.

Sauce 2

1 large onion, diced
2 cloves garlic, diced
1 green pepper, diced
1/4 cup oil
4 ounces mushrooms, sliced and
   drained
1 teaspoon salt
1/2 teaspoon pepper
1 teaspoon oregano
1 6-ounce can tomato paste
2 8-ounce cans tomato sauce
3/4 cup (or more) water

Sauté onion, garlic, and pepper in
oil for 8 minutes. Add remaining
ingredients, cover, and simmer for 30
minutes or until slightly thickened.
Add a little water, if necessary.

Variations

Dairy lasagna: Omit spinach or
broccoli.

Instead of broccoli or spinach,
substitute 2 10-ounce packages of
cooked string beans, or 4 sliced,
sautéed zucchini, or 2 71/2-ounce cans
of tuna, or 2 medium, sliced, fried
eggplants.

Kasha with String Beans

Kasha—sold under the name of buckwheat groats—is a reminder of old-fashioned home cooking for generations of European Jews. Kasha was usually mixed with pasta bow ties and chicken fat in a dish called kasha varnishkes. This variation uses string beans instead of pasta.

1 pound string beans, cut into 1-inch
    pieces, or 1 10-ounce package
    frozen string beans
1¹/₂ cups uncooked kasha
1 egg, beaten
4 tablespoons (1 envelope) powdered
    onion soup
3 cups water
3 tablespoons margarine
salt and pepper, to taste

Cook string beans in a small amount of lightly salted water until just tender-crisp. Drain and set aside. Combine kasha with egg in a medium-sized saucepan. Cook over medium heat for 2 minutes, while stirring constantly, until kasha is dry and separates into individual kernels. In another saucepan, boil onion soup in water for 7 minutes and stir into kasha. Cover and cook for 10-15 minutes. Stir in margarine, salt, pepper, and string beans. Serve hot. Serves 8.

Variations

For a more colorful version, use half the amount of string beans and add 1 medium zucchini and 2 medium carrots, cut into sticks. Cook until tender-crisp.

Turn this into a hearty dairy dish by sprinkling 1 cup of grated yellow cheese on top. Cover and cook for an additional 1-2 minutes.

Add 1 10-ounce can of cream of celery soup to mixture. Pour into a 2-quart casserole and bake uncovered in a 350° oven for 30 minutes.

Rice with Lentils

Two complementary proteins, making a complete protein dish. Lentils are referred to in the Bible in the Book of Genesis; this was the dish for which Esau gave up his birthright to Jacob. This dish is traditionally served by Sephardi Jews during the nine days preceding the fast day of Tisha B'Av, which marks the destruction of the Holy Temple.

1 cup uncooked brown rice
$^1/_2$ cup lentils, soaked in water to cover
    for at least 2 hours
2 large onions, thinly sliced
4 tablespoons oil
$^1/_4$ pound mushrooms, sliced
3 cups water
$^3/_4$ teaspoon salt
$^1/_4$ teaspoon pepper
2 tablespoons margarine
sour cream, for garnish, optional

Wash and check rice and lentils carefully. In a medium-sized pot, sauté onions in oil until tender. Add mushrooms and sauté until onions are golden. Add rice, lentils, water, salt, and pepper. Bring to a boil. Cover, reduce heat, and cook for 45 minutes, or until all water is absorbed and lentils and rice are tender. If necessary, add a little water. Stir in margarine. For a dairy meal, garnish with sour cream. Serves 6.

Stuffed Zucchini Halves

I used this recipe when I first came to Israel and did all of my cooking on top of the stove. This dish really made a hit with my family and guests. Choose short, fat zucchini, if possible, to hold more stuffing.

4 zucchini, halved lengthwise
1 teaspoon salt
2 large onions
1 sweet red pepper, cut into short thin
    strips
3 tablespoons oil
2 tomatoes, diced
$^2/_3$ cup bread crumbs
dash of garlic powder
2 teaspoons onion soup mix or pareve
    chicken soup mix
$^2/_3$ cup water

Scoop out zucchini with a teaspoon, leaving a $^1/_4$-inch-thick shell. Salt shells lightly. Meanwhile, sauté 1 onion and red pepper strips in oil for about 7 minutes until onion is tender. Add tomatoes and cook for an additional minute. Remove from heat. Combine with bread crumbs, garlic powder, and 1 teaspoon of soup powder. Fill shells with mixture. In a large skillet or low pot, sauté second onion until tender. Place stuffed zucchini in skillet. Combine remaining soup powder with water and pour into pan. Cover and steam for about 35 minutes until tender, basting once or twice.

Variation

Sprinkle tops with half a cup of grated Parmesan cheese during last 5 minutes of cooking.

Neapolitan Eggplant

A delicious way of preparing eggplant.

3 small eggplants
1 teaspoon salt
1/3 cup oil
2 large onions, diced
3 medium tomatoes, diced
2 cloves garlic, minced
1 teaspoon salt
1 teaspoon oregano
2/3 cup bread crumbs
1 cup grated cheddar cheese

Cut eggplants in half lengthwise. Sprinkle with salt and let stand for 20 minutes. Rinse with cold water. With a sharp paring knife, cut out pulp, leaving about a 1/4-inch-thick shell. Chop pulp and sauté in oil in a skillet with onions for about 7 minutes. Add tomatoes, garlic, and salt, and cook for an additional 2 minutes. Add oregano. Fill shells with mixture, sprinkle with bread crumbs, and place in a large greased baking pan. Pour 1/2 inch of water into baking pan. Cover and bake in a preheated oven for 40-50 minutes until tender. Sprinkle cheese on top and return to oven uncovered for 10-15 minutes. Serves 6.

Skillet Eggplant Italiano

A delightful dish made right on top of the stove with eggplant, cheese, and tomatoes.

1 large onion, cut into 1-inch cubes
1 large green pepper, diced
oil
dash of garlic powder
salt, to taste
1/4 teaspoon pepper
1 large or 2 medium eggplants, sliced
    or cubed
4-5 large tomatoes, cut into cubes
1 cup shredded cheddar or Muenster
    cheese
1 teaspoon oregano

Sauté onion and green pepper in oil for 5 minutes. Add garlic powder, salt, pepper, and eggplant, and continue sautéing for 5 minutes, stirring occasionally. Add tomatoes, cover, and cook for 15-20 more minutes until eggplant is tender. Stir in cheese and oregano, and cook for 5 more minutes until cheese melts. Serves 5.

Variation

A 20-ounce can of tomatoes can be substituted for fresh tomatoes.

Vegetable Burgers

These vegetable burgers are always a hit—and not just with vegetarians. Try them as a side dish, a main dish, or as different fare for the barbecue.

1 large onion, diced
$^1/_2$ green pepper, diced
1 stalk celery, diced
2 medium carrots, shredded
4 tablespoons oil
1 zucchini, shredded
1 cup cooked cauliflower or string
   beans, chopped
1-1$^1/_2$ teaspoons salt, to taste
$^1/_8$ teaspoon pepper
3-4 large eggs, beaten
$^1/_2$ cup matzo meal
$^1/_3$ cup chopped nuts, optional
oil, for frying or baking
1 teaspoon oregano, optional
$^1/_2$ cup grated cheese, optional

Sauté onion, green pepper, celery, and carrots in oil until onions are light brown. Remove from heat. Combine with remaining ingredients (except cheese) and mix well. Let stand for 10 minutes. Shape into burgers and fry in a small amount of oil on both sides until golden brown. Alternatively, place in a well-greased baking pan, coating top of each with 1 teaspoon of oil. Cover and bake in a preheated 350° oven for 45 minutes. If desired, sprinkle with grated cheese or spread with sauce before baking. Yields 10 burgers.

Sauce

$^2/_3$ cup tomato sauce
1 teaspoon sugar
$^1/_3$ cup water
$^1/_4$ teaspoon thyme
$^1/_2$ teaspoon oregano
1 clove garlic, minced
1 tablespoon oil

Combine all ingredients and simmer for 2 minutes.

To keep cauliflower white, cook it in water with a little vinegar or milk. To eliminate cabbage or cauliflower odor, place a piece of bread in the water while cooking.

Savory Cabbage Squares

This is like a cabbage pie or quiche.

Dough
2 cups unsifted flour
1 teaspoon baking powder
1/4 teaspoon salt
1 cup margarine, room temperature
2/3 cup plain yogurt or sour cream

Filling
1 large onion, diced
1/3 cup oil
1 medium cabbage, shredded
3 tablespoons flour, sifted
1 cup milk
6 ounces cheddar cheese, grated
salt, to taste
white pepper, to taste
5 eggs, beaten
4 tablespoons bread crumbs
1 tablespoon caraway seeds

Sift together flour, baking powder, and salt. Cut in margarine with a pastry blender or 2 knives, until mixture resembles coarse crumbs. Mix in yogurt last. Form dough into a ball. Refrigerate for at least 2 hours. Roll out and pat into a 9x13-inch baking pan. To make filling, sauté onion in oil until soft. Add cabbage and cook for 10 minutes, stirring occasionally. Stir in flour, milk, cheese (reserving 1/3 cup), salt, and pepper. Remove from heat and let cool slightly. Stir in eggs, bread crumbs, and caraway seeds. Pour into unbaked crust. Sprinkle with remaining cheese. Bake in a preheated 350° oven for 1 hour until golden brown. These squares freeze well. Yields about 15 squares.

Green Beans with Sweet Red Peppers

The bland-tasting string beans are enhanced by the addition of the onions, sweet red peppers, and almonds. A colorful and delicious dish.

1 pound fresh or frozen string beans
2 large onions, diced
1-2 sweet red peppers, cut into thin strips
2 tablespoons oil
salt and pepper, to taste
1/3 cup slivered almonds, optional

Steam string beans in a little salted water until just tender-crisp. Uncover during last 2 minutes of cooking to retain fresh green color. Drain. Sauté onions and peppers in oil for 7 minutes. Combine with string beans and seasonings. If desired, add slivered almonds. Serve hot. Serves 6.

For fresher-tasting vegetables, add a touch of sugar when cooking them.

Feta Cheese and Spinach Diamonds

Delectable!

1¹/₂ **portions Easy Flaky Dough (see page 226)**

Filling
2 **medium onions, finely chopped**
4 **green onions, thinly sliced**
¹/₃ **cup oil**
3 **10-ounce packages frozen chopped spinach, thawed and drained**
¹/₄ **cup chopped fresh dill, or 1¹/₂ teaspoons dry dill**
¹/₂ **teaspoon cinnamon**
¹/₄ **teaspoon black pepper**
¹/₃ **cup milk**
5 **eggs, well beaten**
³/₄ **pound feta cheese, crumbled**
2 **tablespoons melted margarine**
sesame seeds, for sprinkling top

In a large skillet, sauté white and green onions in oil until tender. Stir in spinach. Cover and cook over low heat for 5 minutes. Remove cover and continue cooking while stirring for about 1-2 minutes, until liquid evaporates. Stir in dill, cinnamon, and pepper. Transfer mixture to a large bowl. Let cool slightly and stir in milk, eggs, and feta cheese. Divide Easy Flaky Dough into 2 parts. Roll out each part ¹/₈ inch thick and large enough to cover a greased, 11x17-inch cookie sheet with a slight overlap on sides. Brush with margarine. Spread filling evenly over dough. Cover filling with a second layer of dough, overlapping pastry edges. Crimp to seal. Brush with margarine. Sprinkle sesame seeds on top and score halfway down into diamond shapes. Do not cut through to bottom crust. Bake in a preheated 375° oven for 30 minutes, then reduce heat to 325° for 25 minutes. Yields 32 pieces.

Variation

Farmer cheese or ricotta cheese may be substituted for feta cheese, but add 1 teaspoon of salt.

To remove the strong smell of onions from hands, rub hands with cut end of celery stalk.

and Mushroom Soufflé

... easier to prepare than it
... makes an elegant side dish
...uncheon main course. Time it carefully.
Serve as soon as baking is completed.

¹/₄ cup (¹/₂ stick) margarine
4 tablespoons flour, sifted
1¹/₄ cups hot water or milk
5 eggs, separated
1 teaspoon salt
¹/₄ teaspoon pepper
2 cups cooked cauliflower or broccoli,
** diced**
¹/₂ cup cooked fresh or frozen green
** peas**
²/₃ cup sliced mushrooms, sautéed
¹/₂ sweet red pepper, diced and sautéed

Melt margarine in a skillet. Stir in flour until light golden. Slowly stir in hot water or milk until sauce is smooth and thick. Remove from heat and let cool slightly. Stir in beaten egg yolks, seasonings, and vegetables. Beat egg whites until stiff. Fold into vegetable mixture. Pour into a greased 2-quart casserole and bake in a preheated 350° oven for 50-60 minutes. Serve immediately. Serves 6-8.

Variation

Instead of cauliflower or broccoli, use 2 cups of any other cooked vegetable or a mixture of cooked vegetables.

Overnight Soufflé

A delicious soufflé with a special touch.

¹/₂ loaf (8 ounces) challah or white
** bread, cubed**
8 ounces cheddar cheese, grated
4 eggs, beaten
2¹/₂ cups milk
1 tablespoon prepared mustard
¹/₂ teaspoon salt
pinch of pepper
pinch of thyme
pinch of nutmeg

Place half of the bread cubes in a greased 7x11-inch baking pan. Sprinkle half of the grated cheese on top. Repeat with remaining bread and cheese. Beat eggs, milk, and remaining ingredients together. Pour over bread cubes and cheese. Press down to help bread absorb liquid. Refrigerate or freeze overnight. Bake in a preheated 350° oven for 1 hour. Serves 12.

One teaspoon dry herbs equals 1 tablespoon fresh.

Old herbs and spices aren't very flavorful. They should be replaced each year.

A Variety of Quiches

Try these recipes for these delicious quiches: mushroom, onion, tuna-mushroom, and tomato-mushroom.

Crust

$^1/_3$ cup margarine
$1^1/_4$ cups flour, sifted
$^1/_4$ teaspoon salt
3 tablespoons iced water

To make the crust, cut margarine into flour and salt until pea-sized chunks. Add water, a tablespoon at a time. Form into a ball and refrigerate. Roll out dough to fit on bottom and sides of a 9-inch quiche pan. Bake in a 350° oven for 10 minutes. Meanwhile make filling.

Mushroom Filling

1 large onion, thinly sliced
3 tablespoons vegetable oil
$^1/_2$ pound fresh mushrooms, sliced, or 1 cup canned sliced mushrooms, drained
$1^1/_2$ cups milk
6 eggs, beaten
$^3/_4$ cup shredded Swiss cheese
1 scant teaspoon salt
pinch of pepper

Sauté onion in oil until tender. Add mushrooms and sauté for about 10 minutes until onions are nearly golden. Remove from heat. Let cool slightly and stir in remaining ingredients. Pour mushroom filling into quiche crust. Bake in a 375° oven for 35 minutes.

Onion Filling

Omit mushrooms. Sauté 3 large sliced onions in 3-4 tablespoons of oil for about 20 minutes until golden. Add remaining ingredients and proceed as directed.

Tuna-Mushroom Filling

Reduce mushrooms to $^1/_4$ pound or 1 4-ounce can. Add 1 $7^1/_2$-ounce can of drained and flaked tuna fish and $^1/_4$ cup of mayonnaise. Reduce salt to $^1/_4$ teaspoon. Proceed as directed.

Tomato-Mushroom Filling

Add 2 medium thinly sliced tomatoes and place on bottom of prebaked crust. Proceed as directed.

Spinach Quiche

Choose between 2 fillings for this quiche: one with sharp cheese (Swiss or cheddar), the other with salty cheese (feta). If using the latter, omit the salt.

1 large onion, diced
2 tablespoons oil
1 pound fresh spinach, checked and chopped, or 1 10-ounce package frozen chopped spinach, drained
3 eggs, beaten
1 1/2 cups milk
1/2 teaspoon salt
1/4 teaspoon pepper
8 ounces Swiss or cheddar cheese, shredded, or feta cheese

Sauté onion in oil until tender. Add spinach, cover, and cook for 5 minutes. Combine with remaining ingredients and pour into a well-greased 9-inch quiche pan. Bake in a 350° oven for 40 minutes. Serves 6 as a main dish, 8 as an appetizer.

Variation

Add 1 2 1/2-ounce can of fried onion rings to feta cheese mixture and eliminate onion and salt.

Noodle-Cheese Soufflé

A marvelous kugel-type soufflé.

4 ounces cream cheese
1 cup (8 ounces) sour cream
1/2 cup margarine
1/2 cup sugar
1 teaspoon vanilla extract
1 teaspoon salt
4 eggs
4 ounces fine noodles, cooked and drained

Place all ingredients except noodles in a blender, food processor, or electric mixer and blend until fluffy. Combine mixture with noodles and pour into a well-greased 1 1/2-quart casserole. Bake in a preheated 350° oven for 1 hour. Serves 6.

Potato Knishes

Knishes with this tasty potato filling are probably the most popular among Ashkenazi Jews, with meat filling a runner-up. In Israel all kinds of knishes can be seen at outdoor kiosks and cafes which specialize in filled flaky pastries.

Special Knish Dough
2¼ cups flour, sifted
½ teaspoon baking powder
¾ teaspoon salt
1⅓ cups margarine, room temperature
2 small egg yolks
1 tablespoon lemon juice
⅓ cup water

Combine flour, baking powder, and salt. Add remaining ingredients. Mix until smooth. Form into a ball, place in a plastic bag, and refrigerate for at least 2 hours or overnight. Divide dough into quarters. Roll and fill as directed in individual knish recipes. Bake in a preheated 350° oven until golden. Yields 26-28 knishes.

Filling
6-8 medium potatoes
2 large onions, diced
¼ cup oil
1 teaspoon salt (or more), to taste
pepper, to taste
2 eggs, well beaten
oil, for brushing dough

Glaze
1 beaten egg yolk, combined with 1
   teaspoon water

Peel and slice potatoes and boil until tender. Drain very well in a colander and mash while hot. While potatoes are cooking, sauté onions in oil until golden. Add sautéed onions, salt, pepper, and eggs to mashed potatoes. Divide Special Knish Dough into 3 or 4 parts. On a lightly floured surface (a slab of marble is excellent), roll each part into a 9x12-inch rectangle, ⅛ inch thick. Place a 2-inch-wide row of potato filling on edge of dough closest to you and roll. Place on a greased baking sheet. With a sharp knife, cut halfway down at 1½-inch intervals. Brush with glaze, and bake in a preheated 450° oven for about 40-45 minutes or until golden brown. Yields 25 knishes.

Variations

Liver and potato knishes: Place a 1½-inch-wide row of mashed potatoes on edge of rolled out dough. Top with a row of 1½ cups of ground koshered liver or cooked meat combined with a sautéed onion and a beaten egg.

Potato cheese knishes: Stir in 1½ cups of grated cheddar or Swiss cheese.

Borekas

A savory filled pastry popular in the Middle East.

Use Special Knish Dough (see page 149), Easy Flaky Dough (see page 226), phyllo dough (following instructions on package), or puff pastry dough (following instructions on package). Roll out dough into a thin, rectangular shape. Leave whole and place 2 inches of filling along inside edge of dough, then roll. Cut into top of roll at 2-inch intervals, marking slices. Alternatively, cut into 3-inch squares or 3-inch rounds using a cookie cutter or a glass dipped in flour. Put a teaspoonful of filling on each square or round, moisten edges with egg white or water, and fold over filling. Press edges firmly together. Place on a greased baking sheet and brush with glaze: 1 egg yolk combined with 1 teaspoon of water. Sprinkle with sesame seeds, if desired. Prick top with a fork. Bake Special Knish Dough at 350° for about 35-40 minutes and Easy Flaky Dough at 450° for about 40-45 minutes until golden brown. (High heat makes Easy Flaky Dough flaky and puffy.)

Spinach Cheese Filling

1 onion, diced
3 tablespoons margarine
1 10-ounce package frozen chopped spinach, thawed
$^{1}/_{4}$ cup grated Parmesan cheese, optional
$^{3}/_{4}$ pound cottage cheese
2 eggs, beaten
4 tablespoons wheat germ or bread crumbs
1-2 cloves garlic, minced
$^{1}/_{2}$ teaspoon salt
$^{1}/_{8}$ teaspoon pepper

Sauté onion in margarine until soft. Add chopped spinach and cook for 5 more minutes. Let cool and combine with remaining ingredients. Bake as directed.

Broccoli Filling

3 eggs, separated
2 10-ounce packages frozen chopped broccoli
$^{1}/_{2}$ cup mayonnaise
$^{1}/_{2}$ envelope onion soup mix

Beat egg whites until stiff. Combine all remaining ingredients and fold in egg whites. Fill, roll, and bake.

Meat, Liver, or Lung Filling

1 onion, diced
3 tablespoons oil
3 cups cooked ground meat, liver, or
    lung
salt and pepper, to taste
1-2 eggs

Sauté onion in oil until soft. Stir in meat, liver, or lung, and sauté for an additional 5 minutes. Remove from heat and combine with remaining ingredients. Fill rounds, squares, or rolled out dough with a thin layer of filling. Bake as directed.

Kasha Filling

1 medium onion, diced
3 tablespoons oil
$^1/_4$ pound mushrooms, sliced
3 cups kasha, cooked
salt and pepper, to taste
2 eggs, beaten

Sauté onion in oil. Add mushrooms and sauté for 3 more minutes. Add kasha and seasonings. Remove from heat and stir in eggs. Bake as directed.

Savory Cheese Filling

1 pound farmer cheese
2 eggs, beaten
1 cup grated Swiss or sharp cheddar
    cheese
3 tablespoons grated onion
salt, to taste
$^1/_4$ teaspoon pepper

Combine all ingredients. Bake as directed.

Kugels
& Latkes

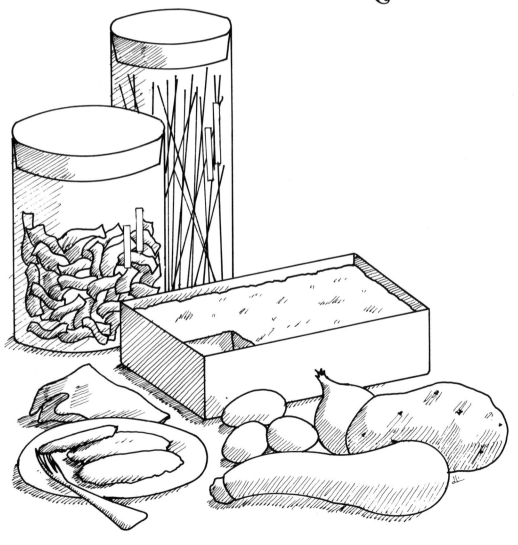

Kugels & Latkes

Classic Potato Kugel

I still recall my mother's Shabbat potato kugel—yaptzug she called it—baked in a cast-iron pot and left on the metal stove cover (blech) overnight. What a marvelous taste it had the next morning! The following potato kugel is easy to make—a flavorful side dish for Shabbat or any time.

8 medium potatoes
1 medium onion
4 large eggs
¹/₄ cup matzo meal or sifted flour, optional
¹/₄ cup oil
1¹/₂ teaspoons salt
¹/₄ teaspoon pepper
¹/₄ cup oil, for pan

Grate potatoes and onion together, either by hand or in a food processor. Let stand for 5 minutes. Squeeze out excess liquid. Stir in remaining ingredients except oil for the pan. Pour the ¹/₄ cup of oil into a 9x13-inch baking pan or a 2¹/₂-quart casserole. Place pan or casserole in oven, while preheating to 350° for about 15 minutes to prevent kugel from sticking. Remove and pour in potato mixture. Return to oven and bake at 350° for 1 hour or until brown. Serves 12.

Variations

Make potato kugelettes by spooning mixture into muffin tins, greased and lined with fluted paper cups. Pour a teaspoon of oil on top of each and bake in a preheated 350° oven for 40 minutes or until golden brown. Serves 18.

For a low-calorie version, substitute raw, grated cauliflower—about half a medium head—for half the amount of potatoes.

Zucchini potato kugel: Use raw, shredded zucchini in place of half the amount of potatoes.

Carrot Kugel and Kugelettes

A tasty change from the classic potato kugel.

2 eggs, well beaten
³/₄ cup brown sugar, packed
1 cup margarine, melted and cooled
juice and grated rind of ¹/₂ lemon
2 cups flour, sifted
1¹/₂ teaspoons baking powder
1 teaspoon baking soda
3 cups shredded carrots
¹/₂ teaspoon salt
1 teaspoon vanilla extract
¹/₂ teaspoon cinnamon

Combine all ingredients in order given. Pour into a well-greased 9x13-inch baking pan or 8-inch springform pan. Bake in a preheated 350° oven for 1 hour. Yields 15 squares. For kugelettes, pour into greased muffin tins lined with greased, fluted paper cups. Bake in a 350° oven for 35-40 minutes.

Tsimmes Kugel

A modern version of two traditional Shabbat favorites—tsimmes and kugel—makes a hit every time. A wonderful combination of sweet potatoes, apples, and carrots. Imagine! A kugel without eggs.

1 small, whole, unpeeled orange, cut into pieces and ground in a food processor
2 cups shredded raw, sweet potatoes
2 cups raw, shredded carrots
2 cups shredded tart apples
1 cup brown or white sugar
1 teaspoon cinnamon
¹/₂ teaspoon salt
1 cup flour, sifted
¹/₂ cup oil
²/₃ cup light raisins

Combine all ingredients. Pour into a greased 1¹/₂-quart casserole, cover, and bake in a 350° oven for 40 minutes. Uncover and continue baking for an additional 20-30 minutes. Serves 10-12.

Variation

Place halved pitted prunes, cherries, or pieces of pineapple on top of kugel before baking, or add 1 cup of chopped dates, pitted prunes, or pineapple to mixture.

Traditional Jerusalem Kugel

A Jerusalem classic. Many old-time Jerusalem families pride themselves on their versions of this kugel, with its unique taste combination of caramelized sugar and pepper. It can be left on the stove overnight and served piping hot for Shabbat Kiddush or lunch. The variation for apple kugel—given to me by the Ariston Hotel in Tiberias—is great.

1 pound medium-fine noodles
$^1/_2$ cup oil
1 cup sugar
4 eggs, beaten
$1^1/_2$ teaspoons salt
1-2 teaspoons pepper, to taste

Boil noodles in a large pot of water for 5 minutes. Drain but do not rinse. Caramelize sugar by pouring oil and $^3/_4$ cup of sugar into a large heavy pot. Stir occasionally over medium-low heat until it is deep brown and bubbles (make sure that it does not burn). Remove from heat immediately and add to hot cooked noodles, stirring vigorously until thoroughly combined. Stir in the eggs, remaining sugar, salt, and pepper. Line a broad 4- or 5-quart pot with wax paper. Pour in noodle mixture. Cover and bake in a preheated 325° oven for $1^1/_2$ hours. To keep it warm over Shabbat, leave on covered stove top (*blech*) near burner or in a 200° oven until ready to serve the next day. Serves 10-12.

Variation

Apple kugel: Stir in 4-5 large, thickly sliced tart apples with rest of ingredients.

Broccoli Kugel

The delicate taste of the broccoli makes this an unusual kugel.

5 large eggs
3 10-ounce packages frozen chopped broccoli, defrosted but uncooked
2 heaped tablespoons onion soup powder
$^3/_4$ cup mayonnaise

Beat eggs in an electric mixer until frothy. Stir in remaining ingredients. Pour into a well-greased 9x13-inch baking pan. Bake in a preheated 350° oven for 45 minutes. Serves 12.

Zucchini Kugel

A kugel made with a vegetable low in calories. A tasty change from the heavier potato kugel.

2 pounds zucchini, shredded
4 eggs, well beaten
1 teaspoon salt
1/4 teaspoon pepper
1/4 cup matzo meal or flour
3 tablespoons grated onion
2 tablespoons margarine, for dotting top

Mix all ingredients together, and pour into a well-greased 1 1/2-quart casserole. Dot with margarine. Bake in a preheated 350° oven for 1 hour. Serves 6.

Variations

For a fluffier version, separate eggs. Beat egg whites until stiff. Beat yolks and add to other ingredients. Fold in beaten egg whites. Pour into a well-greased 1 1/2-quart casserole and bake as above.

Slice and steam zucchini in slightly salted water for 10-15 minutes. Drain, mash, and combine with remaining ingredients. Pour into a well-greased casserole and bake for 45 minutes.

Cheese Kugel

A delicious dairy kugel—a thin batter on the bottom and top, with a delicious, tangy, cheese mixture in the middle. A special recipe.

Batter
1/2 cup margarine, melted
1/4 cup sugar
2 eggs
1 cup flour, sifted
2 teaspoons baking powder
1/4 cup milk
1 teaspoon vanilla extract

Filling
2 pounds cottage cheese
3 eggs, beaten
1/4 cup sugar
juice of 1 lemon

In a food processor or blender, mix ingredients for batter. Then mix filling ingredients together until well blended. Pour 1/2 of batter mixture into a greased 11x7-inch baking dish. Spoon cheese mixture on top. Pour and spread remaining batter evenly over cheese mixture. Bake in a preheated 325° oven for 1 hour.

Gourmet Noodle Kugel with Meringue Nut Topping

A sweet and delectable pareve side dish.

6 eggs, separated
1 pound noodles, boiled and drained
2/3 cup sugar
1/2 cup oil
1 teaspoon salt
2 teaspoons vanilla extract
2/3 cup apricot jam
1/3 cup finely chopped nuts

Beat egg yolks until light and fluffy. Stir in noodles, 1/3 cup of the sugar, oil, salt, and vanilla extract. Pour into a greased 9x13-inch baking pan. Bake in a preheated 350° oven for 40-50 minutes. Remove from oven and spread with apricot jam, then with Meringue Nut Topping.

Meringue Nut Topping

Beat egg whites until frothy. Gradually add remaining 1/3 cup of sugar and beat until stiff. Fold in nuts. Spread over kugel. Return to oven for an additional 20 minutes at 350°. Serves 12.

Variation

Instead of spreading jam on baked kugel, mix it into batter before baking.

Spinach Noodle Kugel

Looks and tastes like a spinach soufflé.

8 ounces fine noodles
1 large onion, diced
1/4 cup oil
1 pound spinach, chopped, checked, and cooked 5 minutes, or 1 10-ounce package frozen spinach, thawed, but not cooked
1 teaspoon salt, or to taste
1/2 teaspoon pepper
4 eggs, well beaten

Cook noodles in lightly salted boiling water, according to directions on package. Rinse with cold water and drain. Sauté onion in oil until tender. Combine all ingredients. Pour into a greased 7x11-inch baking dish and bake in a preheated 350° oven for 1 hour. Yields 12-15 squares.

Variation

For a fluffier kugel, separate eggs. Beat egg whites until stiff and fold into mixture. The beaten yolks are combined with spinach mixture.

Fruity Apple Challah Kugel

A marvelous-tasting side dish. It can even be served as a dessert topped with whipped cream.

3/4 loaf dry challah or white bread, sliced
water for soaking
6 large tart apples, peeled, and chopped or shredded
2 cups pineapple tidbits, drained
1 cup light raisins
1 cup strawberry jam
5 eggs, well beaten
1 1/2 teaspoons cinnamon
juice and grated rind of 2 lemons
1/2 cup oil
1/3 cup brown sugar, for top
2 tablespoons margarine, for top

Soak bread in water to cover for 2 minutes. Drain, squeezing out excess liquid. Add remaining ingredients except brown sugar and margarine. Pour mixture into a greased 10x15-inch pan (or a 9x13-inch pan, for a thicker kugel). Bake in a preheated 350° oven for 1 hour. Sprinkle with brown sugar, and dot with margarine. Then bake for an additional 20 minutes until golden brown. Serves 18-20.

Variations

Add about 2 cups of dried quartered apricots, soaked first in boiling water for 20 minutes.

Cherry kugel: In place of apples, add 1 can of cherry pie filling to mixture. Reduce jam to half a cup.

Substitute 4-5 cups of other fruit—apricots or peaches—for apples and pineapple tidbits.

Caramel Pecan Rice Kugel

A side dish with a delicious caramel flavor to enliven a special meal.

1/4 cup margarine, melted
1 cup pecan halves
1 cup brown sugar
3 cups rice, cooked
4 large eggs, well beaten
2/3 cup sugar
1 teaspoon salt
2 teaspoons vanilla extract
3 1/2 cups hot water or milk
1/2 teaspoon cinnamon
1/8 teaspoon nutmeg

Pour margarine into a 2-quart casserole or a 9x13-inch baking pan. Spread pecans evenly on bottom. Sprinkle with brown sugar. Combine rice and eggs with remaining ingredients and spread evenly on top. Bake in a preheated 350° oven for 1 hour. Serves 15.

Rice and pasta come out sticky if overcooked or if boiled in very little water. To prevent sticking, add one tablespoon oil to boiling water, and rinse well after cooking.

Cranberry Noodle Kugel

A side dish or dessert. Rich and delicious!

8 ounces medium noodles, cooked, drained, and rinsed
1 cup sour cream or yogurt
4 eggs
1 cup milk
$1/3$ cup sugar
$1/2$ pound cream cheese or cottage cheese
$1/2$ teaspoon salt
$1/2$ cup margarine, melted
$1/2$ teaspoon cinnamon
1 teaspoon vanilla extract
1 16-ounce can whole, jelled cranberries

Combine all ingredients except cranberries. Mix well. Pour into a greased 7x11-inch baking pan. Bake in a preheated 350° oven for 40 minutes. Remove from oven and spoon cranberries over top. Bake for an additional 20 minutes. Serves 6-8.

Variation

Fruit noodle kugel: Omit milk and cranberries and add a 16-ounce can of drained, pitted cherries and a $7^{1}/2$-ounce can of crushed pineapple. Sprinkle top with 3 tablespoons of sugar combined with 1 teaspoon of cinnamon. Bake in a 9x13-inch pan.

Apricot Noodle Streusel Kugel

This is a special recipe which I received 30 years ago. Everyone's favorite. Make it for Shavuot or Chanukah or when you have friends over for lunch.

8 ounces medium noodles
$1/2$ teaspoon salt
$1/4$ cup melted margarine
$1/2$ cup sugar
3 eggs, well beaten
1 cup milk or pareve cream
1 cup apricot juice
1 teaspoon vanilla extract

Streusel-Type Topping
1 cup crushed corn flakes
$1/3$ cup brown or white sugar
$1^{1}/2$ teaspoons cinnamon
$1/4$ cup margarine

Cook noodles in lightly salted water until tender. Drain and rinse. Combine noodles with remaining ingredients and pour into a well-greased 7x11-inch baking pan. Combine corn flakes, sugar, and cinnamon, and sprinkle evenly over noodles. Cut margarine into small pieces and scatter evenly over corn flake mixture. Bake in a preheated 350° oven for 1 hour. Yields 15-20 squares.

Traditional Potato Latkes

Potato pancakes—or latkes as they are known in Yiddish—are popular during Chanukah. The oil used in frying them echoes the theme of the holiday, which recalls the oil in the Holy Temple that miraculously lasted for eight days.

5 medium potatoes
1 small onion
2 large eggs
3 tablespoons flour, sifted, optional
salt and pepper, to taste
1 tablespoon oil
oil, for frying

Grate potatoes and onion finely. Let stand for 5 minutes and squeeze out excess liquid. Stir in remaining ingredients. Fry in hot oil on both sides until golden brown. Yields 15-18 latkes.

Zucchini Latkes

A delightful latke variation made with shredded zucchini.

2 medium zucchini, shredded
2 tablespoons wheat germ or matzo meal
5-6 tablespoons whole wheat flour, sifted
3 large eggs, well beaten
1/2 teaspoon salt, or to taste
generous pinch of pepper
2 cloves garlic, minced, or 1/4 teaspoon garlic powder
oil, for frying

Combine all ingredients, mixing well. Drop by tablespoonful into hot oil in a skillet and fry on both sides until golden brown. Yields 10-12 latkes.

Variations

Zucchini and carrot latkes: Stir 2 medium, shredded carrots into mixture. Add 1 more egg and an additional tablespoon of flour.

Apple latkes: Substitute 2-3 shredded apples for zucchini. Omit pepper and garlic.

Spinach Latkes

Your guests will just love these.

3/4 pound fresh spinach, or 1 10-ounce
   package frozen spinach
3 eggs, beaten
6 tablespoons matzo meal or bread
   crumbs
salt and pepper, to taste
3 tablespoons grated onions
oil, for frying

Wash and check spinach carefully. Steam in a tiny amount of lightly salted water for 5 minutes. Drain well. Chop. Mix with remaining ingredients and let rest for 10 minutes. Form patties. Drop by tablespoonful into hot oil and fry on both sides until golden brown.

Variation

Leek pancakes: Wash and thinly slice 1/2 pound of leeks. Proceed as above.

Rice Latkes

A variation on traditional Chanukah latkes.

2 cups brown or white rice, cooked
2 eggs, well beaten
3 tablespoons wheat germ or whole
   wheat flour
2 tablespoons sugar
generous pinch of cinnamon
oil, for frying

Combine all ingredients, mixing thoroughly. Drop by tablespoonful into hot oil and fry on both sides until golden brown. Yields 8-12 latkes.

Scrumptious Cheese Latkes

Dairy foods echo one of the themes of Chanukah, making these cheese latkes especially welcome. They are also easily adaptable into cheese muffins.

4 eggs, well beaten
1 cup farmer cheese or cottage cheese
³/4 cup flour, sifted
2 tablespoons sugar
¹/2 teaspoon salt
¹/2 teaspoon baking soda
¹/2 teaspoon vanilla extract
¹/3 cup raisins, plumped in boiling
**   water for 5 minutes**
1 large tart apple, peeled and grated,
**   optional**
oil, for frying

Combine all ingredients. Drop by tablespoonful into hot oil and fry on both sides until golden brown. Yields about 20 latkes.

Variation

Cheese muffins: Add ¹/2 cup of yogurt or sour cream and an additional ¹/4 cup of sifted flour. Pour into greased muffin tins and bake in a preheated 350° oven for 25 minutes until golden. Yields 12-15 muffins.

Blintzes

Blintzes

Classic Blintz Leaves

Blintzes are popular on Shavuot, when dairy dishes are eaten. These basic blintz leaves—thin pancakes—can be filled with a variety of sweet or savory fillings, then fried to a crisp golden brown or baked with a variety of sauces. They can also be frozen, taken straight from the freezer, and fried in hot margarine or oil over low heat. The first variation is made with fewer eggs, resulting in a thin, soft, pliable, but firm, pancake. Be sure to refrigerate batter for at least 2 hours—to prevent rubberiness—then stir briefly.

Blintz Batter 1

2 eggs
1¹/₄ cups flour
1¹/₂ cups water or milk
2 tablespoons oil
¹/₄ teaspoon salt

Blintz Batter 2

4 eggs
¹/₄ teaspoon salt
2 tablespoons oil
1 cup flour, sifted
1¹/₄ cups water or milk

Mix together all ingredients in a food processor, blender, or electric mixer for about 1 minute until smooth. Scrape sides down using a spatula. Mix for 10 more seconds. Refrigerate for 2 hours. Stir slightly before using. Batter should have the consistency of cream. Lightly oil a 7- or 8-inch frying pan and heat. Pour in 2-3 tablespoons of batter, tilting pan quickly from side to side to distribute a thin coating evenly on bottom. Pour back any excess batter. Cook over medium-high heat until top of blintz is dry. Turn blintz out of pan and stack on a clean, dry tea towel. Yields about 16-18 blintz leaves.

Variations

Chocolate blintz leaves: Add 4 tablespoons of cocoa and 4 tablespoons of sugar to batter.

Whole wheat blintz leaves: Substitute 1 cup of whole wheat flour for white flour, and add ¹/₈ cup more water.

Dessert blintzes: Add to either batter 2 tablespoons of sugar, 1 tablespoon of brandy, and ¹/₂ cup of orange juice in place of ¹/₂ cup of water.

If batter thickens slightly while frying blintz leaves, add a few tablespoons of water to batter until it becomes the proper consistency.

Batter should be beaten at low or medium speed. High speed mixing causes bubbles in the blintz. If the edge of the blintz cracks, the batter is too thin.

Cheese Blintzes

The flavor of these blintzes is greatly enhanced by adding one of the various toppings.

16-18 Classic Blintz Leaves (see page 171)

Cheese Filling

1 1/2 pounds farmer cheese (or use 2 pounds farmer cheese, but omit cream cheese)
1/2 pound cream cheese
3-4 tablespoons sugar, to taste
1 teaspoon vanilla or almond extract
2-3 eggs
1/4 teaspoon cinnamon
grated rind of 1 lemon
1/2 cup raisins or chopped nuts
butter or oil, for frying

Combine all ingredients, and place 1-2 tablespoons of mixture on each blintz leaf. Fold in top and sides to form an envelope, then roll up; or just roll, leaving sides open. Fry in butter or oil on both sides until golden brown. Top with sour cream, yogurt, applesauce, or apricot jam thinned with a little warm water. Yields 16-18 blintzes.

Chicken or Meat Blintzes

16-18 Classic Blintz Leaves (see page 171)
1 medium onion, diced
3 tablespoons oil
2-3 cups cooked ground chicken or meat
1 large beaten egg
oil, for frying
tomato sauce, for topping

Sauté a medium diced onion in 3 tablespoons of oil. Stir in 2-3 cups of cooked ground chicken or meat and 1 large, beaten egg. Sauté for an additional 3 minutes. Place 2 tablespoons of mixture on each blintz leaf. Fold over and fry in oil on both sides, or bake, topped with tomato sauce, in a shallow pan.

Blintz Soufflé

Here is a good way of serving blintzes without many last-minute preparations. Make them beforehand, and bake in this delicious dairy sauce.

14-16 Cheese, Blueberry, or Cherry Blintzes (see pages 172 and 174)
1¹/₂ cups plain yogurt or sour cream
¹/₂ teaspoon cinnamon
¹/₄ cup margarine, melted
¹/₄ teaspoon salt
4 eggs, well beaten
1 teaspoon grated orange rind
¹/₃ cup sugar
2 tablespoons orange juice
1 teaspoon vanilla extract

Arrange blintzes in a greased 9x13-inch pan. Combine remaining ingredients and pour over blintzes. Bake for 40 minutes in a preheated 350° oven. Serve hot. Top with crushed berries or hot fruit compote, if desired. Serves 8.

Baked Cheese Pillows with Sour Cream Pastry

These delicious cheese pillows look like baked blintzes, although they are made with sour cream dough. I sometimes double this recipe and freeze half.

Dough
1 cup margarine, room temperature
2¹/₂ cups flour, sifted
¹/₂ teaspoon baking powder
2 tablespoons sugar
¹/₂ teaspoon salt
1 cup sour cream
¹/₃ cup oil or melted margarine, for brushing

Filling
1 pound farmer cheese (or ¹/₂ pound farmer cheese and ¹/₂ pound cream cheese)
3-4 tablespoons sugar
2 eggs, beaten
¹/₂ teaspoon cinnamon
pinch of salt

To make dough, cut margarine into flour with a pastry blender, until dough is consistency of peas. Add remaining ingredients, mixing only until combined. Refrigerate for 2 hours. Divide dough into 3 parts. On wax paper, roll each part into a rectangle ¹/₄ inch thick. Brush with margarine or oil. Combine ingredients for filling, and place a 1-inch-wide row of filling along inside edge of dough. Roll and cut at 3-inch intervals to resemble blintzes. Place on a greased baking sheet, and brush tops with margarine or oil. Bake in a preheated 375° oven for 35 minutes. Yields about 24 "pillows."

Apple and Nut Blintzes

Serve as a dessert, sprinkled with cinnamon and sugar or a dollop of whipped cream.

16-18 Classic Blintz Leaves (see page 171)

Filling
5 tart apples, finely chopped or shredded
¹/₃ cup bread crumbs
¹/₂ cup chopped walnuts
³/₄ teaspoon cinnamon
¹/₃ cup sugar
2 egg whites, slightly beaten, optional margarine or oil, for frying

Stir together all ingredients. Place 2-3 tablespoons of mixture on each blintz leaf. Fold in top and sides to form an envelope, then roll up; or just roll, leaving sides open. Fry in hot margarine or oil on both sides until golden brown. Yields 16-18 blintzes.

Variation

For quick apple and poppy seed blintzes, combine 5 apples with an 8-ounce can of poppy seed filling and 3-4 tablespoons of raisins.

Strawberry Dessert Blintzes

These are delightful when eaten with a sour cream topping.

10-12 Classic Blintz Leaves (see page 171)

Filling
1 quart fresh strawberries, washed and hulled
¹/₂ cup orange juice
¹/₂ cup sugar
2 tablespoons cornstarch
a few drops red food coloring

Sour Cream Topping
1 cup sour cream, combined with 3 tablespoons sugar

Slice 3 cups of larger strawberries and set aside. In a saucepan, crush 1 cup of smaller strawberries, and combine with orange juice and sugar. Stir in cornstarch until dissolved. Cook over medium-low heat while stirring until thickened. Remove from heat. Stir in food coloring. Let cool. Combine mixture with 3 cups of sliced strawberries. Spoon 2-3 tablespoons of mixture onto center of each blintz leaf. Fold sides over. Serve topped with sweetened sour cream topping. Yields 10-12 blintzes.

Variation

Cherry or blueberry dessert blintzes: Fill blintz leaf with 2 tablespoons of cherry or blueberry pie filling. Fold sides over and top with whipped cream.

Spinach Blintz Cups

With variations for fried or baked spinach blintzes sprinkled with grated cheddar cheese, and many others.

16-18 Classic Blintz Leaves (see page 171)

Filling

2 10-ounce packages frozen chopped spinach, cooked and drained
1$\frac{1}{2}$ cups ricotta cheese
$\frac{1}{2}$ teaspoon salt
$\frac{1}{8}$ teaspoon pepper
1 small onion, finely chopped
2 large eggs, beaten
3 tablespoons bread crumbs
$\frac{1}{2}$ teaspoon thyme or oregano
$\frac{2}{3}$ cup grated cheddar cheese, for sprinkling on top

Tuck blintz leaves into greased cupcake pans. Tops will be ruffled. Combine all filling ingredients, mixing well. Spoon 3-4 tablespoons of mixture into each blintz cup. Sprinkle with cheese. Bake in a 350° oven for 15 minutes. Serve with a dollop of yogurt or sour cream.

Variation

Fill blintz cups with your favorite savory or dessert filling—cheese, tuna or salmon salad, creamed spinach, creamed fish with peas, creamed chicken, broccoli, cherry pie or blueberry pie filling, or mousse—and bake as directed.

Spinach blintzes: Fill blintzes. Fold, tucking in sides, and fry on both sides until golden; or place in a shallow baking pan, topped with a 10$\frac{1}{2}$-ounce can of cream of celery soup combined with $\frac{1}{2}$ cup of milk or water; or top with tomato sauce and sprinkle with grated cheddar cheese. Bake in a 350° oven for 20 minutes.

If blintzes are to be fried after filling, place filling on browner side; if baked or served cold, fill light side so brown side will show.

Tuna Blintzes with Mushroom Sauce

Tuna blintzes are popular among Italian Jews, who often mix anchovies with the tuna in a similar dish.

10 Classic Blintz Leaves (see page 171)

Filling

2 7½-ounce cans of tuna fish, or 1
   16-ounce can salmon
⅓ cup mayonnaise
1 small onion, chopped
3 tablespoons green pepper, finely
   chopped
¼ teaspoon pepper
salt, to taste

Sauce

1 10½-ounce can condensed cream of
   mushroom soup
½ cup milk
¾ cup grated cheddar cheese, for
   sprinkling on top, optional

Mix together all ingredients for tuna filling. Fill blintz leaves. Roll up and place in a shallow baking pan. In a saucepan, combine mushroom soup with milk. Pour sauce over blintzes, sprinkle with cheese, and heat in a 350° oven for 20 minutes. Yields 10 blintzes.

Variation

Fill blintzes with fish salad. Place in a shallow pan. Pour tomato sauce or a can of cream of celery soup on top. Bake as directed.

Gourmet Mushroom Blintzes

Included is a variation for the more-filling mushroom-potato blintzes. Serve either one as an appetizer, with a sauce. To keep the mushrooms light in color, sprinkle with lemon juice, if desired.

12 Classic Blintz Leaves (see page 171)

Filling

1 large onion, diced
2 stalks celery, diced
3 tablespoons oil
½ pound fresh mushrooms, sliced, or 1
   10-ounce can mushrooms, sliced
   and drained
½ teaspoon (or more) salt, to taste
⅛ teaspoon pepper
2 tablespoons flour
1 cup water
margarine or oil, for frying

Sauté onion and celery in oil for 5 minutes. Add mushrooms, salt, and pepper and sauté for an additional 10 minutes. Push vegetables to side of skillet, and stir in flour. Slowly stir in water, and cook for an additional minute until smooth and thick. Place 1-2 tablespoons of mixture on each blintz leaf. Fold in top and sides to form an envelope, then roll up. Or just roll, leaving sides open. Fry in margarine or oil until golden brown. Serve with Mushroom Sauce (see page 84). Yields 12 blintzes.

Variation

Mushroom-potato blintzes: Add 2 cups of seasoned, hot mashed potatoes to mushroom filling. Will fill an additional 8 blintz leaves.

Broccoli-Cheese Blintzes

The combination of broccoli and cheese is simply delightful.

16-18 Classic Blintz Leaves (see page 171)

Filling
1 medium onion, diced
2 tablespoons margarine
3 tablespoons flour, sifted
1 cup water
$^1/_2$ teaspoon salt, or to taste
$^1/_4$ teaspoon pepper
2 cups chopped broccoli, or 1 10-ounce package frozen chopped broccoli, cooked and drained
$^1/_2$ cup grated cheddar cheese
1 cup cottage cheese (half feta cheese can be used)

Sauté onion in margarine for about 5 minutes until tender. Stir in flour until smooth. Slowly stir in water until mixture is smooth, and cook for about 2 minutes until thickened. Stir in seasonings and broccoli. Remove from heat and let cool slightly. Stir in cheddar cheese and cottage cheese. Place 1-2 tablespoons of broccoli-cheese filling on each blintz leaf. Roll up and fry on both sides, or bake in a 350° oven for 15-20 minutes. Yields about 16-18 blintzes.

Italian Blintzes

Savory and different.

16-18 Classic Blintz Leaves (see page 171)

Filling
1$^1/_2$ pounds farmer cheese
3 ounces cream cheese
2 eggs, beaten
pinch of salt and pepper
1 tablespoon margarine, melted
3 tablespoons chopped green onion
$^1/_2$ cup grated Parmesan cheese, for sprinkling top

Sauce
1 8-ounce can tomato sauce
$^1/_2$ cup water
$^1/_2$ teaspoon oregano
2 teaspoons sugar
dash of pepper
salt, to taste

In a mixing bowl, combine all ingredients for filling except Parmesan cheese. Stir well. Combine sauce ingredients thoroughly. Place 1-2 tablespoons of mixture on each blintz leaf. Roll up and place in a greased 9x13-inch baking pan. Pour sauce down center of blintzes. Sprinkle with Parmesan cheese. Bake in a preheated 350° oven for approximately 20 minutes. Yields 16-18 blintzes.

Desserts

Desserts

Dried Fruit and Nut Fritters

Everyone always loves these.

Batter

3 eggs, well beaten
3 tablespoons sugar
1 cup orange juice
1½ tablespoons vegetable oil
1¾ cups flour, sifted
2 tablespoons Sabra liqueur or brandy
oil, for deep-frying
powdered sugar, for sprinkling

Fruit and Nuts

3 tablespoons cut-up dried apricots
3 tablespoons chopped dried figs or
    dates
3 apples, peeled, cored, and diced
2 tablespoons raisins
⅓ cup coarsely chopped walnuts

Blend first 6 ingredients for batter in a blender or food processor for a few seconds until smooth. Refrigerate for 1 hour. Fold fruit and nuts into batter and drop by tablespoonful into deep hot oil. Fry on both sides until golden brown. Drain on paper towels and sprinkle with powdered sugar. Serve warm. Serves 6.

Use less sugar when cooking fruit by adding a pinch of salt.

Crumb-Coated Baked Apples

Bright red apples filled with nuts and plum jam, coated with a crumb mixture and baked.

4 tablespoons cookie crumbs
4 tablespoons brown sugar
½ teaspoon cinnamon
1 egg white
6 large (red) Roman Beauty apples,
    peeled and cored halfway
5 tablespoons plum jam
½ cup chopped pecans
1½ cups water
3 tablespoons white sugar
2-3 drops red food coloring
whipped cream, for garnish, optional

Combine cookie crumbs, brown sugar, and cinnamon. Set aside. Beat egg white until frothy, but not stiff. Dip each apple into egg white, then in crumb mixture. Place apples in a baking pan. Combine plum jam and pecans and spoon into hollowed-out apple cores. Combine water, white sugar, and food coloring, and pour into pan around apples. Bake in a preheated 350° oven for 50-60 minutes until apples are soft, but still hold their shape. Serve hot or cold. Garnish with a dab of whipped cream. Serves 6.

Parfait Rice

This different and delightful dessert recipe was given to me by a cousin almost 40 years ago! Presenting it in tall parfait glasses adds a gala touch.

1^1/$_4$ cups cooked rice
2 7^1/$_2$-ounce cans crushed pineapple, drained
1 cup diced marshmallows
1 tablespoon lemon juice
^{1}/$_2$ cup toasted slivered almonds, optional
1 cup whipped cream or whipped pareve topping
6 strawberries for garnish, optional

Combine all ingredients, folding in cream or pareve topping last. Serve in tall parfait glasses, topped with a fresh strawberry, if desired. Serves 6.

Variation

Fold in ^{1}/$_2$ cup of sliced strawberries after folding in whipped cream or pareve topping.

Cheese Balls

Serve for dessert or as a side dish.

Cheese Balls
1 pound cream cheese or farmer cheese
4 eggs, beaten
6-8 tablespoons matzo meal
2 tablespoons sugar
pinch of salt

Crumb Mixture
4 tablespoons oil or margarine
^{1}/$_4$ cup matzo meal
4 tablespoons sugar
^{1}/$_8$ teaspoon cinnamon

Bring a medium-sized pot of water to a boil. Meanwhile combine ingredients for cheese balls. Let stand for 10 minutes. Roll into balls the size of walnuts. Drop gently into boiling water. Cover and simmer for 5-6 minutes. Remove with a slotted spoon and allow to cool. For crumb mixture, heat oil and matzo meal in a skillet until mixture is golden brown. Remove from heat. Stir in sugar and cinnamon. Roll cheese balls in crumb mixture until well coated all over. Serve warm. Serves 6-8.

Pareve Chocolate Ice Cream

Make it for Pesach or any time. Can also be made in a variety of flavors.

6 large eggs, separated
pinch of salt
³/4 cup sugar
¹/2 cup oil, scant
¹/4 cup water
4 tablespoons cocoa, or 2 ounces
** chocolate, melted**
¹/2 cup chopped pecans, optional
2 packets vanilla sugar

Beat egg whites and salt until frothy. Gradually add sugar and beat until stiff. In a separate bowl, beat egg yolks until light and fluffy. Stir in oil, water, and cocoa or chocolate. Fold egg white mixture into yolk mixture. Fold in pecans. Freeze in a covered container or in individual serving dishes. Yields about 1 quart (serves 8-10).

Variations

Lemon ice cream: Omit cocoa and water. Add ¹/3 cup of lemon juice.

Coconut ice cream: Omit cocoa. Fold in ¹/2 cup of shredded coconut.

Strawberry ice cream: Omit water and cocoa. Fold in 1 cup of crushed or sliced strawberries.

Mocha ice cream: Add 1 tablespoon of instant coffee.

Chocolate chip ice cream: Omit cocoa. Add 2 ounces of chocolate chips.

Raisin or nut ice cream: Fold in ¹/2 cup (or more) of raisins or coarsely chopped nuts.

Fantastic Burnt-Almond Ice Cream

The almonds add a wonderful touch to this ice cream. Particularly delightful when served with a chocolate or caramel sauce.

1³/4 cups brown sugar, tightly packed
1¹/4 cups water
10 eggs
1¹/2 cups margarine, softened
1 tablespoon vanilla extract
³/4 cup toasted ground almonds

In a medium-sized saucepan, cook sugar and water until bubbly. Mix eggs, margarine, and vanilla extract in a blender on high speed for 5 minutes. Add hot sugar mixture to blender and blend again until margarine is well combined. Freeze until firm. Thaw partially (about 15-20 minutes) and beat in an electric mixer on high speed for 8-10 minutes until volume increases. Carefully fold in almonds. Refreeze until firm. Serve with chocolate or caramel sauce. Serves 15.

Whole almonds can be roasted in the oven for 10-15 minutes, stirring occasionally, then ground in a food processor.

Pareve Strawberry Ice Whip

A light, fluffy, and creamy dessert. A favorite during Pesach when strawberries are in season.

2 cups fresh strawberries, hulled
1 cup sugar
2 teaspoons lemon juice
2 egg whites

Combine all ingredients in a large bowl. Beat in an electric mixer on high speed for 20 minutes until mixture triples in volume. Freeze until firm. Serves 8-10.

For juicier lemons, place them in hot water for 10 minutes before squeezing. For easy removal of white membrane, soak oranges in boiling water.

Fruit Crystal Ice Dessert

I served this refreshing dessert at a tea party given for friends of Ohel Hava, a home for girls from disadvantaged backgrounds, a favorite charity of mine, which a group of English-speaking women and I organized about 12 years ago.

2 cups water
$2/3$ cup sugar
$3/4$ cup orange juice
$1/4$ cup lemon juice
strawberries, orange slices, or black grapes, for garnish

In a saucepan, bring water and sugar to a boil. Remove from heat and add orange juice and lemon juice. Pour into a medium-sized bowl and freeze. Remove from freezer, scrape with a large spoon, and separate into crystals. Spoon iced crystals into dessert glasses and top with a fresh strawberry, a thin twisted orange slice, or a large black grape.

Quick Chocolate Mousse

Refreshing and scrumptious.

6 ounces chocolate chips
1/8 cup boiling water
1 tablespoon Sabra or rum liqueur
1 teaspoon peppermint, vanilla, or rum
   extract
3 eggs, separated
3 tablespoons sugar
1/2 cup walnuts, coarsely chopped
orange slices or walnuts, for garnish

Process chocolate chips in a food processor for about half a minute. Pour boiling water through feed tube while processing for another half a minute until chocolate melts. Add liqueur, extract, and egg yolks, and process for a few more seconds. With an electric mixer, beat egg whites until frothy. Slowly add sugar and beat until stiff. Fold stiffly beaten egg whites into chocolate mixture. Fold in walnuts. Chill in 6 serving dishes. Garnish with a twisted half-slice of orange or half a walnut.

To grate chocolate, leave at room temperature, hold in palm of your hand, and grate with a potato peeler, using short strokes.

Apple Cranberry Cobbler

Try preparing this cobbler with other fruits in season. They're all delicious.

4 large apples, peeled and sliced
1 16-ounce can whole, jelled
   cranberries
1/2 cup margarine, room temperature
1/2 cup flour, sifted
1 teaspoon baking powder
1 cup oatmeal
1/4 teaspoon salt
3/4 cup brown sugar, packed
1 teaspoon cinnamon
pinch of nutmeg

Combine apples and cranberries. Pour into a greased 2-quart casserole. In a bowl, combine remaining ingredients. Sprinkle over apple-cranberry mixture. Bake in a preheated 350° oven for 1 hour. Serves 12-15.

Variation

In place of apples and cranberries, use 4-5 cups of fresh cut-up fruits in season: peaches, plums, apricots, berries, etc.

Challah, Bread & Rolls

Challah, Bread & Rolls

Traditional Challah

There is nothing like the aroma of baking challah to bring warmth and comfort into a home. Be sure to separate challah from the dough in accordance with halachah.

2 ounces yeast
1 teaspoon sugar
2^1/$_2$ cups very warm water
1 cup sugar
1 cup oil
1 tablespoon salt (plus 1 teaspoon extra)
1 tablespoon vanilla extract
^{1}/$_2$ teaspoon baking powder, optional
4 eggs
12 cups flour
^{1}/$_2$ cup raisins, optional
cinnamon, for sprinkling on baking
    sheet

Glaze
1 egg yolk, beaten with 1 teaspoon
    water
sesame seeds

In a small mixing bowl, dissolve yeast and 1 teaspoon of sugar in ^{1}/$_2$ cup of the water. Let stand for 10 minutes until foamy. In a large mixing bowl, pour remaining 2 cups of water, sugar, oil, salt, vanilla extract, yeast mixture, baking powder, eggs, and 4 cups of the flour. Beat well. Add flour two cups at a time, beating well after each addition, leaving last cup or two to knead in with a dough hook or by hand. Add raisins, if desired. Knead for 10 minutes until dough is smooth and elastic. Dough should be soft. Place dough in a large, greased bowl, turning over to grease all sides. Cover with a clean, damp towel. Let rise in a warm place until double in bulk—about 1^1/$_2$-2 hours. Punch down, cover, and let rise again until double in bulk. (Letting it rise a second time is optional.) Punch down once again.

Divide dough into 3 parts. From each part, make 3 or 4 ropes about 10 inches long. Attach ends of ropes securely and braid. Place braided loaves on a well-greased baking sheet sprinkled with cinnamon. Cover with a damp cloth, and let rise in a warm place for about 1 hour. Brush with glaze and sprinkle with sesame seeds. Bake in a preheated 350° oven for 40-45 minutes. When challah is done, it has a hollow sound when tapped on bottom. If not, return to oven for several minutes. Yields 3 challahs.

Dough should no more than double in bulk, lest it overrise and become toxic. Overrising also gives a yeasty taste. Punching the dough down stops its rising and prevents a coarse loaf of bread. Beaten eggs, a correct amount of honey or sugar, and a warm room all aid rising. Salt, oil, butter or margarine, and a cold kitchen slow rising.

Challah Basket

An eye-catching way of serving rolls at a simchah. It will be a conversation piece on any table.

1 Traditional Challah (see page 193)

Glaze
1 egg yolk, beaten with 1 teaspoon water

Reserve ⅛ of dough for handle. Form remaining dough into 3 long ropes, ¾ inch wide. Braid. Turn a 5-6-quart ovenproof bowl upside down on a table and grease outside generously. Beginning at top edge of bowl, coil braid around until it reaches the bottom, keeping parts of the strand about 1 inch apart to allow for rising. With dough still wrapped around bowl, brush with beaten egg yolk and place on a well-greased cookie sheet. Bake in a preheated 350° oven for 35 minutes. Remove and let cool. Loosen edges with a knife and carefully remove bread from bowl. Place on a greased baking sheet and return to oven for an additional 5 minutes. To make handle, use reserved dough. Form 3 ropes, long enough to arch over basket. Braid the 3 together (or braid 2 of them, arranging third rope in a figure-8 to form a bow. Attach bow to center of handle before baking it). Make an arch with braid of the right size to fit over basket. Remove handle from basket and place on cookie sheet. Bake in a preheated 350° oven for 20-30 minutes. Let cool. Carefully fasten handle to basket with

toothpicks. Fill basket with rolls or small challahs. Use any leftover dough to make knotted rolls. Roll into 6-8-inch ropes and form a knot with each one. Bake for 15-20 minutes.

Bake challah dough in preheated oven for about 35 minutes. Remove and tap; if challah doesn't sound hollow, bake for another 5-10 minutes.

Round Honey Challah

On Rosh Hashanah and Sukkot we use round, sweet challahs instead of the traditional long, braided ones. The round shape is a reminder of the cycle of the seasons and expresses our fervent hope that the coming year be one of fulfillment. The sweet taste signifies the hope for a sweet year. The extra little braid in the center of the loaf, in the shape of a ladder, is a symbol that our destiny should climb upward in the new year.

2 packages active dry yeast, or 2 cakes
   fresh compressed yeast
1 teaspoon sugar
2 cups warm water
8-9 cups flour, sifted
$3/4$ cup honey
$1/3$ cup sugar
1 tablespoon salt
1 teaspoon baking powder, optional
$3/4$ cup margarine, room temperature
3 eggs, beaten
$1 1/2$ teaspoons vanilla extract
$1/8$ teaspoon nutmeg
$1/2$ cup raisins

Glaze

1 egg yolk, beaten with 1 teaspoon
   water
sesame or poppy seeds, optional

In a large mixing bowl dissolve yeast and 1 teaspoon of sugar in $1/2$ cup of warm water. Cover and let stand for 5-10 minutes until it foams. Beat in 4 cups of flour and remaining ingredients, except raisins, until smooth—about 5 minutes. Add remaining flour 2 cups at a time, beating well after each addition. Add raisins. Knead with a dough hook or by hand for 10 minutes. Place in a greased bowl and turn dough to grease all over. Cover with a damp cloth and allow to rise until double in bulk—about $1 1/2$-2 hours. Punch down. Divide dough into 3 equal parts, setting a handful aside for the ladder. Roll each part into a rope 18 inches long. Taper ends. Coil rope around itself (there should be no hole in the center) and tuck ends under. Place in a round, 9-inch springform pan.

To make ladder, make 2 pencil-thin strips, 4 inches long, for sides; and 4 thin strips, 2 inches wide, for rungs. Fasten securely to top center of each challah. Cover and place in a warm place for 50 minutes to rise again. Brush with glaze. Sprinkle with sesame or poppy seeds, if desired. Bake in a preheated 350° oven for 40-45 minutes. When challah is done, it has a hollow sound when tapped on bottom. Yields 3 challahs.

Variations

Substitute $3/4$ cup of sugar for honey.

Mix 1 tablespoon of anise seeds or 2 tablespoons of sesame seeds into batter.

Whole Wheat Challah

Try making a challah with whole wheat flour for a change. Your family will love it.

8 cups whole wheat flour, sifted
2 cups warm water
2 cakes compressed yeast, or 2
  packages dry yeast
¹/₂ cup honey, or ³/₄ cup brown or
  white sugar
2 eggs, well beaten
¹/₂ cup oil
1 tablespoon salt

Glaze
1 egg yolk, beaten with 1 teaspoon
  water
sesame or poppy seeds

Put 7 cups of flour in a large mixing bowl. Make a well, and pour 1 cup of warm water into it. Crumble yeast and 1 teaspoon of the honey into the well. Let stand for 5-10 minutes until it foams. With your fingers, work yeast mixture into flour. Add honey, eggs, oil, and salt, and mix by hand or with an electric beater. Gradually add more water—a little at a time— beating well after each addition. Beat for 5 minutes. Dough will be sticky. Knead dough for 10 minutes, adding remaining flour. Place in a greased bowl, turn, and cover with a towel. Let rise in a warm place until double in bulk. (Optional: Punch down, cover, and allow to rise again until double—about 1¹/₂ hours.) Punch down again and divide dough into 3 parts. Braid into loaves. Place each loaf on a well-greased baking sheet. Cover and let rise for 1¹/₂ hours. Brush with glaze. Sprinkle with sesame or poppy seeds. Bake in a preheated 350° oven for 45 minutes until golden brown. Yields 3 challahs.

Variation

Substitute white flour for part of whole wheat flour. If half white flour is used, add ¹/₈ cup more water.

In whole wheat bread, raw bulgur can be substituted for an equal amount of flour.

Food Processor Challah

I've found that using a food processor makes the softest and most pliable dough. It is quick and easy to make one batch after another, with a minimum of mess to clean up afterward.

1 package fresh or dry yeast
1 teaspoon sugar
³/₄ cup warm water
3 cups flour
¹/₃ -¹/₂ cup sugar
1 teaspoon salt
1 egg
¹/₄ cup oil

Glaze
1 egg yolk, beaten with 1 teaspoon oil
   and 1 teaspoon sugar
sesame or poppy seeds, optional

Dissolve yeast and 1 teaspoon of sugar in warm water. Let stand for 5 minutes until foamy. Put flour, sugar, and salt in a food processor. Add egg, oil, and yeast mixture. Process until the dough leaves sides of container and forms a ball—about 40 seconds. Place dough on a lightly floured board and knead until smooth—about 2 minutes. Place in a greased bowl and turn. Cover with a cloth. Let rise in a warm place until double in bulk—about 1¹/₂-2 hours. Punch down and shape into 2 loaves. Place in a greased pan. Cover and let rise again in a warm place for about 1 hour. Brush with glaze. If desired, sprinkle with sesame or poppy seeds. Bake in a preheated 375° oven for about 40 minutes. Yields 2 medium-sized loaves.

Variation

Shape dough into small rolls, and bake in a preheated 375° oven for about 20 minutes.

The challah dough should touch both ends of the loaf pan, enabling it to rise upward rather than outward.

Eggless Challah

The added vinegar results in a lighter challah.

2 cakes compressed yeast, or 2 packages active dry yeast
1 teaspoon sugar
2¼ cups warm water
8-9 cups flour, sifted
½-¾ cup sugar
⅓ cup oil
1 tablespoon salt (plus 1 teaspoon extra)
1 tablespoon anise seeds
¼ cup vinegar, optional

Glaze
1 egg yolk, beaten with 1 teaspoon water
sesame seeds

Dissolve yeast and 1 teaspoon of sugar in ½ cup warm water. Let stand for 5 minutes until it foams. In a mixing bowl, combine 4 cups of flour, yeast mixture, and remaining ingredients. Beat for about 3 minutes until smooth. Beat in remaining flour one cup at a time, leaving one last cup. Knead in last cup by hand or with a dough hook for 8-10 minutes. Place in a greased bowl, turn, cover, and set in a warm place to rise until double—1½-2 hours. Punch down. Braid into 3 challahs. Cover with a damp cloth and let rise until double—about 1 hour. Brush with glaze and sprinkle with sesame seeds. Bake in a preheated 350° oven for 45 minutes. When challah is done, it has a hollow sound when tapped on bottom.

Israeli Bagels

These chewy bagels can be seen strung around poles at just about every kiosk in Israel. They are thinner, but larger in circumference, than American bagels—crispier, with more salt on the outside and less on the inside. Chewing these pretzel-like bagels is a good outlet for excess energy!

2 packages dry granulated yeast, or 2 cakes compressed yeast
2 tablespoons sugar
2½ cups lukewarm water
8 cups of flour, sifted
2 teaspoons salt

Glaze
1 egg yolk, beaten with 1 teaspoon water
coarse salt

Dissolve yeast and sugar in water. Combine with remaining ingredients. Beat well. Knead until smooth and soft. Let rest for 10 minutes, but do not let rise. Shape into bagels by pinching off pieces of dough. Roll each piece into a rope ½ inch thick and 6 inches long. Attach ends. Place on a greased cookie sheet, brush with yolk-water mixture, and sprinkle with coarse salt. Bake in a preheated 425° oven for about 20 minutes until golden brown.

Variation

Dough can be rolled into pencil-thin strips, shaped into pretzels or different letters of the alphabet, and baked at 425° for 15 minutes.

Homemade Bagels

An American-Jewish classic unknown in Israel, of all places! (For Israeli Bagels, see page 198.)

1 cup hot water
¼ cup margarine
2 tablespoons sugar
½ teaspoon salt
1 package dry granular yeast, or 1 cake
   compressed yeast
1 egg, well beaten
4 cups flour, sifted

Glaze
1 egg yolk, beaten with 1 teaspoon
   water
½ cup sesame or poppy seeds, optional

In a large mixing bowl, combine water, margarine, sugar, and salt. Let stand for several minutes until lukewarm. Stir in yeast, egg, and flour. Beat until smooth. Cover and let rise in a warm place for 1 hour. Punch down. Roll into ropes the width of a finger and about twice the length. Taper ends and join them together firmly, wetting if necessary, to form bagels. Place on a floured board and let rest for about 10-12 minutes. Drop carefully, one at a time, into a pot of very hot—but not boiling—water. Simmer over very low heat for 2 minutes. Turn and simmer for another 1-2 minutes. Bagels are ready to remove from water when they feel light but firm. Remove from water with a slotted spoon and drain on absorbent paper. Place on a well-greased baking sheet. Brush with glaze for a shiny top. Sprinkle with sesame or poppy seeds, if desired. Bake in a preheated 425° oven for 15 minutes or until golden brown. Yields about 12-15 bagels.

Variations

Onion bagels: Chop very finely, or grate, 1 raw onion and sprinkle on bagel before dropping into water. Onion may also first be sautéed in oil until golden.

Whole wheat bagels: Use 3½ cups of whole wheat flour in place of 4 cups of white flour.

Dough should be adequately mixed or kneaded for a smoother-grained challah or kuchen. Beat with electric mixer at least 10-15 minutes at medium speed after ingredients are combined. Add liquid ingredients alternately with flour and beat several minutes after each addition. Use a food processor for extra-smooth dough. Process in small batches of up to 3 cups flour each.

Dinner Rolls in All Shapes and Sizes

A wide variety of shapes in which to fashion the dough.

**1 Traditional Challah (page 193), or
1 Whole Wheat Challah (page 196), or
1 Round Honey Challah (page 195), or
Mezonot Rolls (page 201)**

Prepare dough as directed in respective recipes, but instead of forming into challah loaves or buns, form dough into any of the following shapes. Let rise for last time on a greased cookie sheet. Before baking, brush with glaze (1 egg yolk, beaten with 1 teaspoon of water). Unless otherwise indicated, bake in a preheated 400° oven for 15-20 minutes or until golden.

Parker House Rolls

Roll out dough ¼ inch thick. Cut into 30 4-inch rounds. Spread with ½ teaspoon of melted margarine or butter. Fold each roll in half. Let rise for about 40 minutes.

Onion Rolls

Roll out dough ½ inch thick and cut into 4-inch rounds. Prick with a fork. Cover and let rise until double. Brush tops with oil. Combine 2 chopped onions, 1 teaspoon of salt, ⅓ cup of poppy seeds, and ¼ cup of melted margarine. Sprinkle on top. Bake in a preheated 400° oven for 20 minutes or until golden brown.

Clover Leaf Rolls

Place 3 small balls of dough into muffin tins. Brush well with melted margarine. Cover and let rise.

Rose Knots

Roll dough between your hands into ropes ½ inch thick and 10 inches long. Tie into a knot. Cover and let rise.

Bread Sticks

On a floured board, divide dough into 4 parts. Roll out each part into a rectangle ¼ inch thick and 8 inches wide. Cut into strips 2 inches wide. Roll each strip between your hands to form sticks. Place in a greased baking pan. Sprinkle with coarse koshering salt and sesame seeds. Let rise until not quite double.

Store flour in a cool, dry place or in the refrigerator. Use unbleached flour for fresher-tasting bread.

Mezonot Rolls

Mezonot rolls are convenient on buffet tables or in picnic baskets and lunch boxes. Many authorities maintain that they do not require the washing of the hands beforehand or the long blessing for bread afterwards. The reason is that they are made with fruit juice, in addition to water—unlike bread, which contains only water.

**2 packages active dry yeast, or 2 cakes
    compressed yeast**
1 teaspoon sugar
³/₄ cup warm water
8 cups flour, sifted
2 teaspoons salt
1¹/₂ cups grape or orange juice
¹/₂ cup oil
¹/₃ cup sugar
oil, for brushing top

Glaze
**1 egg yolk, beaten with 1 teaspoon
    water**
sesame seeds

In a large mixing bowl, dissolve yeast and 1 teaspoon of sugar in warm water. Cover and let stand for 10 minutes until foamy. Add 4 cups of flour and remaining ingredients. Beat until smooth, by hand or with an electric mixer. Beat in remaining flour. Knead until smooth and shiny—about 10 minutes. Brush with oil and place in a large plastic bag (to allow room for rising) or in a large greased bowl, and cover with a damp cloth. Allow to rise in a warm spot until double in bulk—about 1¹/₂ hours. Punch down and let rest for 10 minutes. Form into small round buns or other shapes (see Dinner Rolls, page 200). Place 3 inches apart on a large greased baking sheet. Brush with glaze and sprinkle with sesame seeds. Put in a warm place, cover, and let rise until almost double—about 1 hour. Bake in a preheated 400° oven for 15 minutes or until golden brown. Yields about 40 small rolls.

For more flavorful coffeecakes and sweet rolls, sprinkle a few drops of vanilla or almond extract on rolled out dough. Dot or smear rolled out dough with softened margarine or vegetable oil.

English Muffins

Make your own English muffins, sprinkled with cornmeal to enhance their flavor. Spread muffins with margarine, chopped dill, and a dash of garlic, or use the Pizza Sauce listed here to create a quick mock pizza.

1 package active dry yeast, or 1 cake
    fresh compressed yeast
1 teaspoon sugar
1$^{1}/_{2}$ cups warm water
4 cups flour
2 tablespoons sugar
4 tablespoons margarine, room
    temperature
1 egg, beaten
1$^{1}/_{2}$ teaspoons salt
$^{1}/_{2}$ cup cornmeal, for sprinkling

Dissolve yeast and 1 teaspoon of sugar in $^{1}/_{2}$ cup of the water. Let stand for 5 minutes until foamy. In a large mixing bowl, combine 2 cups of flour, 2 tablespoons of sugar, remaining water, yeast mixture, margarine, egg, and salt. Beat at medium speed until dough leaves side of bowl. Beat in remaining flour until smooth. Knead by hand or with a dough hook for 10 minutes. Dough should be soft, but not sticky. Place in a greased bowl, turning to grease all over. Cover with a clean damp towel and let rise until double in bulk—1$^{1}/_{2}$-2 hours. Punch down. Pat or press carefully on a lightly floured surface. With a cookie cutter, cut into 3-inch rounds and place on a greased baking sheet sprinkled with cornmeal. Cover and let rise until double in bulk—about 1$^{1}/_{2}$ hours. Cook on a hot, greased griddle pan over medium heat for 7 minutes per side. When ready to eat, place in a preheated 300° oven to warm for 5 minutes. Yields 15 muffins.

Variation

For a quick, miniature, mock pizza, split the muffins in half and spread with Pizza Sauce and grated Parmesan cheese.

Pizza Sauce

1 8-ounce can tomato paste
$^{1}/_{8}$ cup water
$^{1}/_{4}$ cup vegetable oil
1 cup chopped olives
1 large onion, grated
$^{1}/_{2}$ green pepper, diced
$^{1}/_{2}$ teaspoon oregano
$^{1}/_{4}$ teaspoon salt
2 cloves garlic, or $^{1}/_{2}$ teaspoon garlic
    powder
$^{3}/_{4}$ pound grated Parmesan cheese

Mix all ingredients together, except cheese. Spread on muffins. Top with cheese. Heat in a preheated 400° oven until cheese bubbles—about 5-7 minutes.

For more professionally uniform dinner rolls and challahs, use dough balls of equal weight.

French Bread

French bread is very popular in America and Israel as well as in Europe. These long, thin, crusty loaves can be used in a variety of ways.

4 cups flour
1¹/₂ cups lukewarm water
1 cake compressed yeast
2 tablespoons sugar
1¹/₂ teaspoons salt
3 tablespoons margarine, softened
2 large egg whites
1¹/₂ teaspoons cornstarch

Put 3¹/₂ cups of flour in a mixing bowl. Make a well in center and pour in 1 cup of lukewarm water. Crumble yeast and 1 teaspoon of sugar in water. Let stand for about 10 minutes until foamy. Mix until combined. Beat in 1 teaspoon of salt and margarine until smooth. Add remaining sugar, and beat for another 3-4 minutes. In a separate bowl, beat egg whites until stiff and fold into dough. Knead in remaining flour. Place in a greased bowl, turn, and cover. Let rise until double. Punch down. Knead for 1-2 more minutes. Divide in half. Shape into 2 long, narrow loaves, tapering ends. Place on a greased baking sheet. Cover and let rise for about 1-1¹/₂ hours. Meanwhile in a saucepan, cook cornstarch, remaining ¹/₂ teaspoon of salt and ¹/₂ cup of water until thick, stirring constantly. Let cool and brush mixture thickly on surface of loaves. Cut into loaves about ¹/₂ inch deep at 3-inch intervals. Bake in a preheated 400° oven—with a pan of water on bottom of oven—for about 15 minutes. Reduce heat to 350° and bake for about 30 more minutes.

Savory Onion Sticks

Savory and different sugar-free onion sticks. They disappear quickly.

1 cup margarine
4 cups white flour, sifted
4 cups whole wheat flour, sifted
1 cup oil
1 large onion, finely chopped
6 teaspoons baking powder
2 teaspoons salt
¹/₄ cup water
3 ounces sesame seeds

Cut margarine into flour until pieces are the size of peas. Stir in remaining ingredients, adding a little more water if necessary, to make a soft dough. Using your hands, roll pieces of dough into thin rolls about 8 inches long. Flatten slightly with palm of your hand. Cut into strips 2 inches long, 1 inch wide and ¹/₂ inch thick. Place 1 inch apart on a well-greased cookie sheet. Bake in a preheated 350° oven for 45-50 minutes. Yields about 60 onion sticks.

Variation

Onion crackers: Roll out dough on a floured surface. Cut with a round cookie cutter or use rim of a small glass dipped in flour. Brush with oil. Bake as above.

Cakes & Icings

Cakes & Icings

One-Bowl Chocolate Cake

A large, moist, creamy cake that couldn't be easier, but disappears fast.

2 eggs
1³/4 cups sugar
1 cup oil
2 teaspoons vanilla extract
³/4 teaspoon salt
³/4 cup cocoa
1 cup hot, strong coffee
³/4 cup hot water
3 cups cake flour, sifted
2 teaspoons baking powder
2 teaspoons baking soda
²/3 cup raisins, optional

Beat the eggs until light, gradually adding the sugar. Stir in oil, vanilla extract, salt, and cocoa. Stir in coffee and water alternately with flour, baking powder, and baking soda. Stir only until smooth, adding raisins if desired. Pour into a greased, 9x13-inch baking pan. Bake in a preheated 350° oven for 1 hour. When cool, top with Chocolate Glaze Icing (see page 229).

French Chocolate Cream Cake

A thick, creamy, chocolate top enhances this delicious cake, baked in a rectangular pan and cut into rectangles.

6 ounces semi-sweet chocolate
1 cup margarine
6 eggs, separated
1¹/2 cups sugar
1 cup flour, sifted
4 tablespoons sweet red wine
1 teaspoon baking powder
¹/4 teaspoon salt

Melt chocolate with margarine over low heat. In a mixing bowl, beat egg yolks until light and fluffy. Gradually beat in half of the sugar. Stir in melted chocolate-margarine mixture, reserving 1 cup of this mixture for top of cake. To remaining mixture, stir in flour, wine, baking powder, and salt. In another bowl, beat egg whites until stiff, gradually adding remaining sugar. Fold egg whites into chocolate-flour mixture. Pour into a greased, 9x13-inch baking pan. Bake in a preheated 350° oven for 40 minutes. Let cool and spread top with reserved cup of chocolate mixture. Cut into 1¹/2 x 2-inch rectangles. Yields 24.

Chocolate Chip, Date and Nut Cake

This recipe was given to me when chocolate chips first became available on the market. Some of the chocolate chips blend into the cake, while others remain on the top for a satisfying chocolatey crunch. The chopped dates help keep it moist.

1 cup dates, chopped
1 teaspoon baking soda
1 cup hot water
1 cup margarine, room temperature
1 cup sugar
2 eggs
1 teaspoon vanilla extract
1³/₄ cups flour, sifted
¹/₄ teaspoon salt
2 tablespoons cocoa
6 ounces chocolate chips
¹/₂ cup nuts, chopped

Place dates in a small bowl. Add baking soda and cover with hot water. Let cool. Cream margarine and sugar. Stir in eggs and vanilla extract and beat well. Sift together flour, salt, and cocoa. Add alternately with date mixture. Pour into a greased, 9x13-inch baking pan. Sprinkle with chocolate chips and chopped nuts. Bake in a preheated 350° oven for 45 minutes.

Classic Chocolate Chiffon Cake

A light, airy cake.

¹/₂ cup cocoa
³/₄ cup boiling water
6 eggs, separated
¹/₂ teaspoon cream of tartar
1³/₄ cups sugar
1 tablespoon baking powder
1 teaspoon salt
1 teaspoon vanilla extract
¹/₂ cup vegetable oil
1³/₄ cups flour, sifted

Dissolve cocoa in boiling water. Let cool. Sift together dry ingredients. Beat egg whites with cream of tartar until frothy. Gradually add sugar and beat until mixture forms stiff peaks. Set aside. Beat egg yolks until light. Stir in rest of ingredients, leaving egg whites for last. Gently and thoroughly fold egg whites into cocoa mixture. Pour into an ungreased, 10-inch tube pan. Bake in a 325° oven for 1 hour, 10 minutes. Ice with Royal Mocha Cream Icing (see page 231) and decorate with ¹/₂ cup of slivered almonds.

Five-Egg Orange Chiffon Cake

A marvelous, light chiffon cake with only 5 eggs, which are used at room temperature for greater volume. Be sure to beat the egg whites until they can hold stiff peaks. This versatile recipe lends itself to many variations.

5 large eggs, room temperature, separated
1¹/₂ cups sugar
¹/₂ cup oil
2 teaspoons vanilla extract
³/₄ cup orange juice
2¹/₄ cups cake flour, sifted
3 teaspoons baking powder
¹/₂ teaspoon salt
grated rind of 1 orange

Beat egg whites until frothy, gradually adding half of the sugar. Beat until able to hold quite stiff peaks. In another bowl, beat the yolks until light and fluffy, adding remaining sugar. Stir in oil, vanilla extract, and orange juice. Sift together flour, baking powder, and salt, and stir into yolk mixture until combined. Do not over-mix. Lastly, fold in stiffly beaten egg whites and orange rind. Pour into a 10-inch tube pan, greased on bottom only. Bake in a preheated 350° oven for 1 hour or until top springs back when touched lightly. Invert pan over neck of bottle to cool. Top with Royal Mocha Cream Icing (see page 231).

Variations

Mocha flake chiffon cake: Fold into batter 2 ounces of coarsely grated semi-sweet chocolate, 1 tablespoon of instant coffee, 1 teaspoon of vanilla extract, and 1 teaspoon of cinnamon. Top with Royal Mocha Cream Icing.

Pineapple coconut chiffon cake: Substitute ³/₄ cup of pineapple juice for orange juice. Fold in ¹/₂ cup of shredded coconut. Frost with Pineapple Butter Cream Icing (see page 230).

Maple chiffon cake: Replace white sugar with brown sugar. Add 2 teaspoons of maple flavoring in place of vanilla extract. Fold in ²/₃ cup of finely chopped nuts. Omit orange juice and rind.

Marble chiffon cake: Remove ¹/₄ of batter and carefully blend in 3 tablespoons of cocoa. Pour half of white batter into a 10-inch tube pan. Pour cocoa mixture on top, then add remaining white batter. Cut through batter at 3-inch intervals to marbleize.

Lemon chiffon cake: Instead of orange juice and rind, use ¹/₂ cup of lemon juice, ¹/₄ cup of water, and grated rind of 1 lemon.

Egg whites will keep for three or four weeks in a covered, refrigerated jar.

Honey Chiffon Cake

This cake is particularly tasty when topped with the icing.

6 eggs, room temperature, separated
³/₄ cup white sugar
³/₄ cup brown sugar (or white, if preferred)
6 tablespoons honey
³/₄ cup oil
³/₄ cup very strong coffee
2 tablespoons cognac or brandy
juice and finely grated rind of ¹/₂ lemon
finely grated rind of 1 orange
¹/₂ teaspoon salt
1¹/₂ teaspoons cinnamon
¹/₂ teaspoon ground cloves
¹/₂ teaspoon ginger
2¹/₂ cups flour, sifted
2¹/₂ teaspoons baking powder
1 teaspoon baking soda
¹/₂ cup raisins, optional

Beat egg whites until frothy. Gradually add white sugar and beat with a mixer on high speed until they form stiff peaks. Set aside. Beat egg yolks and brown sugar until light and fluffy. Stir in remaining ingredients in order given. Lastly, fold egg whites into mixture. Pour into a greased, 10-inch tube pan and bake in a preheated 350° oven for 1 hour. Ice with Silky Beige Icing (see page 230).

Nechama's Classic Honey Cake

This is an old recipe, handed down from generation to generation.

3 eggs
1 cup brown sugar (half white may also be used)
1 cup honey
juice and grated rind of ¹/₂ lemon
¹/₂ orange, ground with peel
³/₄ cup strong black coffee
3 cups flour
¹/₂ teaspoon salt
2 teaspoons baking powder
1 teaspoon baking soda
4 tablespoons brandy or cognac
²/₃ cup raisins
1 cup dates, cut up, optional
1 cup broken walnuts

Beat eggs until light, gradually adding sugar. Stir in remaining ingredients in order given. Pour into a greased, 9x13-inch baking pan. Bake in a 350° oven for 1 hour.

Mock Honey Cake

A honey cake on a budget! The combination of ingredients gives a real honey flavor.

2 eggs
2 cups sugar
1 cup oil
$1/2$ teaspoon ginger
1 teaspoon vanilla extract
$2^1/2$ cups flour, sifted
$1/2$ cup strong coffee
1 teaspoon baking soda
4 large apples, grated

Beat together eggs and sugar. Stir in oil. Blend in remaining ingredients. Pour into a greased, 10-inch tube pan or a 9x13-inch baking pan. Bake in a preheated 350° oven for 50-60 minutes for the tube pan or 45 minutes for the baking pan. When cool, spread with Silky Beige Icing (see page 230).

If an egg lies on its side or sinks when placed in a bowl of water, it is fresh. If it stands at an angle, it is 3 days old. If it stands on its end or rises, it is 10 days old.

Evelyn's Marble Cake

This cake always gets raves.

2 cups flour, sifted
$1/2$ teaspoon salt
3 teaspoons baking powder
6 eggs, separated
$1^1/2$ cups sugar
$3/4$ cup orange juice
$1/2$ cup oil
1 teaspoon almond extract
1 teaspoon vanilla extract

Chocolate Syrup
$1/4$ cup cocoa
$1/4$ cup sugar
$1/4$ cup boiling water

Combine flour, salt, and baking powder. Set aside. Beat egg whites until they form stiff peaks. Beat egg yolks until light and fluffy, adding sugar gradually. Stir in orange juice, oil, and almond and vanilla extracts. Add dry mixture. Fold in stiffly beaten egg whites. In a bowl, combine all Chocolate Syrup ingredients until smooth, and blend into $1/3$ of the batter. Pour half of remaining white batter into a greased, 10-inch tube pan. Layer with chocolate batter, then with remaining white mixture. To marbleize, cut through batter with a knife at 3-inch intervals. Bake in a preheated 350° oven for 1 hour.

Basic Kuchen Yeast Dough

*This is a marvelous yeast dough recipe,
handed down from generation to
generation. It is easy to mix by hand or, for
a smooth lighter dough, in an electric mixer.
Fill it with your favorite filling, or fit
one-third of it into a loaf pan or square
pan. Top with streusel or fill it with a
cheese mixture.*

8-9 cups flour
1³/₄ cups warm water
2 cakes compressed yeast, or 2
   packages dry yeast
¹/₂-³/₄ cup sugar
3 eggs
³/₄ cup oil
1 tablespoon salt
grated rind of 1 lemon
¹/₂ cup raisins, optional

Glaze
1 egg yolk, combined with 1 teaspoon
   water

Put 7 cups of the flour into a large
mixing bowl. Make a well in
center and pour in 1 cup of the warm
water. Crumble yeast, with 1
teaspoon of sugar on top. Let stand
for 5-10 minutes until yeast foams.
With your fingers, mix yeast mixture
into flour. Add sugar, eggs, oil, salt,
lemon rind, and raisins, if desired.
Beat in remaining water, a little at a
time, beating well after each addition.
Dough will be sticky. Knead for 10
minutes, adding remaining flour.
Dough should be very soft. Place in a
greased bowl, turn, and cover with a
towel. Set in a warm place to rise
until double in bulk—about 1¹/₂-2
hours. Punch down. (If desired, let

rise again until double and punch
down.) Divide into 3 parts for 3
cakes. After shaping and filling each
cake, cover and let rise for only 30-40
minutes. Brush with egg glaze. Bake
in a 375° oven for 30-35 minutes
until golden brown.

*For crusty challah or coffeecake, place a pan
of hot water in the bottom of the oven while
baking.*

Cheese-Filled Kuchen

Delicious every time.

**¹/₃ portion Basic Kuchen Yeast Dough
(see page 214)**
2 tablespoons margarine, softened
2 tablespoons apricot jam, optional

Cheese Mixture
**1 pound farmer cheese (or half cream
cheese, if desired)**
¹/₃ - ¹/₂ cup sugar
**2 tablespoons instant vanilla pudding,
optional (use only ¹/₃ cup sugar)**
juice and grated rind of ¹/₂ lemon
2 eggs, beaten
1 teaspoon vanilla extract
¹/₄ teaspoon cinnamon
¹/₃ cup raisins

Glaze
**1 egg yolk, combined with 1 teaspoon
water**

Roll out dough into a
¹/₄-inch-thick rectangle. Spread
with margarine and apricot jam.
Spread with cheese mixture leaving a
margin 2 inches from outer edge. Roll
and pinch ends together. Place, seam
side down, on a greased, 11x17-inch
cookie sheet. Cover and let rise for
30-40 minutes. Brush with egg glaze.
Bake in a preheated 375° oven for
30-35 minutes until golden brown.

Cherry Cake

A luscious dessert any time.

³/₄ cup margarine
³/₄ cup sugar
2 eggs
2¹/₄ cups flour, sifted
1¹/₂ teaspoons baking powder
¹/₄ teaspoon salt
1¹/₂ teaspoons vanilla extract

Topping
2 1-pound cans sour cherries, with juice
1 cup sugar
3 tablespoons cornstarch
1 teaspoon almond extract

Cream margarine and sugar. Stir in
eggs. Add remaining ingredients
and blend well. Spread into a greased,
9x13-inch baking pan. To make
topping, combine all ingredients in a
medium-sized saucepan. Bring to a
boil. Cook while stirring constantly
for 1-2 minutes until thickened. Let
cool and pour over cake batter in
pan. Alternatively, top with 1 can of
cherry pie filling. Bake in a 350° oven
for 40-45 minutes.

*Substitute potato flour for cornstarch. Un-
like cornstarch, potato flour is loaded with
nutrients and has half the calories of flour.*

Classic Sponge Cake

A hit every time.

**6 large eggs, room temperature,
   separated**
1 tablespoon lemon juice
1 cup sugar
1/4 cup orange juice
1 cup cake flour, sifted
1 teaspoon baking powder
1/4 teaspoon salt
1 teaspoon vanilla extract
grated rind of 1 orange

Beat egg whites and lemon juice until frothy, very gradually adding sugar. Beat until mixture holds stiff peaks. Set aside. In a separate bowl, beat yolks until light and thick—about 5 minutes. Add orange juice. Blend in flour, baking powder, salt, and vanilla extract. Do not over-mix. Fold whites gently but thoroughly into yolks, with orange rind. Pour into an ungreased (or greased on bottom only), 10-inch tube pan. Bake in a preheated 350° oven for 45-50 minutes or until golden brown. Top with Easy Raspberry Sauce. Serves 12.

Easy Raspberry Sauce
1 10-ounce package frozen raspberries
1 tablespoon cornstarch
3-4 tablespoons cold water

Defrost raspberries over low heat. Add remaining ingredients, stirring until thick. Spoon over individual pieces of sponge cake.

Variations

Filled sponge cake: To fill sponge or chiffon cake, cut off top 1 inch of cake. With a sharp knife, cut out center of cake, leaving a 1 1/2-inch shell on bottom and sides of cake. Fill with flavored whipped cream. Place top of cake over whipped cream. Ice with your favorite icing or sweetened whipped cream. Refrigerate. Alternatively, fill cake with softened ice cream and freeze. Serves 14.

Whole wheat sponge cake: Use half whole wheat and half white flour instead of all cake flour.

Carob sponge cake: Use 1/4 cup of sifted carob powder in place of 1/4 cup of the cake flour.

To get greater volume out of beaten egg whites, allow eggs to reach room temperature. Then begin beating slowly. Cream of tartar or a pinch of salt helps maintain volume.

My Favorite Apple Cake

I make this cake often. It can also be made with fresh apricots, plums, or sliced peaches: separately, or in combinations. Apricots give it an especially interesting flavor.

4 eggs
2 cups granulated sugar
1 cup oil
2 teaspoons vanilla extract
¼ cup orange juice
½ teaspoon salt
3 cups cake flour, sifted
4 teaspoons baking powder
5-6 large apples, sliced
½ cup brown or white sugar
2 teaspoons cinnamon

Beat eggs and granulated sugar until light and fluffy. Stir in oil, vanilla extract, orange juice, and salt. Blend in flour and baking powder. Pour half of mixture into a greased, 9x13 inch baking pan. Scatter apples on top. Combine sugar and cinnamon and sprinkle ⅔ of it on top of apples. Pour remaining batter on top. Sprinkle with remaining cinnamon and sugar. Bake in a 350° oven for 1 hour. If you prefer to bake in a 10-inch tube pan, add ¼ cup more orange juice to batter. Mix 3 teaspoons of cinnamon and ⅓ cup of sugar and combine with sliced apples. Into a greased pan, pour ⅓ of batter, ⅓ of apple mixture, then another ⅓ of batter, and ⅓ of apple mixture. Pour remaining batter with remaining apple mixture on top. Bake for 1 hour, 20 minutes at 350°.

Variation

Use 4-5 cups of sliced peaches, or sliced or halved apricots or plums, in place of apples.

Applesauce Cake

This is a perennial pleaser that I enjoy making again and again. As a neighbor's little girl once said of this cake: "It has sugar and spice and everything nice."

2 eggs
2 cups sugar
1 cup oil
2 cups applesauce
3 cups flour, sifted
1½ teaspoons baking powder
1½ teaspoons baking soda
½ teaspoon ground cloves
1 teaspoon cinnamon
½ teaspoon nutmeg
½ teaspoon allspice
1 cup nuts, chopped
¾ cup raisins
½ teaspoon salt
juice and grated rind of 1 lemon

Beat eggs until light and thick, gradually adding sugar. Stir in oil and remaining ingredients. Pour into a greased, 9x13-inch pan or 2 15x3x4½-inch loaf pans. Bake in a preheated 350° oven for 1 hour for the first pan or 45 minutes for the loaf pans.

Cakes usually fall if their batter is too liquidy, or if they are baked at the wrong temperature or removed from the oven too soon.

Angel Food Cake

A winner every time.

10-12 egg whites (1¹/₂ cups)
¹/₂ teaspoon salt
1¹/₂ teaspoons cream of tartar
1¹/₂ cups fine granulated sugar
1¹/₂ teaspoons vanilla or almond extract
1¹/₄ cups cake flour, sifted 3 times

In a large mixing bowl, beat egg whites with salt and cream of tartar until soft peaks are formed. Gradually add granulated sugar. Beat until stiff but not dry. Stir in vanilla or almond extract. Fold in flour thoroughly, a little at a time. Gently pour batter into an ungreased, 10-inch tube pan. Cut through in a few places to release air bubbles. Bake in a 350° oven for about 50-60 minutes. Let cool and remove from pan. Spread with slightly sweetened whipped cream, and sprinkle top with ¹/₄ cup of toasted slivered almonds or flaked chocolate, or simply sprinkle cooled cake with powdered sugar.

Variations

Angel food nut cake: Reduce flour to 1 cup. Fold ³/₄ cup of chopped nuts into batter.

Chocolate angel food cake: Reduce flour to 1 cup. Add ¹/₄ cup of cocoa, sifted with flour.

Mocha angel food cake: Add 2 teaspoons of instant coffee powder to chocolate angel food cake and sift with cocoa and flour.

Coconut Cloud Cake

This unusual cake caught my eye at a Kiddush one Shabbat. It is so named because that's just how the white coconut meringue looks in between the two layers of fluffy chocolate.

8 eggs, separated
1¹/₂ cups sugar
²/₃ cup flour, sifted
1 teaspoon baking powder
3 tablespoons oil
4 tablespoons cocoa
3 tablespoons sweet wine
6 ounces (2 cups) shredded coconut

Beat egg whites until frothy. Gradually add 1 cup of the sugar and beat until able to hold stiff peaks. Set aside. In another bowl, beat yolks until light, gradually adding remaining sugar. Stir in flour, baking powder, oil, cocoa, and wine. Gently fold the coconut into egg-white mixture. Pour half of the cocoa mixture into a greased, 10-inch tube pan. Pour coconut mixture on top. Cover evenly with remaining cocoa mixture. Bake in a preheated 350° oven for 1 hour. Ice with Continental Chocolate Icing (see page 229).

Variation

Coconut cloud squares: Spread half of cocoa mixture into a greased, 9x13-inch pan. Pour coconut-meringue mixture on top. Cover evenly with remaining cocoa mixture. Bake for 45-50 minutes.

Carrot Cake

I first tasted this carrot cake at a gala tea party hosted for a young bride who had just escaped from Iran. Someone whispered to me that the cake was so full of nutritious ingredients, it made her feel less guilty about having a second piece.

4 eggs
2 cups sugar
1 cup oil
$^1/_2$ teaspoon nutmeg
1 teaspoon cinnamon
$^1/_2$ teaspoon salt
2 cups shredded carrots
$^1/_3$ cup hot water
2 cups flour, sifted
$2^1/_4$ teaspoons baking powder
$^1/_2$ teaspoon baking soda
1 cup chopped nuts
$^2/_3$ cup raisins

Beat eggs until light and fluffy, adding sugar gradually. Stir in oil, nutmeg, cinnamon, salt, carrots, and water. Sift together flour, baking powder, and baking soda, and beat into mixture until smooth. Blend in nuts and raisins. Pour into a well-greased, 10-inch tube pan or a Bundt pan. Bake in a preheated 350° oven for 55-60 minutes.

Zucchini Cake

When you taste this cake, you'll never guess that it is made with zucchini!

3 eggs
$1^1/_3$ cups sugar
$^1/_2$ cup oil
2 medium zucchini, shredded
1 teaspoon vanilla extract
$^1/_2$ teaspoon salt
$1^1/_2$ cups flour, sifted
2 teaspoons baking powder
$^1/_2$ cup nuts, coarsely chopped
$^1/_2$ cup chocolate chips

Beat eggs until light and thick, gradually adding sugar. Stir in oil and remaining ingredients. Pour into a well-greased, 9x4-inch loaf pan. Bake in a preheated 350° oven for 40-45 minutes. (For a larger cake, double recipe and bake in a 9x13-inch pan.)

Surprise Lemon Torte

Layers of lemon filling surround bite-size pieces of cake. You'll love this light and refreshing dessert.

6 eggs, separated
1¹/₂ cups sugar
³/₄ cup lemon juice
grated rind of 1 lemon
1 envelope plain gelatin, dissolved in ¹/₄ cup cold water
1 Classic Sponge Cake (see page 216) or Angel Food Cake (see page 218)
whipped cream, optional
strawberries, for garnish, optional

In a medium-sized saucepan, beat egg yolks until light, gradually adding ³/₄ cup of the sugar. Stir in lemon juice and rind and cook over low heat until mixture coats the spoon. Remove from heat and allow to cool. Add gelatin to mixture. Beat egg whites until frothy, gradually adding remaining sugar. Beat until able to hold stiff peaks. Fold into cooled yolk mixture. Tear cake into bite-size pieces. Alternate layers of cake pieces with layers of cooked lemon mixture in a well-greased, 10-inch tube pan. Refrigerate for at least 3 hours or overnight until set. Remove carefully from pan. If desired, cover top and sides with whipped cream and garnish with strawberries.

Viennese Almond Torte

This is similar to the famous Sacher Torte—made with only 1 tablespoon of flour—which has become almost synonymous with rich, luxurious desserts.

6 ounces semi-sweet chocolate
¹/₂ cup margarine
8 eggs, separated
³/₄ cup sugar
juice of 1 lemon
1 teaspoon vanilla extract
3 tablespoons Sabra liqueur
1 cup ground almonds
1 tablespoon flour

Melt chocolate and margarine over low heat. Beat egg yolks and ¹/₂ cup of the sugar until light and fluffy. Stir in melted chocolate and margarine, lemon juice, vanilla extract, liqueur, almonds, and flour. Beat egg whites until frothy, gradually adding remaining sugar. Beat until whites form stiff peaks. Fold into chocolate-egg yolk mixture. Pour into a greased, 9-inch spring form pan and bake in a preheated 350° oven for 15 minutes. Lower heat to 325° and continue baking for an additional 45 minutes. When cool, spread with Continental Chocolate Icing (see page 229).

Supreme Nut Torte

A light torte made without flour, but with
¹/2 cup of dry, toasted bread crumbs. The
combination of cinnamon and lemon juice
gives it a wine flavor.

6 large eggs, room temperature,
    separated
1 cup granulated sugar
1 teaspoon cinnamon
3 tablespoons lemon juice
¹/2 cup dry, toasted bread crumbs or
    graham cracker crumbs
1 cup finely chopped walnuts
¹/4 teaspoon salt
1 teaspoon almond extract

Beat egg whites until frothy.
Gradually add half of the sugar
and continue beating until stiff peaks
are formed. Set aside. In another
bowl, beat egg yolks until light.
Gradually add remaining sugar and
beat until fluffy. Stir in remaining
ingredients. Fold beaten egg whites
into egg-yolk mixture gently but
thoroughly. Pour into a 9-inch
springform pan or a 10-inch tube pan
greased on bottom only. Bake in a
350° preheated oven for 50-60
minutes. When cool, frost with Super
Orange Icing (see page 230).

Elegant Cake Roll with Mocha Filling

A real party cake.

4 eggs, room temperature, separated
³/4 cup sugar
¹/4 teaspoon salt
¹/4 cup orange juice
³/4 cup flour, sifted
1 teaspoon baking powder
¹/3 cup powdered sugar, for dusting
toasted almonds, for garnish

Beat egg whites until frothy,
gradually adding sugar. Beat until
stiff. In another bowl, beat egg yolks
with salt until light and thick. Stir in
orange juice, flour, and baking
powder. Fold egg whites into yolk
mixture. Pour into a greased,
11x17-inch jelly roll pan, lined with
greased wax paper. Bake in a
preheated 375° oven for 12-15
minutes or until cake springs back
when touched lightly. While still
warm, turn cake upside down on a
large clean towel sprinkled with
powdered sugar. Carefully peel away
wax paper and use the towel to roll
up the cake, jelly roll-style. Let cool
and unroll. Make Mocha Filling (see
page 263). Set aside ¹/3 cup of filling.
Use the rest to spread evenly on cake.
Re-roll and cover top with reserved
filling. Sprinkle with toasted almonds.
Freeze.

Variation

Strawberry cream cheese filling: Mix
well 1 pound of cream cheese, at
room temperature, 3 tablespoons of
Sabra liqueur, and 4 tablespoons of
sugar. Scatter with sli
strawberries. Roll as fc

Rogelach

These small, individually rolled yeast pastries, filled with cinnamon, sugar, and chopped nuts, are called rogelach, which, in Yiddish, means "little rolled cakes."

Dough

1 package dry yeast
$^1/_2$ cup warm water
1 cup margarine
5 tablespoons sugar
3 cups flour
$^1/_2$ teaspoon salt
3 egg yolks
1$^1/_2$ teaspoons vanilla extract
melted margarine, or oil, for brushing
    dough

Filling

1$^1/_2$ cups brown or white sugar
2 teaspoons cinnamon
1 cup chopped nuts

Glaze

1 egg yolk, combined with 1 teaspoon
    oil, 1 teaspoon sugar, and 1 teaspoon
    water

To make the dough, combine yeast and water. Set aside. Meanwhile mix together margarine, sugar, and flour. Stir in remaining ingredients, including yeast mixture. Put dough in a plastic bag and refrigerate for 2 hours. Divide dough into 5-7 balls. Roll each ball into a 7-inch circle. Spread generously with melted margarine or oil. Combine filling ingredients and sprinkle generously on top of circles. Cut each one into 8 pie-shaped wedges. Roll up each wedge, starting at wide end. Place on a greased baking sheet. If desired, curve ends slightly inward for crescent shape. Combine ingredients for glaze and brush tops. Do not let rise. Bake in a 350° oven for about 35 minutes.

Variation

Cheese dough: Combine 1 cup of margarine with 1 cup ($^1/_2$ pound) of cream cheese, 2 cups of flour, and 3 tablespoons of sugar. Refrigerate overnight. Roll, fill, and bake.

Strawberry Trifle

A popular English dessert.

2 cups vanilla custard (use 1 package
    instant vanilla pudding mix, or
    recipe below)
1 medium-sized sponge cake, cut into
    strips
2/3 cup sherry or raspberry or cherry
    brandy
4 cups fresh strawberries, sliced
1 cup whipped cream
1/2 cup toasted slivered almonds
a few whole strawberries, for garnish

Prepare Vanilla Custard or combine
1 package of instant vanilla
pudding mix with 2 cups of milk.
Chill until firm. Line a large serving
bowl with thin strips of cake. Sprinkle
with sherry or brandy. Arrange
alternate layers of sliced strawberries,
chilled custard, and cake strips until
bowl is full. Spread whipped cream on
top. Sprinkle with almonds and
garnish with strawberries. Serve
chilled.

Variations

Use instant chocolate pudding mix,
prepared according to package
directions. Add 1 cup of chocolate
chips.

Use blueberries, raspberries, jam, or
cut-up canned fruit in place of
strawberries.

Vanilla Custard (dairy or pareve)
2 1/2 cups milk or pareve cream
1/3 sugar
1/4 cup cornstarch
4 tablespoons cold water
2 egg yolks
1 teaspoon vanilla extract
3 tablespoons margarine

Bring milk to a boil. Add sugar.
Dissolve cornstarch in cold water
and stir into hot milk. Cook until
thick and smooth. In a small bowl,
beat egg yolks. Stir in a few
tablespoons of the hot mixture. Then
pour egg yolks into hot mixture.
Cook over low heat for 2 more
minutes while stirring constantly.
Remove from heat and stir in vanilla
extract and margarine.

Old-Fashioned Taiglach

Taiglach—"little pieces of dough" in Yiddish—are honey-coated knotted pastries with nuts and raisins, cooked in syrup. It's not surprising that they are served on holidays when sweetness and joy are the keynotes: Sukkot, Simchat Torah, and Purim. Save the syrup and use it in recipes calling for honey.

Dough

3 eggs
3 tablespoons oil
2 tablespoons cognac
1 teaspoon ground ginger
3 cups flour, sifted
1 teaspoon baking powder
$1/2$ cup raisins, optional
$1/2$ cup pecan halves
chopped nuts or shredded coconut, for
    coating

Syrup

1 cup honey
$1^1/2$ cups sugar
2 teaspoons ground ginger
$1/4$ teaspoon cinnamon

Make dough first: Beat eggs. Stir in next 5 ingredients to make a smooth, soft dough, just firm enough to handle (add a little water, if necessary). Divide dough into 6 parts. Roll each part into a long, pencil-thin rope. Cut into 3-inch lengths. Tie in knots and tuck ends in, or roll into $1^1/2$-inch balls. Press a pecan half and a few raisins into the center. Make syrup by bringing all ingredients to a boil in a large pot. Drop balls into pot. Simmer in syrup uncovered for 25-30 minutes. Stir occasionally to bring bottom balls to top. Cook until all are brown and give a hollow sound when removed and tapped. Add 2 tablespoons of water. Allow taiglach to cool slightly in pot. Remove with a slotted spoon onto wax paper. Roll in chopped nuts or shredded coconut. Yields 36 taiglach.

Hungarian Jerbo

The Hungarians are known for their extravagant pastries. This jerbo consists of three layers of delicious pastry, with a tangy filling of chopped nuts and ground lemon, which gives it a marvelous flavor. Another layer of prune lacqvar or other jam and a creamy chocolate icing complete this mouth-watering recipe. You'll want to make it for special occasions and holidays.

Dough
1 cup margarine
$^1/_2$ cup sugar
6 egg yolks
$^1/_2$ cup orange juice
3 cups all-purpose flour
2 teaspoons baking powder

Filling
1-1$^1/_2$ cups chopped nuts
3 tablespoons bread crumbs
1 cup sugar
2 teaspoons vanilla extract
1 whole lemon, ground with peel in food processor

Second Layer of Filling
1$^1/_2$ cups prune lacqvar (prune jam) or other jam

Cream margarine and sugar. Add yolks, and cream until fluffy. Stir in orange juice, flour, and baking powder. Divide into three parts and refrigerate for 1 hour. Combine filling ingredients and set aside. Roll out each part of dough to fit a greased, 9x12-inch baking sheet. Place one layer on the bottom. Spread with whole amount of nut filling. Place second layer of dough over nut filling. Spread with second layer of filling. Place third layer of dough on top. Bake in a 350° oven for 40 minutes. When cool, ice with Chocolate Icing.

Chocolate Icing
$^1/_3$ cup cocoa
1 cup powdered sugar
2 tablespoons oil
2 tablespoons hot water
1 teaspoon vanilla extract

Combine ingredients and spread on cooled jerbo. Slice into diamond shapes or small squares. To serve, place in fluted paper cups.

Mock Strudel

Lovely for a tea party.

Dough

$^1/_2$ cup oil, or 1 cup margarine
$^3/_4$ cup sugar
2 eggs
$^1/_4$ cup orange juice
$3^1/_2$ cups flour
2 teaspoons baking powder
$^1/_4$ teaspoon salt
1 teaspoon vanilla extract
oil, for brushing

Cream together oil or margarine and sugar. Stir in eggs and remaining ingredients except oil for brushing. Chill.

Filling

1 cup orange marmalade or apricot jam
1 cup shredded coconut
$^1/_2$ cup raisins
$^3/_4$ cup coarsely chopped nuts
4 tablespoons orange juice

Combine all ingredients. Divide dough into 3 parts. Roll out each part into a thin rectangle. Spread filling until 2 inches from outer edge, or place a $1^1/_2$-inch-thick row of filling on inside edge of dough. Roll as for jelly roll. Brush top with oil. Bake in a 350° oven for 35-40 minutes until lightly browned.

Variations

Instead of orange juice, add 1 whole, unpeeled orange ground in a food processor with a blade.

Use any of the fillings used for Hamantaschen (see page 246).

Easy Flaky Dough

This is a simple, yet versatile, dough—for knishes, strudels, rogelach, and turnovers—which can be used instead of puff pastry or phyllo dough. It should be mixed or handled as little as possible. It stays fresh for several days in the refrigerator, or keeps for months in the freezer.

1 cup margarine, cold
2 cups flour, sifted
$^1/_3$ cup cold water
2 tablespoons vinegar
1 egg yolk, beaten
$^1/_2$ teaspoon salt

With a pastry blender or 2 knives, cut margarine into flour until mixture resembles peas. Combine cold water with vinegar, egg yolk, and salt. Stir into mixture, a little at a time. Mix with your fingers or a fork until combined. Do not over-mix or handle too much. Dough should be soft but not sticky. Wrap in a plastic bag and refrigerate for 2 hours or overnight. Remove from refrigerator and let rest for 10 minutes. Roll, fill, and bake in a hot oven, about 450-475°, to ensure a flaky texture.

Variation

Omit egg yolk, but increase water to $^1/_2$ cup.

When baking with artificial sweeteners, bake at low temperatures. If at all possible add sugar substitutes after removing foods from heat. They work best in foods that require no cooking.

Apple Strudel

Popular on Sukkot and Simchat Torah, when stuffed foods—symbolizing plenty—are eaten. The dough is spread with a thin layer of orange marmalade to enhance the flavor.

Easy Flaky Dough (see page 226)
4 tablespoons orange marmalade

Filling
5-6 large apples, peeled and thinly
**   sliced**
$^1/_2$ cup white or brown sugar
$^2/_3$ cup raisins
$^1/_2$ cup walnuts, coarsely chopped
$^1/_4$ cup bread crumbs
1 teaspoon cinnamon
melted margarine, for brushing top

Glaze
1 egg yolk, combined with 1 teaspoon
**   water**

Divide dough into 3 parts. Roll each part into a $^1/_8$-inch-thick rectangle. Spread with orange marmalade. Combine remaining ingredients and spread over dough, leaving a 2-3-inch margin at the edges. Roll and place in a greased, 11x17-inch baking pan. Brush with melted margarine; then brush with egg glaze. Cut through top at 1-1$^1/_2$-inch intervals to mark slices. Bake in a preheated 475° oven for 20 minutes, then in a 350° oven for 20 more minutes until golden brown. Yields 24 1$^1/_2$-inch slices.

Variations

Cherry strudel filling: Combine 5 cups of pitted sour cherries, $^1/_2$ cup of bread crumbs, 1 cup of sugar, $^1/_2$ teaspoon of cinnamon, and $^2/_3$ cup of chopped nuts. Alternatively, combine 1 can of cherry pie filling, $^2/_3$ cup of shredded coconut, and $^1/_2$ cup of chopped nuts. Prepare as directed.

Nut strudel filling: Combine 1 unpeeled, ground orange, 1 cup of raisins, 1 cup of chopped nuts, $^2/_3$ cup of shredded coconut, 1 cup of jam, and 4 tablespoons of bread crumbs. Prepare as directed.

To prevent apples and bananas from discoloring, sprinkle with lemon juice.

Sesame Strudel

The toasted sesame seeds add just that extra touch to this delicious strudel.

Easy Flaky Dough (see page 226) or cookie dough

Filling
3 1/2 ounces toasted sesame seeds
1 1/4 cups bread crumbs
3/4 cup sugar
1 cup shredded coconut
1/2 cup wine
orange marmalade or apricot jam, for spreading on dough

Glaze
1 egg yolk, combined with 1 teaspoon water

Combine all filling ingredients in a bowl. Set aside. Divide dough into 3 equal parts. Roll out each part into a 1/8-inch-thick rectangle. Spread thinly with marmalade or jam. Place filling near inside edge of dough in a roll 1 1/2 inches wide. Roll as for jelly roll. Place on a greased, 11x17-inch cookie sheet. Mark by cutting into top layer of dough with a sharp knife. Brush with egg glaze. Bake in a preheated 450° degree oven for about 20 minutes. Reduce heat to 350° and bake for an additional 20 minutes until golden brown. Yields 28-30 pieces.

Venetian Nut Cake with Chocolate Topping

When we lived in Chicago, a friend sent us this special cake to welcome our children from Israel. Everyone enjoyed this unusual cake, with its rich chocolate topping and all-nut filling.

12 egg whites
1 1/4 cups sugar
3/4 pound ground filberts, walnuts, or pecans
juice and rind of 1 large lemon
4 teaspoons vanilla extract
pinch of cinnamon, optional

Beat egg whites until frothy. Add sugar gradually and beat until able to form stiff peaks. Fold in nuts and remaining ingredients. Pour into a greased, 10-inch tube pan. Bake in a preheated 350° oven for 50 minutes. When cooled slightly, spread with Special Chocolate Topping.

Special Chocolate Topping
8 ounces semi-sweet chocolate
12 egg yolks
2 tablespoons of your favorite liqueur

In a double boiler, or in a pan set over boiling water, melt chocolate. In a medium-sized bowl, beat egg yolks and combine with melted chocolate. Stir in liqueur. Spread on top and sides of cooled cake. Refrigerate.

Sugar-Free Cake

A light, tasty cake, with variations. You'd never guess it was sugar-free. You can double the recipe and pour batter into a 9x13-inch Teflon or lightly greased pan.

3 eggs, separated
¹/₄ cup vegetable oil
¹/₂ cup frozen apple or orange juice concentrate
10 tablets sugar substitute, dissolved in 2 tablespoons hot water
1 teaspoon grated orange rind, optional
¹/₄ teaspoon salt
1 cup flour
1¹/₂ teaspoons baking powder

Beat egg yolks until light. Stir in remaining ingredients. In another bowl, beat egg whites until stiff and fold into yolk mixture. Pour into a lightly greased, 8-inch square pan. Bake in a 350° oven for 30-35 minutes.

Variations

Sugar-free chocolate cake: Combine 3 tablespoons of cocoa with 3 additional sugar substitute tablets dissolved in 1 tablespoon of hot water and add to batter.

Sugar-free nut cake: Fold ¹/₃ cup of chopped nuts into batter before baking.

Sugar-free marble cake: Remove ¹/₄ of batter to a small bowl. Stir into it 2 tablespoons of cocoa combined with 2 sugar substitute tablets dissolved in 1 teaspoon of hot water. Pour ¹/₃ of white batter into a lightly greased, 8-inch pan or a 9x5-inch loaf pan. Pour cocoa mixture on top and spread with remaining white mixture. Cut through batter at 2-inch intervals to marbleize. Bake as directed.

My Favorite Icings

A good icing puts the finishing touch on any cake.

Chocolate Glaze Icing

¹/₂ cup cocoa, unsweetened
1 cup sugar
¹/₃ cup water, scant
3 tablespoons margarine
1 teaspoon vanilla extract
2 ounces semi-sweet chocolate, optional

In a saucepan, mix together cocoa, sugar, and water. Bring to a boil and lower heat. Cook for about 10-12 minutes until a few drops form a ball when placed into cold water. Remove from heat and stir in remaining ingredients. Stir vigorously until slightly thickened.

Continental Chocolate Icing

Melt 6 ounces of chocolate chips with 3 tablespoons of margarine. Remove from heat and stir in 2 tablespoons of brandy or wine and ¹/₂ teaspoon of vanilla extract. Spread on cake while quite warm.

Caramel Nut Icing

Cook 2 cups of brown sugar and ²/₃ cup of water over low heat until smooth. Remove from heat. Let cool slightly and stir in 4 tablespoons of margarine, 1 teaspoon of almond extract, and, if desired, ¹/₂ cup of chopped nuts. Beat until thickened. Spread on cake immediately.

Fluffy Boiled Icing

1 1/2 cups sugar
1/3 cup water
1 tablespoon corn syrup
2 egg whites
1 teaspoon vanilla or almond extract
pinch of salt

In a saucepan, bring to a boil sugar, water, and corn syrup. Reduce heat and cook until mixture spins a thread when dropped from a spoon. Do not stir. Meanwhile, beat egg whites until frothy. Slowly, in a thin steady stream, pour hot syrup into beaten egg whites. Continue beating until mixture is thick and holds its shape. Add remaining ingredients. Yields enough for a 10-inch tube cake or a 9-inch layer cake.

Variations

Mocha: Add 1 teaspoon of instant coffee powder.

Peppermint: Add 1/2 teaspoon of peppermint extract and 1/2 teaspoon of vanilla extract.

Silky beige: Substitute brown sugar for white sugar.

Coconut: Sprinkle generously with shredded coconut before icing dries.

Marshmallow: Cut 5 marshmallows into pieces. Combine with 2 tablespoons of water and melt over low heat. Stir into syrup before adding to egg whites.

Butter Cream Icing

Cream together 2 cups of confectioner's sugar, 3 tablespoons of hot water, a pinch of salt, 1/4 cup of margarine, and 1 teaspoon of vanilla or almond extract.

Variations

Pineapple butter cream: Add 1/2 cup of drained crushed pineapple and 3 teaspoons of lemon juice. Omit water.

Mint butter cream: Stir in 1/2 teaspoon of mint extract and 3-4 tablespoons of creme de menthe liqueur in place of hot water. Add a drop of green coloring.

Chocolate butter cream: Stir into mixture 1/4 cup of cocoa or 2 ounces of melted unsweetened chocolate.

Chocolate mint butter cream: Add 1/2 teaspoon of peppermint extract to variation 3.

Coconut Icing

1 cup brown sugar
3 tablespoons soft margarine
pinch of salt
2/3 cup shredded coconut
3-4 tablespoons liqueur

Combine ingredients and spread on cake. Place under broiler, about 5 inches away, until dissolved—about 5 minutes.

Super Orange Icing

2 cups powdered sugar
2-3 tablespoons orange juice
grated peel of 1 large orange
1 teaspoon lemon juice
1 teaspoon grated lemon peel
3 tablespoons soft margarine
1/2 teaspoon vanilla extract

Combine all ingredients and cream together well.

Variation

Lemon icing: Substitute lemon juice for orange juice.

Royal Mocha Cream Icing
1 cup margarine, softened
2 large eggs
1/2 cup sugar
3 tablespoons cocoa
1-2 teaspoons instant coffee powder
2 tablespoons Sabra liqueur or sweet red wine
1 teaspoon vanilla extract

Place all ingredients in a food processor or blender. Blend at high speed for about 8-10 minutes until icing is fluffy and thick.

Chocolate Whipped Cream
2 cups whipping cream
2/3 cup powdered sugar
1/3 cup cocoa

Whip cream until stiff. Fold in sugar and cocoa.

Variation

Mocha whipped cream: Add 1 tablespoon of instant coffee.

Orange Filling
For chiffon, sponge, or layer cakes.

2/3 cup sugar
1 cup orange juice
3 tablespoons flour
2 egg yolks
1 teaspoon grated orange rind
2 tablespoons margarine
1/2 teaspoon vanilla extract
sweetened whipped cream, or 2 teaspoons grated orange rind, optional

Bring sugar, orange juice and flour to a boil, stirring constantly. In a small bowl, beat egg yolks, stir in 2 tablespoons cooked mixture, and add to hot mixture. Cook while stirring for 2 minutes, until thickened. Remove from heat and add 1 teaspoon grated orange rind, margarine, and vanilla extract. Cut cake in half. Spread bottom half with orange filling and replace top half. Top with whipped cream or 2 teaspoons orange rind, if desired.

Variations

Lemon filling: Substitute 1/3 cup of lemon juice for same amount of orange juice, and add 2/3 cup of water.

Date filling: Stir in 1/2 cup of chopped dates to cooked filling.

Chocolate Coconut Filling
This filling is good with cookie dough.

4 tablespoons cocoa, rounded
4 tablespoons shredded coconut, rounded
4 tablespoons chopped nuts, rounded
4 tablespoons sesame seeds
1 1/4 cups sugar
jam, for spreading on dough

Combine all ingredients except jam. Spread rolled out dough thinly with jam. Add filling, roll, and bake.

Cookies, Bars & Confections

Cookies, Bars, & Confections

Regal Chocolate Peanut Butter Squares

One of my favorite recipes.

2/3 cup margarine, room temperature
1 1/2 cups brown sugar
1 1/4 cups white sugar
1 cup peanut butter
4 eggs
1 tablespoon vanilla extract
2 cups all-purpose flour, sifted
2 teaspoons baking powder
1/2 teaspoon salt
6-12 ounces semi-sweet chocolate chips

Cream together margarine with brown and white sugar and peanut butter. Beat in eggs and vanilla extract. Stir in flour, baking powder, and salt. Pour into a well-greased, 9x13-inch baking pan or, for thinner squares, onto a cookie sheet. Scatter chocolate chips evenly over top. Bake in a preheated 400° oven for 5 minutes to melt chocolate. Remove from oven and swirl chocolate through batter with a knife. Lower heat to 350°. Return to oven and bake for an additional 30 minutes. Cut into squares while warm. Yields 30-40 small squares.

Quick and Easy Eclair Cuts

Graham crackers line the pan instead of the hard-to-prepare cream puff pastry. Cut them into squares. Delicious!

22 graham crackers

Custard Filling
2 packages instant French vanilla pudding mix
3 cups milk or pareve cream
8 ounces pareve whipped cream or topping

Chocolate Icing
1 6-ounce package chocolate chips
3 tablespoons margarine
2 tablespoons liqueur or orange juice

Place a single layer of graham crackers on bottom of a 9x13-inch baking pan. Combine instant pudding with milk or pareve cream until smooth. Fold in whipped cream or topping and spread half of mixture evenly over graham crackers. Add another layer of graham crackers. Add remaining custard filling and another layer of crackers. Melt chocolate chips and margarine over very low heat. Remove from heat and stir in liqueur or orange juice. Spread over top layer of graham crackers. Refrigerate overnight or longer. Cut into squares.

Harriet's Chocolate-Filled Rectangles

Layers of chocolate meringue alternated with layers of no-rise yeast dough—rich and delicious.

Dough
1 package dry granular yeast, or 1 cake
   compressed yeast
$^2/_3$ cup lukewarm water
$1^1/_2$ cups margarine
$4^1/_2$ cups flour, sifted
2 teaspoons baking powder
3 tablespoons sugar
4 egg yolks, beaten

Chocolate Meringue Filling
4 egg whites
2 cups sugar
4 tablespoons cocoa

Glaze
1 egg yolk, mixed with 1 teaspoon
   water

Dissolve yeast in lukewarm water. Set aside for 5 minutes. Mix together margarine, flour, baking powder, and sugar. Stir in yeast mixture and egg yolks. Refrigerate for at least 2 hours. Divide dough into 4 equal parts. For the filling: Beat egg whites, gradually adding sugar until stiff. Fold in cocoa. Roll out each part of dough into a 9x13-inch rectangle and place one part on bottom of a greased, 9x13-inch baking pan. Spread with $^1/_3$ of filling mixture. Repeat twice. Place fourth layer of dough on top. Brush with glaze. Bake in a preheated 350° oven for 40 minutes. Cut into rectangles. Yields 24 pieces.

Variation

For a coffee filling, substitute 2 teaspoons of instant coffee for cocoa.

Chocolate Brandy Squares

For a family simchah, these rich chocolate brandy squares are superb.

$^2/_3$ cup raisins
$^2/_3$ cup nuts, coarsely chopped
$^1/_4$ cup brandy
1 cup margarine
7 ounces semi-sweet chocolate
6 eggs, separated
$1^1/_2$ cups sugar
$1^1/_2$ cups flour, sifted

Soak raisins and nuts in brandy. Meanwhile, melt margarine and chocolate over very low heat. Let cool. Beat egg whites until frothy, gradually adding half of the sugar. Beat until stiff peaks are formed. Set aside. In another bowl, beat egg yolks until light. Add remaining sugar, flour, and raisins and nuts plus the brandy. Add cooled margarine-chocolate mixture. Fold in egg whites. Pour into a well-greased, 9x13-inch baking pan. Bake in a preheated 350° oven for a maximum of 35 minutes. Yields 24-36 squares.

Make your own diet margarine by whipping it with water.

Date Diamonds

A light date-nut confection made without shortening and cut into diamond shapes.

2 eggs, beaten
3/4 cup brown sugar, packed
1/2 teaspoon cinnamon
1 teaspoon vanilla extract
2 tablespoons grated orange rind
2/3 cup all-purpose flour, sifted
1 teaspoon baking powder
1 cup dates, chopped
1 cup nuts, coarsely chopped
1/2 cup maraschino cherries, drained
   and quartered

B eat eggs. Add remaining ingredients in order given. Spread in a greased, 9-inch square or 7x11 1/2-inch baking pan. Bake in a preheated 325° oven for 30-35 minutes. While still warm, cut into 1-inch columns, then diagonally into diamond shapes.
Yields 36 "diamonds."

Dream Bars

A dream for coconut lovers.

Bottom Layer
1/2 cup margarine, softened
1/2 cup brown sugar
1 1/4 cups flour

Top Layer
2 eggs
1/2 teaspoon baking powder
1 cup brown sugar
1/2 teaspoon salt
1 cup shredded coconut
1 teaspoon vanilla extract
1/2 cup walnuts, chopped

C ombine ingredients for bottom layer and pat into a 9-inch cake pan. Bake in a 350° oven for 15 minutes. Beat eggs and stir in remaining ingredients for top layer. Spread over the prebaked crust and bake for an additional 20-25 minutes. Cut into squares. Yields about 25 squares.

Brownies

My favorite brownie recipe. Rich, delicious, and easy to make with an electric mixer or by hand. Try these variations, including carob brownies made with whole wheat flour. You can make brownies with oil. They are just as good as those baked with butter or margarine.

1 cup butter or margarine, room
    temperature
2 cups sugar
2 teaspoons vanilla extract
4 eggs
1 cup cocoa, or 4 ounces unsweetened
    chocolate, melted
1¼ cups all-purpose flour, sifted
1 cup coarsely chopped nuts

Cream together butter or margarine and sugar until light and fluffy. Stir in vanilla extract and eggs. Add cocoa and flour. Stir in all the nuts, or reserve ⅓ to sprinkle on top before baking. (If using icing on top, stir all the nuts into batter.) Pour into a greased, 9x13-inch pan. Bake in a preheated 350° oven for 25-30 minutes. Yields 28-32 brownies.

Variations

Chocolate chip brownies: Stir 6 ounces of chocolate chips into batter before baking.

Marshmallow brownies: Stir 1 cup of miniature marshmallows into batter before baking.

Creme de menthe brownies: In place of vanilla extract, use 1 teaspoon of peppermint extract. Frost with a mixture of 2 cups of powdered sugar, 4 tablespoons of creme de menthe liqueur, a few drops of green food coloring, and 2 ounces (½ stick) of margarine. Mix until smooth. Drizzle top with 2 ounces of semi-sweet chocolate melted with 2 tablespoons of margarine.

Carob brownies: Substitute 1 cup of carob powder for cocoa and whole wheat flour for all-purpose flour. Add ¼ teaspoon of baking soda.

White chocolate brownies: Substitute 4 ounces of melted white chocolate for unsweetened chocolate. Reduce sugar to 1¾ cups.

Crunchy Peanut Butter Chocolate Topping

Combine 1 cup of peanut butter, at room temperature, with 12 ounces of melted chocolate chips and 1½-2 cups of Rice Krispies, to spreading consistency. Spread on top.

Mocha Icing

Mix until smooth: 2 cups of confectioner's sugar, 1 teaspoon of instant coffee, ½ teaspoon of vanilla extract, 3-4 tablespoons of hot water, 1 ounce of melted unsweetened chocolate, and 4 tablespoons of margarine. Spread on cooled brownies.

Crunchy Oatmeal Squares

Made with oatmeal, coconut, and honey, but without eggs. Really good.

1 cup margarine
2 tablespoons honey
1 teaspoon baking soda
1 cup flour, sifted
1 cup white or brown sugar
2 cups uncooked oatmeal
1 cup shredded coconut, optional
4 ounces semi-sweet chocolate chips

Melt margarine in a saucepan over low heat. Add honey and baking soda. In a large mixing bowl, combine flour, sugar, oatmeal, and coconut. Add honey mixture and mix thoroughly. Pat evenly into a well-greased, 9x13-inch baking pan. Bake in a preheated 350° oven for about 25 minutes. Remove from oven. Sprinkle with chocolate chips. Return to oven for 3 minutes, then use a knife to spread chocolate evenly over mixture. Cut into squares. Yields 28 squares.

Coconut Pinwheels

A rich, no-rise yeast dough baked with a coconut meringue filling.

Dough
1 package active dry yeast, or 1 cake
   fresh compressed yeast
$1/2$ cup lukewarm water
4 tablespoons sugar
$1^1/8$ cups margarine, room temperature
$3^1/2$ cups flour, sifted
2 egg yolks, slightly beaten

Coconut Meringue Filling
2 egg whites
$3/4$ cup sugar
1 cup grated coconut

Make dough first: Dissolve yeast in lukewarm water. Add 1 teaspoon of the sugar. Cover and let stand for 5 minutes. Place margarine and flour into a large mixing bowl. With a pastry blender or 2 knives, cut margarine into flour until pieces are the size of peas. Stir in remaining sugar, egg yolks, and yeast mixture until smooth. Form into a ball. Place in a plastic bag and refrigerate for 2 hours or overnight. Filling: Beat egg whites until stiff while gradually adding sugar. Gently fold in coconut. Remove dough from refrigerator and divide into 3 parts. Roll out each part into a 9x13-inch rectangle, $1/4$ inch thick. Spread $1/3$ of filling on each part of dough, leaving a 1-inch margin. Roll as for jelly roll. Cut into $3/4$-inch slices and place, cut side down, on a greased cookie sheet, $1^1/2$ inches apart. Bake in a preheated 350° oven for 30 minutes. Yields 36-40 "pinwheels."

Coconut Meringue Squares

This is an old Sisterhood favorite. Once a month on a Shabbat afternoon, we would gather to enjoy tea, conversation, and words of Torah. The pastries each hostess prepared added to the warmth and beauty of celebrating Shabbat—a real Oneg Shabbat.

³/₄ cup margarine, room temperature
1¹/₂ cups brown sugar
¹/₂ cup white sugar
3 eggs, separated
1 teaspoon vanilla extract
2 cups flour, sifted
1 teaspoon baking powder
¹/₄ teaspoon baking soda
¹/₄ teaspoon salt
6 ounces semi-sweet chocolate chips
1 cup flaked coconut
³/₄ cup chopped nuts

Cream together margarine with ¹/₂ cup of the brown sugar and all of the white sugar. Beat in egg yolks and vanilla extract until fluffy. Stir in flour, baking powder, baking soda, and salt. Spread batter in a well-greased, 9x13-inch pan. Sprinkle with chocolate chips, then with coconut and nuts. Beat egg whites until frothy, gradually adding remaining brown sugar. Beat until stiff, but not dry. Spread evenly over top. Bake in a preheated 350° oven for 35-40 minutes. Yields 40 small squares.

Hungarian Nut Meringue Squares

An old Hungarian recipe using a thick layer of nuts on top.

Bottom Layer

¹/₂ cup margarine, room temperature
1 cup sugar
4 egg yolks (reserve whites for top)
2 cups all-purpose flour, sifted
¹/₂ teaspoon baking powder
2 tablespoons water

Top Layer

4 egg whites
1¹/₂ cups sugar
3 cups ground nuts

Make bottom layer first: Cream together margarine and sugar. Beat in egg yolks. Stir in flour, baking powder, and water. Spread evenly in a greased, 11x17-inch baking pan. Bake in a preheated 350° oven for 20 minutes. Remove from oven. Prepare top layer: Beat egg whites until frothy, gradually adding sugar. Beat until stiff. Fold in nuts. Spread evenly over prebaked crust and return to oven for an additional 20 minutes. Let cool. Cut into squares. Yields about 60 squares.

Continental Nut Slices

A delicious pastry with a nut-meringue filling.

Dough

3/4 cup margarine
2 cups all-purpose flour, sifted
1 package dry granulated yeast, or 1
   cake compressed yeast
1/4 cup warm water
1 tablespoon sugar
2 egg yolks (reserve whites for filling)
1/8 teaspoon salt

Filling

2 egg whites
3/4 cup sugar
1 teaspoon vanilla extract
1 cup chopped nuts

Make dough first: Cut margarine into flour with a pastry blender until pieces are the size of peas. Combine with remaining ingredients. Form into a ball, place in a plastic bag, and refrigerate for 1 hour or overnight. To make filling: Beat egg whites until frothy. Gradually add sugar, and beat until stiff. Stir in vanilla extract. Leave chopped nuts aside. Divide dough in half. Roll out each part into a rectangle 1/4 inch thick. Spread with half the filling; sprinkle with half the nuts. Roll as for jelly roll. Place on a greased cookie sheet. Cut down center of roll, only halfway through, to expose filling. Then mark slices by cutting into top of dough at 3/4-inch intervals. Bake in a preheated 375° oven for 25-30 minutes. Let cool and cut into slices. Yields about 32 slices.

Date Bars

A thin pastry crust with a thick, delicious, date-nut topping. A party recipe that the family will also enjoy. A real winner.

Bottom Layer

1 1/2 cups flour, sifted
1/2 cup sugar
1/2 cup margarine

Top Layer

2 eggs
1/3 cup brown sugar
1/2 cup white sugar
1 teaspoon vanilla extract
2 tablespoons all-purpose flour, sifted
1/2 teaspoon baking powder
1/2 teaspoon salt
1/2 teaspoon cinnamon
1 cup nuts
8 ounces dates, pitted and coarsely
   chopped

Bottom layer: Combine flour, sugar, and margarine. Pat into a 9x13-inch pan. Bake in a preheated 350° oven for 20 minutes. Top layer: Beat eggs, and stir in remaining ingredients. Spread evenly over prebaked bottom layer. Bake for an additional 20 minutes. Cut into small bars while still warm. Yields 24 bars.

Creamy Apple Squares

This looks and tastes like apple cake. No one will guess it is made with applesauce. A good and easy-to-prepare recipe. Make a larger quantity of the dough and keep it in the refrigerator for a few weeks or in the freezer for longer.

2¹/₂ cups flour, sifted
2¹/₂ teaspoons baking powder
1 cup margarine, room temperature
1 cup sugar
1 teaspoon cinnamon
grated rind of ¹/₂ lemon
¹/₈ teaspoon salt
1 20-ounce can applesauce

Combine all ingredients except applesauce. Pat half of the mixture into a well-greased, 9x13-inch baking pan. Spread with applesauce. Crumb the remaining dough mixture and sprinkle evenly over top until applesauce is completely covered. Bake in a preheated 375° oven for 30 minutes. Yields about 24 squares.

Variations

Cheese filling: In place of applesauce, combine 1 pound of cream cheese, 2 well-beaten eggs, ²/₃ cup of sugar and 1 teaspoon of lemon or vanilla extract until creamy.

Cherry or blueberry filling: Use a can of pie filling instead of applesauce.

Linzer Diamonds

Linzer Diamonds are a take-off on the Viennese Linzer Torte. Really special.

1 cup margarine
¹/₂ cup powdered sugar
2¹/₂ cups flour, sifted
12 ounces chocolate chips
1 10-ounce jar raspberry jam
1 cup blanched slivered almonds

Cream together margarine and powdered sugar until fluffy. Stir in flour. Spread dough on a greased, 10x17-inch baking sheet. Bake in a 350° oven for 20 minutes. Remove from oven and sprinkle with chocolate chips. Return to oven for about 5 minutes until chocolate chips melt. With a knife, spread melted chocolate evenly. Let cool. Spread with jam and sprinkle with almonds. Cut into diamond-shaped pieces. Yields 45 "diamonds."

Date Oatmeal Squares

Oatmeal crumb crust on the bottom, as well as sprinkled on top. Really good. From my Chicago Sisterhood days.

Bottom Layer
3/4 cup margarine
1 cup brown sugar
1 1/2 cups uncooked oatmeal
1 3/4 cups all-purpose flour, sifted
1/2 teaspoon baking soda
1/8 teaspoon salt

Top Layer
1 pound dates, pitted and chopped
1/3 cup sugar
1/2 cup water
juice and grated rind of 1 orange
2/3 cup nuts, coarsely chopped

Bottom layer: Combine all ingredients until thoroughly blended. Reserve 1/3 of mixture for crumb topping. Spread remaining 2/3 evenly in a greased, 9x13-inch pan. Top layer: Cook dates, sugar, water, and orange juice for 2-3 minutes until dates are dissolved and thick. Let cool, and stir in orange rind and nuts. Spread evenly over bottom layer. Crumb the remaining dough mixture and sprinkle over top. Bake in a preheated 375° oven for 30-35 minutes. Yields 32-36 squares.

Variation

Cranberry squares: Combine a 1-pound can of whole cranberry sauce with 1/2 cup of drained crushed pineapple and 1 teaspoon of vanilla extract. Spread over bottom layer in place of date filling. Bake as directed.

Coconut Oatmeal Cookies

Here is another old favorite. The coconut makes the difference! A rich cookie that is absolutely delicious.

1/2 cup margarine or butter, room temperature
3/4 cup white or brown sugar
1 egg
1/4 cup warm water
1 cup flour, sifted
1 teaspoon baking powder
1/4 teaspoon salt
1 cup uncooked regular or instant oatmeal
1/2 cup nuts
1 cup flaked coconut

Cream together margarine and sugar. Beat in egg. Stir in remaining ingredients until thoroughly combined. Drop by the teaspoonful onto a greased baking sheet. Bake in a preheated 350° oven for 15-20 minutes. Yields about 30 cookies.

Cookies spread too much if their batter is too oily or liquidy, or if the oven temperature is too low.

Hamantaschen

Hamantaschen—Yiddish for "Haman's pockets"—passed into Hebrew as Oznei Haman—"Haman's ears." Filled delicacies, particularly kreplach and hamantaschen, are traditional on Purim. They symbolize the hidden miracles of the day. Make a batch with each of the fillings. This is a marvelous soft dough. Use it for cookies or filled pastries, too.

1 cup margarine, room temperature
1 cup sugar
2 eggs, beaten
$^1/_4$ cup orange juice
$3^1/_2$ cups flour, sifted
$^1/_2$ teaspoon baking powder
$^1/_2$ teaspoon baking soda
1 teaspoon vanilla extract
grated rind of 1 lemon

Cream together margarine and sugar until fluffy. Stir in remaining ingredients in order given. Divide dough into 3 parts and, on a floured surface, roll out each part $^1/_8$ inch thick. Cut into 2-inch rounds. Put a heaped teaspoonful of filling in center of each round. Fold 3 sides over, pinching edges together to form a triangle. Place on a greased cookie sheet and bake in a preheated 350° oven for 25 minutes or until golden. Yields about 36 hamantaschen.

Prune or Apricot Filling
1 pound prunes, pitted, or dried apricots
$^1/_3$ cup raisins
$^2/_3$ cup chopped nuts, optional
4 tablespoons lemon juice
$^1/_2$ cup apricot jam
pinch of nutmeg
pinch of cinnamon

To pit prunes, soak them in boiling water to cover for 20 minutes, then remove pits and drain prunes well. Chop fruit in a food processor or by hand. Stir in remaining ingredients.

Date Filling
2 cups pitted dates, chopped
$^1/_2$ cup raisins
$^1/_2$ cup chopped nuts
grated rind of 1 orange
$^1/_4$ teaspoon cinnamon

Combine all ingredients in a food processor or by hand.

Best Mandelbrot

Mandelbrot—literally, "almond bread"—is an old European Jewish favorite and a traditional treat on Shabbat and holidays. I've made many versions of mandelbrot over the years, but this recipe tops them all.

3 eggs, well beaten
1 cup sugar
1 cup oil
1 teaspoon vanilla extract
3 cups flour, sifted
1 teaspoon baking powder
1 cup ground or finely chopped
  almonds

Beat together eggs and sugar until fluffy. Stir in remaining ingredients. Form into 3-4 long rolls each about 2 inches wide. Place on a lightly greased cookie sheet 2 inches apart. Bake in a preheated 350° oven for 30 minutes until golden. Remove from oven. Cut while warm into diagonal slices about 1 inch thick. Yields about 36 pieces.

Variation

To toast mandelbrot, turn slices on their sides and sprinkle with a mixture of 3 tablespoons of sugar and ¹/₂ teaspoon of cinnamon. Lower heat to 300° and return to oven for an additional 15 minutes until lightly toasted.

Mandelbrot 2

1 medium orange, ground in food
  processor
2 eggs
1 cup sugar
¹/₂ cup oil
2 teaspoons baking powder
3¹/₂-4 cups flour
1 cup chopped almonds
1 teaspoon vanilla extract

Mix together all ingredients. Form into rolls and bake as directed.

Pecan Bars Supreme

Everybody's favorite.

Bottom Layer
$^1/_3$ cup margarine, room temperature
$^1/_3$ cup sugar
1 egg yolk
$1^1/_2$ cups all-purpose flour, sifted
$^1/_2$ teaspoon baking soda
$^1/_8$ teaspoon salt
1 teaspoon vanilla extract
2 tablespoons water

Top Layer
3 eggs
$1^1/_2$ cups brown sugar
3 tablespoons flour, sifted
$^1/_8$ teaspoon salt
1 cup pecans, coarsely chopped
1 teaspoon vanilla extract
$^2/_3$ cup shredded coconut, optional

Make bottom layer first: Cream together margarine, sugar, and egg yolk. Stir in remaining ingredients. Pat down evenly in a greased, 9x13-inch pan and bake in a preheated 350° oven for 15 minutes. Meanwhile prepare top layer: Beat eggs until light, and stir in remaining ingredients. Spread over prebaked crust and return to oven for an additional 25 minutes. Let cool. Cut into squares. Yields about 28-35 squares.

Homemade Marzipan

A sumptuous confection popular in the Middle East and central Europe. Tint them in different colors and shape them to simulate fruits. Use marzipan to stuff dried fruit or to cover whole nuts. Double or triple the recipe for a larger quantity. Can be refrigerated or frozen after shaping.

$1^1/_2$ cups finely ground blanched almonds
1 cup powdered sugar
1 egg white
1 teaspoon almond extract
pinch of salt
red, yellow, and green food coloring
4 ounces semi-sweet chocolate, melted, for dipping, optional
2 tablespoons margarine, melted, for dipping, optional

Mix together first 5 ingredients, in a food processor with a blade, for 1-2 minutes. Alternatively, combine and knead with wet hands for 2 minutes. Divide into desired number of parts to make tiny simulated fruits. Add a few drops of food coloring to each part—red for apple and cherry, yellow for banana, green for pear. With your hands, shape into simulated fruits and serve in fluted paper cups. Or leave uncolored and dip into mixture of melted chocolate and margarine. Yields 20 pieces (about $1^1/_2$ cups of marzipan).

Variation

Use small pieces of marzipan to stuff pitted prunes, dates, apricots, and figs. Dip into melted chocolate-margarine mixture.

Venetian Marzipan Stripes

This rich and elegant marzipan cake has three colors. Great for a party.

Cake

1¹/₈ pounds margarine, room
    temperature
1¹/₂ cups sugar
6 eggs
1¹/₂ cups marzipan paste
1¹/₂ teaspoons almond extract
¹/₄ teaspoon salt
3 cups flour, sifted
red and green food coloring

Filling

¹/₃ cup apricot jam
2 tablespoons water

Icing

9-12 ounces semi-sweet chocolate
¹/₃ cup margarine
3 tablespoons liqueur or wine

Cream together margarine, sugar, and eggs. Beat in marzipan paste, almond extract, and salt. Stir in flour. Line three 10x17-inch cookie sheets with aluminum foil or parchment baking paper and grease well. Divide batter into 3 equal parts. With food coloring, color 1 part red and 1 part green. Leave the third part uncolored. Spread each part thinly and evenly in a separate pan. Bake in a preheated 350° oven for 10-15 minutes. Do not over-bake. Tops should be just dry. Allow to cool. Turn over carefully onto a large platter and remove foil or baking paper. Make filling: Heat jam with water, stirring until smooth. Spread ¹/₃ of filling mixture onto each layer and stack them with uncolored layer in the middle. Make icing: Melt chocolate and margarine over low heat. Stir in liqueur or wine. Cool slightly and spread over cake while icing is still warm. Make a wavy pattern with a fork. Cut into squares. Yields about 60 1¹/₂-inch squares or 90 1-inch squares.

Pastry Swans Filled with Cream

A gala decorative dessert. Simple to make and adds a professional touch to a special dinner. To serve as an appetizer, fill the pastry with chopped liver or fish salad. Can also be prepared on Pesach, substituting matzo meal for flour.

$^1/_2$ **cup margarine**
1 cup water
$^1/_4$ **teaspoon salt**
1 cup flour, sifted
4 large eggs
strawberries, for garnish
powdered sugar, for sprinkling

Place margarine, water, and salt in a saucepan and bring to a boil. Lower heat and add flour all at once, stirring vigorously until mixture leaves sides of pan and is thick. Remove from heat and add eggs one at a time, beating vigorously after each addition. Set aside a small amount of dough to make necks. To make swans: Mound dough into slightly oval-shaped 3-inch cream puff shells. Place on a greased cookie sheet, 2 inches apart. Bake in a 400° oven for 10 minutes. Reduce heat to 350° and bake for an additional 25 minutes. To make necks: By hand or from a pastry bag, place S-shaped pieces of dough on a greased cookie sheet. Bake in a preheated 400° oven for 10 minutes. To make a quick filling: Combine 1 package of chocolate, vanilla, or lemon instant pudding mix with 1 cup of milk until smooth. Fold in whipped cream. To assemble: Cut off top quarter of cream puff shells. Fill with cream filling and top with strawberries. To make wings: Slice cut-off portions into halves and insert into filling on sides at an angle. Insert neck piece in front. Place on plates with doilies and sprinkle with powdered sugar. Yields 8 "swans."

Variation

Fill with ice cream and freeze.

Whole Wheat Cookies

A wholesome and delicious cookie.

1 cup margarine, room temperature
1¹/₂ cups brown sugar
1 whole egg
2 egg yolks
2 tablespoons wheat germ
2 teaspoons vanilla extract
2 cups whole wheat flour, sifted
1¹/₂ cups all-purpose flour, sifted
3 teaspoons baking powder
¹/₂ teaspoon salt
¹/₄ cup lemon juice
grated rind of 1 lemon
¹/₂ cup brown sugar, for sprinkling
1 teaspoon cinnamon, for sprinkling

Cream together margarine and sugar until light. Beat in eggs and add all ingredients except sugar and cinnamon. In a separate bowl, combine sugar and cinnamon for sprinkling. Pinch off walnut-size pieces of dough and roll in sugar-cinnamon mixture. Place 2 inches apart on a greased cookie sheet, flattening slightly. Sprinkle with sugar-cinnamon mixture. Bake in a preheated 350° oven for 20-30 minutes until light brown. Yields about 35 cookies.

Variations

Use all white flour for a richer cookie. Roll out dough ¹/₄ inch thick and cut with a cookie cutter or a glass dipped in flour. Omit wheat germ.

Add ²/₃ cup of coarsely chopped nuts to batter.

Sesame Coconut Cookies

This recipe was given to me by a lovely Yemenite woman when I first came to Israel.

1 cup margarine, softened
1 cup sugar
2 eggs
¹/₄ cup orange juice
4 cups flour, sifted
3 teaspoons baking powder
1¹/₂ cups flaked coconut
1 cup sesame seeds

Cream together margarine and sugar. Beat in eggs. Stir in remaining ingredients. Chill for at least 1 hour. Form into small balls and flatten slightly with tines of a fork. Place on a greased cookie sheet and bake in a preheated 350° oven for 12-15 minutes until lightly browned. Yields 60 cookies.

Variation

Spritz cookies: In a food processor, finely chop coconut before adding to mixture.

Creme de Menthe Bars

A most unusual and delicious treat.

Crust
¹/₂ cup margarine
1 ounce baking chocolate, grated
1 cup flour
¹/₂ cup powdered sugar

Combine all ingredients and pat into a 7x11-inch pan. Bake in a 350° oven for 15 minutes.

Filling
1 can sweetened condensed milk
1¹/₂ cups shredded coconut
¹/₂ cup chopped pecans
2 tablespoons creme de menthe liqueur
few drops of green food coloring

Mix all ingredients and pour over prebaked crust. Bake for an additional 25 minutes until set.

Topping
6 ounces chocolate chips
1 tablespoon margarine
2 tablespoons water
³/₄ teaspoon mint extract

Melt chocolate chips and margarine. Remove from heat. Stir in water and mint extract. Spread on bars.

Sufganiyot

A light, delicious jelly donut, eaten in Israel at Chanukah time.

1¹/₂ ounces fresh compressed yeast
1¹/₂ cups lukewarm water
1 teaspoon sugar
4 cups flour
2 tablespoons cognac
4 tablespoons vegetable oil
5 tablespoons sugar
grated rind of ¹/₂ lemon
2 egg yolks
oil, for frying
¹/₂ cup jelly
powdered sugar, for sprinkling

Dissolve yeast in ¹/₂ cup of lukewarm water and 1 teaspoon sugar. Set aside for about 5-7 minutes. Sift flour into bowl. Add remaining water, cognac, oil, sugar, lemon rind, egg yolks, and yeast mixture. Mix at low speed for 2 minutes, then at medium speed for 5-7 minutes. Cover bowl with dishcloth and put in a warm place to rise for 1¹/₂ hours until double in bulk. Punch down. Divide dough into 3 parts. Roll each into a rectangle ¹/₂ inch thick. Cut into 3-inch circles. Cover and let rise for 1 hour. Drop gently into 2 or 3 inches of hot oil. Fry for 3 minutes until golden brown, turning once. Remove and drain on paper towel. When cool, cut a small slit and fill with 1 teaspoon of jelly. Close tightly. Sprinkle with powdered sugar or roll in granulated sugar. Yields 24 donuts.

Pies & Cheesecakes

Pies & Cheesecakes

Make your own! Form each part of dough for top and bottom pie crust into a round ball. Using a rolling pin, roll out either between two pieces of wax paper or on a slightly floured surface. Roll 1 inch larger than bottom of pie pan. Do not stretch dough, as it might shrink while baking. Fill with desired filling. When using top crust, seal edges by pressing with tines of a fork against rim of pie pan, or flute edges with fingers. Prick crust in several places to keep from rising, or sprinkle with 2-3 tablespoons of dry bread crumbs. To prevent sogginess, brush with a slightly beaten egg white before baking. For a flakier crust, refrigerate dough for 2 hours before rolling out. Most pie crusts should be baked at high temperature. Crusts made with cookie crumbs or graham cracker crumbs should be refrigerated, or prebaked for 8-10 minutes, before filling.

Double Crust Flaky Pie Crust

A delicious, flaky crust that lends itself to many variations.

$2/3$ cup margarine, cold
2 cups all-purpose flour, sifted
$1/2$ teaspoon salt
4-5 tablespoons ice water
(approximately)

With a pastry blender or 2 table knives, cut margarine into flour and salt until pieces are the size of peas. Stir in water, using a fork, a little at a time. Form into 2 balls. Refrigerate for at least 2 hours. Roll out and bake in a 425° oven for 12 minutes. Yields 2 9-inch pie crusts.

Variations

Cream cheese pie crust: Add 4 ounces of cream cheese or $3/4$ cup of sieved cottage cheese.

Whole wheat pie crust: Substitute whole wheat flour for all-purpose flour. Add 1 tablespoon of water.

Sesame or caraway pie crust: Add 3 tablespoons of toasted sesame or caraway seeds.

Nut pie crust: Add $1/2$ cup of finely chopped nuts.

Sharp cheese pie crust: Add $1/2$ - $1/3$ cup of grated cheddar or Muenster cheese.

Vegetable oil pie crust: Substitute $1/2$ cup of vegetable oil for margarine.

Chocolate pie crust: Add $1^1/2$ tablespoons of cocoa, $1^1/2$ tablespoons of sugar, and $1/2$ teaspoon of vanilla extract.

6 Pie Crust Shells in One

An excellent, flaky pie crust recipe for 6 pie crusts. Can be frozen.

5 cups flour
2 tablespoons sugar
1 teaspoon salt, scant
2 cups margarine
$^1/_2$ cup cold water
1 large egg
1 tablespoon vinegar

In a bowl, combine flour, sugar, salt, and margarine, cutting flour into margarine until pieces are the size of peas. In another small bowl, combine water, egg, and vinegar. Combine both mixtures. Do not over-mix. Divide dough into 6 balls. Refrigerate or freeze. Roll out to fit $^1/_2$ inch over rim of pie pan. Press against outside edge of rim so crust will not shrink, and clip edges. Bake in a 425° oven for about 15 minutes. Yields 6 pie crusts.

Famous Pie Crust

Can be made by hand, in a mixer, or in a food processor.

1 cup margarine, cut into pieces
3 cups flour, sifted
1 teaspoon salt
1 egg, beaten
2 tablespoons lemon juice
$^1/_4$ - $^1/_3$ cup ice water

By hand: Cut margarine into flour and salt, with a pastry blender or 2 knives, until pieces are the size of peas. Mix together egg, lemon juice, and ice water. Add to flour mixture until well combined.

In food processor: Place margarine, flour, and salt into container. Process with on-off bursts until crumbly. Through feed tube, pour egg, lemon juice, and ice water, processing until dough leaves sides of container.

After mixing ingredients—for all methods—let dough rest for 10-15 minutes. Divide in half and roll each part into a circle to fit a 10-inch pie pan. Fill and bake as directed in individual pie recipes. Yields enough for 1 double-crust, 10-inch pie or 11-inch flan, or 2 single-crust pies.

Coconut Pie Crust

Fill it with ice cream and freeze. If desired, top with whipped cream.

1 cup flaked coconut
3 tablespoons margarine
2 tablespoons sugar
$^{1}/_{4}$ cup graham cracker or cookie
   crumbs

Combine all ingredients well and press into bottom and sides of a 9-inch pie pan. Bake in a 375° oven for 10-12 minutes.

To avoid soggy pie crusts, brush crust with egg white or sprinkle with bread crumbs, and prick all over with fork.

Meurbe Teig Pastry Dough

A delicious Viennese pastry.

$^{3}/_{4}$ cup margarine or butter
$^{1}/_{2}$ cup sugar
2 egg yolks
2 cups flour, sifted
grated rind of 1 lemon
1 teaspoon vanilla extract
2-3 tablespoons lemon juice

Cream together margarine or butter with sugar. Stir in remaining ingredients. Divide into 2 balls. Chill. Roll out into two 9-inch crusts. Bake in a 350° oven for 15 minutes.

Cookie Pastry Dough

Use it for strudel or hamantaschen.

2 eggs
³/₄ cup sugar
¹/₂ cup vegetable oil
¹/₂ teaspoon salt
1 teaspoon vanilla extract
¹/₄ cup lemon juice
3¹/₂ cups flour
2 teaspoons baking powder

Beat eggs until light. Beat in sugar. Stir in remaining ingredients. Roll out into a rectangle. Fill with desired filling and bake in a 350° oven for 35-40 minutes.

Rice Shell

A novel and scrumptious pie crust.

Press 1¹/₂ cups of cooked brown or white rice into a lightly greased, 9-inch pie pan. Bake in a preheated 375° oven for 5 minutes.

Graham Cracker Crumb or Cookie Crumb Crust

Don't forget to either refrigerate or prebake this crust.

1¹/₂ cups graham cracker or cookie crumbs (chocolate, vanilla, or ginger-flavored)
3 tablespoons brown or white sugar
¹/₃ cup margarine, softened (6 tablespoons)
¹/₂ teaspoon cinnamon

Mix together all ingredients until thoroughly combined. Reserve 3 tablespoons of mixture for top of pie, if desired. Press into a 9-inch pie pan. Before adding filling, refrigerate to set or bake in a 325° oven for 8-10 minutes to prevent crust from becoming soggy.

Variation

Chocolate, vanilla, or ginger flavored wafer crumb crust: Combine 1¹/₃ cups of wafer crumbs with ¹/₄ cup of melted margarine or butter. Prepare as directed above.

My Favorite Apple Pie

This recipe never fails in getting raves.

1 9-inch pie crust, prebaked

Filling
6 large tart apples, peeled and thinly sliced
¹/₂ cup brown sugar
¹/₄ cup bread crumbs
1 teaspoon cinnamon
pinch of nutmeg
¹/₃ cup raisins
3 tablespoons jam
2 tablespoons margarine, melted

Combine all ingredients for filling. Spread over pie crust. Cover with top crust, sealing and fluting edges. Prick with a fork in several places. Bake in a preheated 400° oven for 10 minutes. Lower heat to 350° and bake for an additional 35-40 minutes.

If juice from fruit pies overflows while baking, sprinkle salt into it. The juice will then burn to a crisp, rendering it easily removable.

Yummy Pecan Pie

The classic pecan pie that everyone loves. Can also be made with chocolate chips.

1 unbaked, 9-inch pie crust

Filling
3 eggs
²/₃ cup brown sugar
1 cup corn syrup
3 tablespoons margarine, melted
¹/₄ teaspoon salt
1 teaspoon vanilla extract
1 cup pecan halves

Beat together eggs, brown sugar, corn syrup, and margarine. Stir in salt, vanilla extract, and ²/₃ cup of pecans. Pour into pie crust. Top with remaining pecans. Bake in a 375° oven for 45 minutes until set. Cool before serving. Can be frozen. Serves 8.

Variation

Chocolate chip pecan pie: Fold in 6 ounces of chocolate chips before baking.

Glazed Strawberry Pie

Glazed fresh strawberries in a baked pie crust. Easy to prepare and no baking necessary. An eye-catching dessert.

1 9-inch pie crust, prebaked

Filling
4-5 cups fresh strawberries
1 cup water
1 cup granulated sugar
2 tablespoons cornstarch

To make glaze, crush 2 cups of strawberries. Cook in a saucepan with water and sugar for about 1 minute. Dissolve cornstarch in a few tablespoons of cold water and stir into crushed strawberry mixture while cooking. Stir constantly for about 2 minutes until thickened. Remove from heat and let cool slightly. Place remaining whole strawberries in a prebaked pie crust. Pour cooled glaze on top. Chill.

Frozen Chocolate Mousse Pie

A cake-like crust and a creamy chocolate top all in one mixture—no need for a separate crust. Easy to prepare. Recipe can be doubled or tripled. Pies can be frozen.

6 ounces semi-sweet chocolate
³/₄ cup margarine
6 eggs, separated
¹/₂ cup sugar
¹/₄ cup brandy or rum
5 tablespoons flour, sifted
¹/₂ teaspoon baking powder

Melt chocolate and margarine over low heat. Let cool. Beat egg whites until frothy, gradually adding sugar. Beat until able to hold stiff peaks. Set aside. In another mixing bowl, using same unwashed beater, beat yolks until light and fluffy, adding brandy or rum. Stir in cooled, melted chocolate-margarine mixture. Fold this mixture into beaten egg whites. Remove ¹/₃ of mixture and fold flour and baking powder into it. Pour this into a greased, 10-inch pie pan. Bake in a preheated 350° oven for 15-18 minutes until still soft to the touch, but not dry. Let cool and spread with reserved ²/₃ of mixture. Freeze.

Mocha Whipped Cream Pie

A no-bake recipe. Just prepare the cookie crumb crust and refrigerate for 2 hours before filling.

1 9-inch Chocolate Cookie Crumb Crust (see page 261)

Mocha Filling
1 6-ounce package chocolate chips
2 tablespoons hot water
4 tablespoons sugar, or to taste
3 large eggs, separated
1¹/₂ cups heavy cream, for whipping
3 teaspoons instant coffee
1 tablespoon cherry or rum liqueur
chocolate curls, for garnish, optional

In a saucepan over low heat, melt chocolate chips with water and 2 tablespoons of the sugar. Remove from heat. Meanwhile beat egg yolks and stir into slightly cooled chocolate mixture. Beat egg whites until soft peaks form. Set aside. Whip cream and fold in 2 tablespoons of sugar (or more, to taste) and coffee powder. Remove ²/₃ of whipped cream mixture and fold into cooled chocolate mixture with liqueur. Fold in beaten egg whites. Pour into prepared cookie crumb crust. Spread remaining whipped cream mixture on top. Refrigerate. If desired, decorate with chocolate curls.

A Variety of Cream Pies

Including coconut, butterscotch nut, banana, chocolate, chocolate mint, orange cream, and mocha pie, as well as fruit flan. Serve in individual dessert dishes, with or without whipped cream or meringue topping. Pies can be frozen.

1 8-inch pie crust, prebaked

Filling
1/3 cup flour
1/2 cup sugar
1/4 teaspoon salt
2 cups milk or pareve cream
3 large egg yolks
1 teaspoon vanilla extract
2 tablespoons margarine
1 tablespoon cherry brandy
1 cup whipping cream, whipped, optional

In a saucepan, combine flour, sugar, and salt. Stir in milk gradually until flour is completely dissolved. Cook over low heat or in a double boiler for about 12-15 minutes, stirring until smooth and thickened. Beat egg yolks, using a fork, and stir in 3 tablespoons of hot mixture, then add entire yolk mixture to saucepan. Cook for 2 more minutes. Remove from heat and add vanilla extract, margarine, and brandy. If desired, fold in whipped cream. Pour into prebaked pie crust. If desired, add Meringue Topping.

Meringue Topping
3 large egg whites
1 teaspoon cream of tartar
6 tablespoons sugar

Beat egg whites and cream of tartar until stiff, gradually adding sugar. Brown lightly in a 375° oven for about 10 minutes. Spread on filled pie, covering the edges.

Variations

Substitute water for milk. Fold whipped cream into mixture when somewhat cooled.

Coconut cream pie: Fold in 1/2 -2/3 cup of shredded coconut to mixture before pouring into pie crust. Top with whipped cream or meringue.

Butterscotch nut cream pie: Substitute 2/3 cup of packed brown sugar for white sugar. Fold in whipped cream, if desired. Stir in, or sprinkle on top, 1/2 cup of slivered almonds. Top with meringue, if desired.

Banana cream pie: Place alternate layers of 3 sliced bananas and cooled mixture. Top with whipped cream or meringue.

Chocolate cream pie: Stir into hot custard mixture 3 ounces of chocolate pieces.

Chocolate mint cream pie: Add 1/2 teaspoon of peppermint extract to previous variation. Fold in whipped cream, if desired.

Orange cream pie: Substitute 2 cups of orange juice and 2 teaspoons of grated orange rind for milk.

Mocha cream pie: Add 1 teaspoon of instant coffee to hot mixture. Add another teaspoon of instant coffee to whipped cream.

Fruit flan: Pour a ½-inch-thick layer of cream filling into a prebaked, 11-inch flan shell. Cover with sliced fresh or canned fruits—peaches, apricots, bananas, strawberries, seedless grapes, etc. Brush with glaze: heat ¼ cup of red jelly in a saucepan over low heat. Prepare flan 2-3 hours before serving.

To make chocolate curls, hold a bar of chocolate, at room temperature, in the palm of your hand and peel thin layers of chocolate using a wide potato peeler.

Strawberry Custard Pie

Creamy and refreshing.

1 9-inch pie crust

Filling
1 package instant vanilla pudding
2 cups fresh strawberries, halved or quartered

Glaze
see Glazed Strawberry Pie (page 262)

Fill bottom half of pie crust with pudding, prepared according to directions on package. Chill. Fill top half with strawberries. Pour cooled glaze on top. Chill.

Classic Lemon Meringue Pie

An all-time favorite. There won't be a crumb left.

1 9-inch pie crust, prebaked

Filling
2 cups cold water
1 cup sugar
$^1/_4$ cup cornstarch
3 egg yolks
$^1/_8$ teaspoon salt
1 tablespoon margarine
$^1/_2$ cup lemon juice
1 tablespoon grated lemon rind

Bring water and sugar to a boil in a medium saucepan over medium-low heat. Dissolve cornstarch in a little cold water and stir into simmering mixture. Lower heat and stir constantly until thickened. In a separate small bowl, beat egg yolks and stir in 3 tablespoons of hot mixture. Add yolk mixture to saucepan and cook for 5 minutes. Pour from heat and stir in salt, margarine, lemon juice and rind. Pour into a prebaked crust. Add Meringue Topping.

Meringue Topping
3 egg whites
2 teaspoons lemon juice
4 tablespoons sugar
$^1/_2$ teaspoon vanilla extract

Beat egg whites and lemon juice until stiff, gradually adding sugar. Fold in vanilla extract. Spread meringue over filling, covering edges well. Bake pie in a preheated 350° oven for 15 minutes or until meringue is lightly browned.

Variation

Frozen lemon pie: Fold meringue and/or 1 cup of whipped cream or whipped topping into cooled filling. Pour into a prebaked pie crust and freeze until firm.

Swiss Chocolate Cheesecake with Chocolate Leaves

This is for anyone who loves rich chocolate. The chocolate leaves look real, and no wonder!

Crust
1¼ cups graham cracker or chocolate cookie crumbs
⅓ cup margarine, melted
2½ teaspoons sugar (if using graham cracker crumbs)
½ cup shredded coconut
1 teaspoon almond extract

Mix all ingredients and press evenly on bottom and sides of a greased, 9-inch pie pan or springform pan. Chill for 1 hour.

Filling
1 pound cream cheese
2 eggs
⅔ cup sugar
8 ounces semi-sweet chocolate, melted
2 tablespoons cornstarch
1 teaspoon vanilla extract
⅓ cup chopped pecans, optional
¾ cup whipped cream, optional

In an electric mixer on low speed, beat cream cheese together with eggs, sugar, chocolate, cornstarch, and vanilla extract until smooth. Stir in pecans. Pour into crust and bake in a preheated 350° oven for 1 hour, 10 minutes. Allow to cool and spoon whipped cream around edge of cake. Decorate center with Chocolate Leaves.

Chocolate Leaves
3 ounces semi-sweet chocolate
2 teaspoons margarine
6 medium-sized lemon leaves, or any other firm, non-toxic leaves
glacé cherries for garnish

Over low heat, melt chocolate and margarine. Let cool slightly. With a knife, spread chocolate mixture over bottom of well-washed lemon leaves. Place, chocolate side up, on a platter and refrigerate for about 20 minutes until chocolate is firm. Peel lemon leaves carefully from chocolate. Return leaf-shaped pieces of chocolate to refrigerator until ready to serve cake, then place them in center of cake with edges slightly overlapping. Decorate cake with glacé cherries, placing 1 more in center of cluster of "leaves." Serves 8-10.

Marbleized Cheesecake

Marbleized with chocolate and cream cheese mixture.

Crust
1½ cups chocolate cookie crumbs
4 tablespoons margarine, melted
2 tablespoons ground pecans, optional
2 tablespoons sugar

Mix together all ingredients for crust. Press into bottom and halfway up sides of a 9-inch spring-form pan. Bake in a 325° oven for 10 minutes.

Filling
4-6 ounces semi-sweet chocolate chips
1 pound cream cheese, softened
1 cup sugar
½ cup sour cream
1 teaspoon rum extract
4 eggs
2 tablespoons cornstarch
½ cup chopped pecans, optional

In a double boiler or in a pan set over boiling water, melt chocolate chips. In a mixing bowl, beat cream cheese together with sugar, sour cream, and rum extract. Beat in eggs one at a time. Add cornstarch. Pour half of mixture into crust. Blend chocolate into remaining filling. Spoon evenly over filling in crust. With a table knife, zigzag through filling to give a marbleized effect (but don't mix!). If desired, sprinkle with pecans. Bake in a preheated 350° oven for 50 minutes. If desired, add Topping. Let cool, and refrigerate.

Topping
1½ cups sour cream
2 tablespoons sugar
1 teaspoon vanilla extract
chocolate shavings, for garnish

Mix first 3 ingredients together, spread on baked cheesecake, and return to oven for 5 minutes. Remove from oven and garnish with shaved chocolate pieces.

Variation

For a chocolate-colored top and a white-colored bottom, prepare as above, but without the zigzagging.

No-Crust Angel Cheese Torte

A light, luscious dessert.

6 eggs, separated
1 cup sugar
1¹/₂ pounds cream cheese
1 cup sour cream
2 teaspoons vanilla extract
grated rind of 1 lemon
¹/₂ cup flour, sifted
powdered sugar, for sprinkling, optional

Beat egg whites until frothy, gradually adding sugar. Beat until stiff peaks form. Set aside. In another bowl, beat egg yolks until light and fluffy, then beat in cream cheese, sour cream, and vanilla extract. Stir in lemon rind and flour. Fold beaten whites into yolk mixture carefully but thoroughly. Pour into a greased, 10-inch tube pan or a 9-inch spring-form pan. Bake in a preheated 350° oven for 1 hour. Turn off oven and let cake remain inside for an additional 15 minutes. If desired, sprinkle with powdered sugar, spread with Lemon Glaze, or cover with a topping. Chill before serving.

Lemon Glaze
1 cup powdered sugar
2-3 tablespoons lemon juice
2 tablespoons margarine

Mix all ingredients until creamy. Drizzle over cheese torte.

Luscious Chiffon Cheesecake

This luscious cheesecake combines chiffon cake and a creamy cheese filling—baked in one mixture.

6 eggs, separated
1 cup sugar
¹/₄ teaspoon salt
2 teaspoons vanilla extract
³/₄ cup cake flour
2 teaspoons baking powder
1 pound cream cheese

Beat egg whites until frothy. Gradually add ³/₄ cup of the sugar and beat until stiff. In another bowl, beat 3 of the egg yolks, salt, and 1 teaspoon of the vanilla extract until light. Fold yolk mixture into flour and baking powder, then fold in beaten egg white mixture. Pour half of the batter into center of a greased, 9-inch springform pan. In another bowl, combine cream cheese with remaining egg yolks, ¹/₄ cup sugar, and vanilla extract until creamy. Fold in remaining batter and pour into center of chiffon batter already in pan. Bake in a 350° oven for 45 minutes.

Old-Fashioned Cheesecake with Glazed Strawberry Topping

Made with cottage cheese. Delicious with or without the glazed strawberry topping. With a variation for a low-calorie cheesecake.

1 9-inch unbaked pie crust

Filling
4 large eggs, separated
1 cup sugar
1¹/₂ pounds cottage cheese
1 cup sour cream or milk
4 tablespoons cornstarch
3 tablespoons melted margarine
¹/₄ teaspoon salt
1 teaspoon vanilla extract
grated rind and juice of 1 lemon

Beat egg whites with half of the sugar until stiff. In another bowl, using an electric mixer, cream the cottage cheese. Stir in egg yolks and remaining ingredients, folding in beaten egg whites last. Pour into unbaked pie crust. Bake in a 350° oven for 1 hour.

Glazed Strawberry Topping
¹/₃ cup sugar
2 tablespoons cornstarch
¹/₃ cup water
1 cup crushed strawberries
1 drop red food coloring

In a saucepan, combine sugar, cornstarch, water and crushed strawberries. Cook while stirring continuously until thickened. Cook for 1 more minute. Add a drop of red food coloring. Let cool and spread on cooled cheesecake.

Variation

Low-calorie cheesecake: Before folding in beaten egg whites, stir in 15 sugar substitute tablets dissolved in 2 tablespoons of hot water. Reduce sugar to ¹/₄ cup and add 1 shredded apple. Omit margarine.

Creamy Vanilla Cheesecake

A rich cheesecake.

Crust
1¼ cups flour, sifted
1½ teaspoons baking powder
½ cup margarine, room temperature
¼ cup milk
¼ cup sugar
1 egg yolk

Make crust first by mixing all its ingredients together. Dough will be sticky. With wet hands, spread on a greased, 9x13-inch baking sheet.

Filling
1 pound cream cheese
½ cup milk
½ cup sugar
½ teaspoon vanilla extract
1 tablespoon flour
1 egg yolk

Mix all ingredients together until smooth. Pour onto crust and bake in a preheated 375° oven for 10 minutes. Lower heat to 350° and bake for another 40 minutes until crust is golden. Remove from oven and spread with Vanilla Meringue Topping.

Vanilla Meringue Topping
2 egg whites
¼ cup sugar
2 tablespoons instant vanilla pudding mix

Beat egg whites, gradually adding sugar until they are frothy and hold soft peaks. Fold in pudding mix. Return to oven and bake for an additional 7 minutes until top is golden. Yields 28 1½-inch squares.

Royal Cheesecake

This cheesecake is delicious even without the topping of cherry pie filling.

Crust
½ cup margarine
1¼ cups flour, sifted
1¼ teaspoons baking powder
¼ cup sugar
⅓ cup plain yogurt or sour cream
1 egg yolk
pinch of salt

Using a pastry blender or 2 knives, cut cold margarine into flour, baking powder, and sugar until pieces are the size of peas. Stir in yogurt or sour cream, egg yolk, and salt. Form into a ball and refrigerate for at least 1 hour. Roll out into a circle to cover bottom and halfway up sides of a well-greased, 9-inch springform pan.

Filling
4 eggs, separated
¾ cup sugar
1½ pounds cream cheese, room temperature
⅔ cup sour cream
1 teaspoon vanilla extract
2 tablespoons instant vanilla pudding mix
1 can cherry pie filling, for top

Beat egg yolks until light, adding half of the sugar. Stir in remaining ingredients except egg whites, remaining sugar, and cherry pie filling. Beat egg whites, gradually adding remaining sugar. Beat until able to form stiff peaks. Fold egg white mixture into cheese mixture. Pour into crust. Bake in a preheated 350° oven for 45 minutes. When cool, spread with a can of cherry pie filling. Refrigerate.

Pesach

Pesach

Three Kinds of Charoset

Charoset is one of the important components of the seder plate—a sweet mixture symbolizing the mortar used by the Israelites to make bricks during their slavery in Egypt. Here is the traditional recipe we use in our home—along with two interesting Middle Eastern varieties.

Traditional Charoset
2 large apples, peeled, cored, and cut up
¹/₂ cup walnuts
1 teaspoon cinnamon
¹/₄ cup sweet red wine
2 teaspoons honey or sugar

Combine all ingredients. Chop finely by hand or in a food processor, with on-off bursts. Refrigerate in a covered container until ready to use. Yields about 1¹/₂ cups.

Orange Charoset
1 orange, peeled
1 cup pitted dates
1 banana
¹/₂ cup almonds
1 tablespoon honey or sugar
¹/₂ teaspoon cinnamon
¹/₃ cup wine

Chop the orange, dates, banana, and almonds finely, by hand or in a food processor. Stir in remaining ingredients, and refrigerate in a covered container until ready to use. Yields about 1¹/₂ cups.

Middle Eastern Charoset
¹/₂ pound pitted dates, chopped
2 tablespoons honey
¹/₂ cup water
²/₃ cup chopped nuts
4 tablespoons wine
1 teaspoon cinnamon

Cook dates with honey in water for about 10-15 minutes, stirring frequently until smooth. Stir and combine with rest of ingredients. Yields 1 cup.

Lasagna

Lasagna will be a welcome change during chol hamoed Pesach. It can be made without the eggplant, using other fresh vegetables instead. In this delicious lasagna recipe, Pesach blintz leaves are used in place of lasagna noodles.

1 large onion, diced
2 cloves garlic
1 green pepper, diced
4 tablespoons oil
1 medium eggplant, cut into 1-inch
    cubes
$^1/_2$ pound mushrooms, sliced, optional
3 large tomatoes, cubed
1 10-ounce can tomato-mushroom
    sauce
1 teaspoon salt
$^1/_3$ teaspoon pepper
6 Pesach blintz leaves (see page 286)
$^3/_4$ pound cottage cheese, optional
1 8-ounce package sliced Muenster,
    Swiss, or sharp cheddar cheese

In a skillet, sauté onions, garlic, and green pepper in oil until tender. Add eggplant and stir-fry for about 7 minutes. Add mushrooms, tomatoes, tomato-mushroom sauce, and seasonings. Cover and cook over low heat for about 15 minutes, until eggplant is tender. Add a little water if too thick. In a greased, 7x11-inch baking dish, alternate layers of blintz leaves, sauce, cottage cheese, and cheese slices, ending with sauce and cheese slices. Bake in a preheated 350° oven for 35 minutes. Serves 8.

Variation

Omit eggplant and substitute about 2 cups of cooked spinach, broccoli, or mixed vegetables. Steam vegetables first in a small amount of water for about 5-7 minutes. Drain and combine with cottage cheese, and place between layers—instead of including in sauce.

Vegetable Loaf with Vegetable Gravy

A nutritious, light main course for chol hamoed Pesach. Serve it with or without the vegetable gravy. The gravy also makes a splendid accompaniment to veal or chicken.

1 large onion, diced
4 tablespoons oil
8 stalks celery, diced (about 4 cups)
2 medium carrots, shredded
1 medium green pepper, diced
1 can string beans, drained and
    chopped
$^2/_3$ cup sliced mushrooms
2 teaspoons salt
$^1/_2$ teaspoon pepper
$^1/_2$ cup matzo meal
2 eggs, beaten

Sauté onion in oil until transparent. Add celery, carrots, and green peppers. Sauté until tender-crisp. Remove from heat and combine with remaining ingredients. Pour into a well-greased loaf pan. Bake in a preheated 350° oven for 1 hour. Slice and serve hot with Vegetable Gravy. Serves 6.

Vegetable Gravy

1 large onion, diced
2 tablespoons oil
3 tablespoons potato starch
2 teaspoons pareve vegetable soup mix
2 cups boiling water
1 medium carrot, diced
1 stalk celery, diced
$^1/_4$ pound fresh peas

Sauté onion in oil until transparent. Stir in potato starch until smooth. Dissolve soup mix in water and stir. Simmer and stir over low heat until smooth and thickened. Add carrots and celery and cook over low heat for 20 minutes, adding peas during last 5 minutes of cooking.

Feather-Light Matzo Balls

Matzo balls should be light and fluffy. Boil them in a very large pot of slightly salted boiling water, and watch them swell and grow. Then reheat them in soup. Enjoy them for Pesach—or any time of the year.

Matzo Balls 1

5 eggs
1 cup matzo meal
1 teaspoon salt
$^1/_8$ teaspoon pepper
$^1/_8$ teaspoon ginger, optional

Beat eggs until light and fluffy, preferably in an electric mixer. Gradually stir in matzo meal and remaining ingredients. Let stand for about 15 minutes. With wet hands, form into balls the size of walnuts, and gently drop into a large pot of lightly boiling water. Cover and simmer over low heat for 20 minutes. Yields about 16 balls.

Matzo Balls 2

3 eggs
4 tablespoons water
$^1/_4$ cup oil
1 teaspoon salt
$^1/_8$ teaspoon pepper
pinch of ginger, optional
$^2/_3$ cup matzo meal
fried onions, optional

Beat eggs until fluffy. Stir in remaining ingredients. Let stand for 15 minutes, until firm. Form into balls, and drop into a large pot of boiling water. Cover and simmer for 20-30 minutes. Yields about 20 balls.

Eggplant Parmesan

Rich and delicious.

2 medium eggplants, cut into 1/2-inch
  slices
salt, for sprinkling
2 eggs, beaten
2/3 cup matzo meal or potato flour
oil, for frying
1 11-ounce can tomato-mushroom
  sauce
1/3 cup water, optional
salt and pepper, to taste
1 8-ounce package sliced American or
  Swiss cheese
1/2 cup grated Parmesan cheese

Sprinkle eggplant with salt. Let
stand for 30 minutes. Rinse
slightly. Dip slices in beaten eggs,
then in matzo meal or potato flour.
Fry on both sides until tender.
Combine sauce with water and
seasonings. In a greased, 2-quart
casserole, place a little sauce, a layer
of fried eggplant slices, and a layer of
sliced cheese. Repeat, ending with
sauce. Sprinkle with Parmesan
cheese. Bake in a preheated 350°
oven for 30 minutes. Serves 8.

Shakshuka

*Shakshuka was made popular in Israel by
the Tunisian olim. This recipe is similar to
letcho, a Hungarian dish, but is made with
tomato paste.*

1 large onion, diced
2 cloves garlic, diced
2 large green peppers, diced
4 tablespoons oil
4 large tomatoes, cubed
salt and pepper, to taste
1 cup water
1 4-ounce can tomato paste
6 eggs

Sauté onion, garlic, and green
peppers in oil until onions are
golden. Stir in remaining ingredients
except eggs. Cover and simmer for
about 20 minutes. Remove cover.
Make indentations. Drop a whole egg
into each indentation. Cover and
cook for 5 minutes until eggs are set.
Serves 6.

Variation

This is also good with fish fillets. In
place of eggs, place 2-inch pieces
of fish fillets (1 pound of perch,
halibut, cod, or hake) into vegetables.
Add a little water, if necessary. Cover
and cook over low heat for 12-15
minutes.

Pesach Stuffings

Made with a variety of vegetables.

1 large onion, diced
1 medium green pepper, diced
2 cloves garlic, diced
¼ cup oil
1 cup matzo meal
1-2 carrots, grated
½ cup sliced mushrooms, optional
1 teaspoon salt
¼ teaspoon pepper
2 stalks celery, diced
2 eggs
1 small zucchini, diced

Sauté onion, green pepper, and garlic in oil for about 5-6 minutes until tender. Remove from heat and stir in remaining ingredients. Let cool and stuff chicken loosely. Alternatively, onion, green pepper, and garlic can be combined without sautéing. Enough for a 5-pound chicken.

Giblet Stuffing

Add 1-2 cups of cooked and cut-up chicken or turkey giblets to mixture.

Chicken Liver Stuffing

Add 4-5 koshered chicken livers—cut into bite-size pieces—to mixture.

Prune and Apple Stuffing

Add 1 cup of pitted and quartered prunes, soaked in boiling water for 20 minutes. Add 1 large, peeled and diced apple, ⅛ teaspoon of cinnamon or nutmeg, ½ cup of raisins, and 3 tablespoons of honey. Omit carrots and mushrooms.

Ground Meat Stuffing

Add ½ pound of ground meat. Reduce matzo meal to ½ cup. Omit carrots.

Mushroom Stuffing

Add 1 cup of mushrooms and sauté with onion, green pepper, and garlic. Omit carrots.

If there is too much stuffing for chicken, wrap extra stuffing in aluminum foil and put in a roasting pan or pour into a well-greased, 9x3-inch loaf pan and bake with chicken. Alternatively, add 2 more eggs and 2-3 tablespoons more oil to remaining stuffing, and bake like a kugel.

Pesach Frittata

This is a baked version of the Italian frittata, an omelet filled with assorted vegetables.

1-1¹/₂ pounds unpeeled zucchini, cut into half slices
1 cup cottage cheese
1¹/₃ cups shredded Swiss or sharp cheddar cheese
1 teaspoon salt
¹/₄ teaspoon pepper
4 eggs, beaten
¹/₃ cup matzo meal
2 tablespoons oil

Cook zucchini in water until tender. Drain and combine with other ingredients, reserving ¹/₃ cup of shredded cheese for top. Pour mixture into a well-greased, 1¹/₂-quart casserole. Sprinkle with reserved cheese. Bake in a preheated 350° oven for 40-50 minutes. Serve with sour cream or yogurt. Serves 6-8.

Variation

Use 1 10-ounce package of frozen chopped spinach, cooked and drained, in place of zucchini; or use 1 large, cubed tomato, ¹/₂ cup of mushrooms, and other cooked vegetables.

Liver Kugelettes

A side dish or an appetizer, with gravy spooned on top. These individual portions are very convenient for buffets as well. Double or triple the recipe to serve a crowd.

2 large onions, diced
2 cloves garlic, minced
¹/₃ cup oil
6 matzos, broken, soaked in warm water, and drained
³/₄ pound chicken or beef liver, koshered and cut into small pieces
¹/₈ teaspoon pepper
1 teaspoon salt, or to taste
4 eggs, beaten

Sauté onion and garlic in ¹/₄ cup of hot oil until tender. Combine with remaining ingredients and pour into greased muffin tins (using remaining oil). Bake in a 350° oven for 45 minutes. Yields 12-15 individual kugelettes.

Variation

In place of liver, use 2 cups of cubed chicken.

Vegetable Soup

A pareve vegetable soup for Pesach.

2 large onions, diced
1 small green pepper, diced
3 tablespoons oil
3 tablespoons matzo meal
9 cups water
2 stalks celery, diced
$^1/_2$ pound mushrooms, sliced
2 medium potatoes, cubed
2 carrots, sliced
2 teaspoons salt
$^1/_4$ teaspoon pepper
1 tablespoon pareve vegetable soup
    powder, or to taste, optional

Sauté onions and green pepper in oil until golden. Stir in matzo meal until dissolved. Slowly stir in 1 cup of the water, and cook for about 2 minutes until thickened. Add remaining ingredients, cover and cook over low heat for about 30 minutes. Serves 8.

Vegetable Matzo Kugel

A tasty Pesach kugel. The variation is particularly good.

3 large onions, diced
$^1/_2$ cup oil
2 stalks celery, diced
2 large carrots, shredded
1 large green pepper, diced
6 matzos
1 teaspoon salt
$^1/_4$ teaspoon pepper
$^1/_2$ teaspoon onion powder
5 eggs, well beaten

Sauté onions in oil until soft. Add celery, carrots, and green pepper. Continue sautéing over low heat for an additional 10 minutes, stirring occasionally. Break matzos and moisten with warm water. Squeeze out excess water and combine matzos with vegetables, seasonings, and eggs, mixing well. Pour into a well-greased, 7x11-inch baking pan. Bake in a preheated 350° oven for 45 minutes. Serves 10-12.

Variation

Onion matzo kugel: Add 1 more onion. Omit carrots.

Apple Kugel

Your family will just love this kugel.

8 matzos, broken into pieces
5 eggs, well beaten
²/₃ cup sugar or jam
¹/₃ cup vegetable oil
1 teaspoon salt
1 teaspoon cinnamon
¹/₈ teaspoon nutmeg
¹/₃ cup walnuts, coarsely chopped
5-6 large tart apples, peeled and thickly
    sliced
juice and grated rind of 1 lemon
1 cup raisins, optional

Topping
¹/₃ cup sugar
¹/₄ -¹/₃ cup chopped walnuts
1 teaspoon cinnamon

Soak matzos in warm water for 2 minutes. Drain immediately and squeeze out water. Combine with remaining ingredients, mixing well, and pour into a well-greased, 9x13-inch baking pan. Combine topping ingredients, and sprinkle evenly over surface. Bake in a preheated 350° oven for 1 hour. Serves 8-10.

Variation

Apricot or prune kugel: Add to mixture 1¹/₂ cups of cut-up dried apricots or pitted prunes, soaked in boiling water for ¹/₂ hour. Reduce number of apples to 4. Bake as directed.

Royal Carrot Kugel

You'll want to make this throughout the year as well as on Pesach, it is that good. The ground, unpeeled orange gives this kugel a special flavor.

3 cups carrots, shredded
3 apples, shredded
²/₃ cup raisins
¹/₂ cup pecans, coarsely chopped
4 large eggs
1 small whole orange, ground with peel
²/₃ cup oil
1 teaspoon vanilla extract
1 cup Pesach cake meal
1 cup sugar
1 teaspoon cinnamon
¹/₂ teaspoon salt
¹/₂ teaspoon ginger

Mix together all ingredients thoroughly and pour into a well-greased, 7x11-inch baking dish. Bake in a 350° oven for 1 hour.

Pesach Rolls or Bagels

Yes, there is such a thing as a Pesach bagel.

1 cup water
1 teaspoon salt
$^{1}/_{2}$ cup oil
$1^{1}/_{2}$ cups matzo meal
4 eggs
pinch of pepper
1 tablespoon sugar

In a saucepan, bring to a boil water, salt, and oil. Lower heat and add matzo meal all at once, stirring well until mixture leaves sides of pan. Remove from heat. Add whole eggs one at a time, stirring vigorously after each addition. Stir in pepper and sugar. With greased hands, roll into 2-inch balls and place 2 inches apart on a greased, 10x17-inch baking sheet. For bagels, flatten balls slightly and make a hole in center. Bake in a preheated 400° oven for approximately 35-40 minutes until golden. Let cool. Yields about 12 rolls or bagels.

Variation

For Pesach soup nuts, pinch off marble-sized pieces of mixture. Place on a greased baking sheet and bake in a preheated 400° oven for 15 minutes.

Chremslach

These dried-fruit pancakes are really good—for breakfast, for a snack, or even for dessert—topped with cinnamon and sugar.

3 large eggs, beaten
$^{1}/_{2}$ cup cut-up dried apricots, prunes, or raisins
3 tablespoons walnuts, coarsely chopped
2 tablespoons sugar
2 tablespoons Sabra liqueur or wine
$^{1}/_{2}$ teaspoon cinnamon
$^{1}/_{3}$ cup matzo meal
oil, for frying

Combine all ingredients except oil. Let stand for 10 minutes. Drop from a tablespoon into hot oil and fry on both sides until golden brown. Sprinkle with a sugar-cinnamon mixture. Serve with jam, thinned with a few tablespoons of water and heated to combine. Yields 8-10 pancakes.

Variation

For fluffier chremslach, separate the eggs, and beat whites stiffly. Beat egg yolks, stir in remaining ingredients, and fold in beaten egg whites.

Pesach Blintzes (Non-Gebruchts)

These blintz leaves can be used to make delicious homemade noodles. Stack about two or three, roll, and slice into noodle strips about $1/4$ inch wide. Let stand for 15 minutes to dry. Simmer in soup for a few minutes.

Blintz Leaves
$1/3$ cup potato starch
1 cup cold water
3 eggs
1 tablespoon oil
a little oil, for brushing pan

Combine all ingredients in a food processor or blender until smooth. Refrigerate for half an hour. Brush a 6- or 8-inch frying pan lightly with oil. Heat pan and pour 3 tablespoons of batter into hot pan, tilting from side to side quickly to make a thin, even coating. Pour off any excess batter. Fry for about half a minute until top is dry. Turn over and fry for 10 more seconds. With a knife, loosen edges and turn out, piling blintz leaves in a stack. Yields 12-14 blintz leaves.

Cheese Filling
1 pound farmer cheese
2 eggs
3 tablespoons sugar
grated rind of $1/2$ lemon
2 tablespoons melted margarine
$1/4$ teaspoon cinnamon
$1/3$ cup raisins, optional

Combine all ingredients and mix well. Spoon about 2 tablespoons of filling onto each blintz leaf. Roll and fry in oil on both sides until golden.

Potato Filling
2-3 cups mashed potatoes
2 eggs, beaten
1 onion, diced and sautéed
salt and pepper, to taste

Combine, fill, and fry on both sides.

Potato-Cheese Filling

Add $1/2$ -$2/3$ cup of grated American or cheddar cheese to previous mixture.

Apple Filling
4 large apples, shredded
$1/3$ cup sugar
$1/2$ teaspoon cinnamon
3 tablespoons chopped nuts
2 egg whites, optional

Combine, fill, and fry on both sides.

Meat or Chicken Filling
1 medium onion
2 cups cooked, ground chicken or meat
1 egg

Sauté onion until transparent. Stir in chicken or meat combined with beaten egg. Sauté for about 5 minutes. Prepare as directed.

Pesach Borekas

This recipe was given to me by a cousin who immigrated to Israel from Shanghai years before the Israeli War of Independence. The borekas in this recipe are made from whole matzos—moistened with water to soften and cut carefully into quarters—and filled with a potato or savory cheese filling. They are then folded into triangles, dipped in egg, and fried. A whole matzo can also be folded in half—after being moistened and filled—then fried, baked with cheese melted on top, and served with seasoned tomato sauce.

5 whole matzos

Potato Filling
1 large onion, diced
3 tablespoons oil
3 cups mashed potatoes
1 egg, beaten
1 teaspoon salt
$^1/_4$ teaspoon pepper
2 eggs, beaten with 3-4 tablespoons
    water or milk, for dipping
oil, for frying

Sauté onion in oil until soft. Combine with next 4 ingredients. Set aside. Soak whole matzos in warm water for 3 minutes. Let drain and put on a paper towel. With a sharp knife, carefully cut each matzo into quarters. Fold over into triangles. Place a tablespoonful of potato mixture on bottom of each triangle, and fold over again into a triangle, pressing edges slightly together. Combine eggs with water or milk, and dip filled matzo triangle into mixture. Fry in oil on both sides until golden brown. Serve topped with yogurt or sour cream. Yields 20 borekas.

Variations

Add 1 cup of shredded Swiss or American cheese to potato filling.

Cheese filling: Combine 1 pound farmer cheese, 2 eggs, $^2/_3$ cup grated cheddar or American cheese, salt and pepper to taste, and 3 tablespoons grated onion. Fill and fry as directed.

Seasoned Tomato Sauce
1 6-ounce can tomato paste or sauce
2-3 cloves garlic, minced
salt and pepper, to taste
$^1/_3$ cup water

Bring to a boil and cook for 3 minutes. Prepare as directed in introduction.

Bubele

Bubele—a large, puffy pancake my mother used to make on Pesach—stands out in my mind among many fond holiday memories. I recall how we children used to hover around my mother, trying to be helpful, as she made it for breakfast.

3 eggs, separated
3 tablespoons matzo meal
pinch of salt
oil, for frying
sugar and cinnamon, for sprinkling top

Beat egg whites until stiff. Set aside. With the same unwashed beater, beat yolks until light. Fold whites into yolks, then gradually fold in matzo meal and salt. Heat oil in a large skillet. Pour entire mixture into hot skillet, and cook on both sides over low heat until golden. Sprinkle with sugar and cinnamon. Serves 2.

Traditional Matzo Brei

A light meal—and a Pesach classic.

4 matzos, broken
warm water, to cover
3-4 large eggs
salt and pepper, to taste
oil, for frying
cinnamon and sugar, for sprinkling
     top, optional
strawberry or raspberry jam, optional

Pour warm water over matzos. Drain, squeezing out water. Beat eggs and seasonings, and stir together with the matzos. Heat oil and fry matzo mixture on both sides until golden. Serve sprinkled with cinnamon and sugar, and spread with jam.

Variation

Onion matzo brei: Sauté 1 medium, diced onion in 3 tablespoons of oil until tender. Add matzo-egg mixture. Stir-fry until golden.

Matzo Farfel with Mushrooms

A savory, pasta-like Pesach dish that your family will surely relish.

2 large onions, diced
1 green pepper, diced
$1/4$ cup oil
1 cup sliced mushrooms
2 cups matzo farfel or crumbled matzo
1 teaspoon salt
$1/4$ teaspoon pepper
$1^1/2$ cups water or chicken soup

Sauté onions and green pepper in oil until onions are tender. Add mushrooms and sauté for about 5 more minutes until onions are lightly browned. Over low heat, stir in matzo farfel, and cook until lightly browned, stirring constantly. Add seasonings and water or chicken soup, and cook over low heat until all liquid is absorbed and farfel is soft. If necessary, add a little water. Serves 8.

Variations

Add $1/2$ pound of broiled, koshered chicken livers—cut into eighths—to mixture, and beat in.

Kugel: Stir into mixture 4 beaten eggs and $1/4$ cup of oil, and pour into a greased, 2-quart casserole. Bake in a preheated 350° oven for about 50 minutes.

Knishes

A hit every time I make them.

1 large onion, diced
$1/4$ cup oil
5 medium potatoes, cooked, drained, and mashed
2 eggs, beaten
$1/2$ cup matzo meal or potato flour
1 teaspoon salt
$1/4$ teaspoon pepper
1 cup cooked meat (chicken, beef, or liver), finely chopped
oil, for frying

Sauté onion in oil until tender. Mix with mashed potatoes. Add eggs, matzo meal, and seasonings. Form into balls and make an indentation with your thumb in center of each. Fill hole with chicken, beef, or liver. Cover with potato mixture. Slightly flatten into patties and fry on both sides until golden brown. Yields 15-18 knishes.

Varenya

Your great-grandmother would have recalled this delicacy, which was eaten with a teaspoon and accompanied by a hot glass of tea and good conversation. This is an easy and delicious homemade variety of orange marmalade, for Pesach or any time. Good to spread on matzo as a snack.

4 oranges
2¹/₄ cups sugar
1 tablespoon lemon juice

Peel oranges thinly, and cut into chunks with on-off bursts of a food processor. Cook diced oranges and sugar in a medium-sized covered pot over low heat for 1¹/₂ hours. Stir in lemon juice. If mixture is too thin, remove cover and cook for several minutes more over medium heat until liquid cooks down. It should have the consistency of jam. Pour into a jar, cover, and refrigerate; or let stand at room temperature. If a milder taste is desired, remove white pith from oranges after peeling.

Pesach Brownies

Delightful. Try the mocha variation for a change.

4 eggs
1¹/₂ cups sugar
²/₃ cup oil
1 tablespoon orange juice
¹/₂ cup cocoa
1 cup Pesach cake meal
2 tablespoons potato starch
³/₄ cup walnuts, coarsely chopped

Beat eggs, gradually adding sugar until fluffy. Stir in remaining ingredients. Pour into a greased, 9x13-inch baking pan. Bake in a 350° oven for about 25-30 minutes. Cut into squares. Yields 24-32 brownies.

Variation

Mocha brownies: Add 2 teaspoons of instant coffee.

Classic Pesach Sponge Cake

This is my favorite basic sponge cake for Pesach. For a special occasion, scoop out the inside of the cake, fill it with mocha cream filling or ice cream, and freeze it. It can also be cut in half horizontally, filled with lemon filling, and topped with fresh sliced strawberries.

8 large eggs, room temperature,
    separated
1/4 teaspoon salt
1 1/2 cups sugar
juice and grated rind of 1/2 lemon
juice and grated rind of 1/2 orange
1/2 cup Pesach cake meal
1/2 cup potato starch, scant

Beat egg whites and salt until frothy. Gradually add half of the sugar, and continue beating until stiff peaks are formed. In another bowl, beat yolks until light. Add remaining sugar slowly, and beat until very fluffy. Stir in lemon and orange juice and rinds, cake meal, and potato starch. Fold in beaten egg whites carefully. Pour mixture into a 10-inch tube pan (after greasing only bottom) and bake in a preheated 350° oven for 1 hour. Invert over neck of bottle to cool. Let cool, slice in half horizontally, and spread with Lemon Filling. Ice top and sides with Chocolate Glaze Icing (see page 229). Serves 12.

Lemon Filling
1 1/2 cups water
1 cup sugar
juice of 2 lemons
grated rind of 1 lemon
3 eggs, separated
4 tablespoons potato flour
pinch of salt

In a saucepan, boil water, 1/2 cup of the sugar, and the lemon juice and rind. In a separate bowl, beat yolks with remaining sugar until light and thick. Stir 3 tablespoons of hot mixture into egg yolks, then add entire yolk mixture to saucepan and simmer while stirring for about 2 minutes. Dissolve potato flour in water and add to simmering mixture, stirring until thickened. Let cool slightly. Beat egg whites and salt until they hold stiff peaks. Fold whites into mixture.

Variations

Chocolate cake: Use 9 eggs. Use juice and rind of a whole orange. Omit lemon juice and rind. Add 6 tablespoons of cocoa and 1/3 cup of chopped nuts along with egg yolks.

Banana cake: Add 1 cup of ripe, mashed bananas. Omit orange and lemon juice and rind.

Chocolate banana cake: Add 2/3 cup of grated semi-sweet chocolate and 1 cup of ripe, mashed bananas.

Chocolate flake cake: Fold in 2 ounces of grated semi-sweet chocolate.

Pesach Cream Puffs

These cream puffs can be served as dessert, with a sweet cream filling, or as an appetizer—with a savory filling.

Cream Puff Shells

1 cup water
$^1/_2$ cup margarine or oil
$^1/_4$ teaspoon salt
1 cup Pesach cake meal
4 eggs

Cream Filling

$^1/_3$ cup sugar
2 cups water or milk
$^1/_4$ cup potato starch
2 eggs
1 teaspoon margarine
1 teaspoon vanilla extract

Shells: In a medium-sized saucepan, bring water, margarine, and salt to boil. Stir in cake meal all at once. Remove from heat. Beat in eggs one at a time, beating vigorously after each addition. Drop, by 2-3 tablespoonsful, onto a greased cookie sheet, 2 inches apart. Bake in a preheated 450° oven for 15 minutes. Reduce heat to 325° and bake for an additional 30 minutes. Let cool.

Filling: In a medium-sized saucepan, combine sugar and water or milk. Bring to a boil. Combine potato starch with a little cold water, and pour into simmering sugar-water mixture. Cook, stirring constantly until thickened. In a small bowl, beat eggs with a fork. Stir 3 tablespoons of hot mixture into beaten eggs, then add egg mixture to saucepan. Cook for 2-3 more minutes. Remove from heat, and stir in margarine and vanilla extract. Let cool.

To assemble: Slice $^1/_3$ from top of cream puff shells. Fill with cooled filling. Fill shells as close to serving time as possible, unless frozen. Drizzle with Chocolate Glaze Icing (see page 229) on top, if desired. Yields 8-10 puffs.

Variation

Fill with ice cream and freeze. Top with chocolate sauce. Fill shells as close to serving time as possible, unless frozen.

Shells can be used for appetizers. Fill with chopped liver, chicken livers with mushrooms, chicken salad, egg salad, cream cheese, or anchovies.

Marga's Pesach Coconut Cake

A chocolate cake with a thick layer of coconut. A real favorite for Pesach.

6 eggs, separated
1¼ cups sugar
1¼ cups shredded coconut
3 tablespoons oil
½ cup potato flour, sifted
¼ cup sweet red wine
⅓ cup cocoa

Beat egg whites until frothy, gradually adding ¾ cup of the sugar. Beat until they hold stiff peaks. Divide beaten egg whites into 2 equal parts. Fold coconut into 1 of the parts. Beat egg yolks with remaining sugar until light and thick. Stir in oil, potato flour, wine, and cocoa. Fold in the portion of the egg whites without coconut. To create a sandwich effect, pour ½ of the cocoa mixture into a 10-inch springform, or tube pan. Pour egg white-coconut mixture on top, spreading evenly. Spread remainder of cocoa batter evenly over coconut mixture. Bake in a preheated 350° oven for 45-50 minutes. Let cool, and frost with Continental Chocolate Icing. Serves 10-12.

Continental Chocolate Icing
4 ounces semi-sweet chocolate
2 tablespoons margarine, softened
2 tablespoons Sabra liqueur
1 teaspoon vanilla extract

Melt chocolate and margarine over low heat. Remove from heat and stir in Sabra liqueur and vanilla extract. Spread while warm.

Apple Matzo Charlotte

A real treat.

3 matzos, crumbled
6 eggs
½ cup sugar
1 teaspoon salt
½ teaspoon cinnamon
¼ cup margarine, melted
½ cup raisins
4 tart apples, shredded
grated rind of 1 orange
4 tablespoons sugar, for sprinkling on top
½ teaspoon cinnamon, for sprinkling top
melted shortening, for pouring on top

Soak crumbled matzos in water for 3 minutes. Squeeze out excess water. Beat eggs, sugar, salt and cinnamon. Stir in next 4 ingredients. Spread into a well-greased, 7x11-inch baking pan. Sprinkle with a mixture of 4 tablespoons sugar and ½ teaspoon cinnamon. Pour melted shortening on top. Bake in 350° oven for 45-50 minutes. Serves 8.

If cake meal is unavailable, use well sifted matzo meal.

Gan Eden Layer Cake

A simply heavenly recipe.

8 eggs, separated
1 cup sugar
$^1/_4$ cup honey
$^1/_3$ cup orange juice
$^1/_4$ cup sweet wine
1 tablespoon grated lemon rind
2 ounces semi-sweet chocolate, grated
$^3/_4$ cup almonds, ground or finely chopped
1 cup Pesach cake meal
2 teaspoons cinnamon

Beat egg whites until frothy. Gradually beat in sugar, and continue beating until stiff, but not dry. Set aside. With same unwashed beaters, beat egg yolks until thick. Stir in remaining ingredients. Fold stiffly beaten egg whites into yolk mixture. Pour into 2 greased and wax paper-lined 9-inch layer cake pans. Bake in a 350° oven for 35 minutes. Let cool, and remove cake from pans. Spread $^1/_3$ cup of apricot jam, thinned with 3 tablespoons of hot water, between layers, if desired. Frost with Mocha Icing.

Mocha Icing
1 cup margarine, softened
2 large eggs
$^1/_2$ cup sugar
3 tablespoons cocoa
2 teaspoons instant coffee
2 tablespoons sweet red wine
1 packet vanilla sugar

Place all ingredients in a food processor or blender, and blend on high speed for about 10 minutes until thick. Frost top and sides of cake.

Pesach Streusel Apple Cake

A kosher-for-Pesach streusel crumb topping. You can use this recipe during the entire year—it is that good.

6 tart apples, peeled and sliced
4 tablespoons lemon juice
2 teaspoons cinnamon
$^3/_4$ cup sugar
pinch of nutmeg
6 eggs
1$^1/_2$ cups sugar
1 teaspoon vanilla extract
$^3/_4$ cup oil
2 cups Pesach cake meal
2 tablespoons potato starch
$^1/_4$ teaspoon salt

Streusel Topping
$^1/_4$ cup sugar
1$^1/_2$ teaspoons cinnamon
$^1/_4$ cup chopped nuts

Toss apples with lemon juice. Mix together cinnamon, sugar, and nutmeg, and combine with apples. Set aside. Beat eggs until light and fluffy, slowly adding sugar and vanilla extract. Stir in oil, cake meal, potato starch, and salt. Put half of batter into a greased, 9x13-inch baking pan. Spread apple mixture on top. Cover with remaining batter. Combine streusel ingredients, and sprinkle on top of batter. Bake in a preheated 350° oven for 1 hour, 10 minutes. Yields 18-24 squares.

Pesach Chocolate Nut Torte

A rich, delicious torte, made without matzo meal.

10 eggs, separated
1 cup sugar
6 ounces semi-sweet chocolate
2 cups walnuts, finely chopped
1/4 teaspoon salt

Beat egg yolks until light and thick, adding sugar gradually. Melt chocolate in a double boiler. To egg yolk mixture, stir in melted chocolate, nuts, and salt. Beat egg whites until they form stiff peaks, and fold carefully into yolk mixture. Pour into a 10-inch tube pan, greased on bottom only, and bake in a preheated 350° oven for 1 hour. Invert to cool. Serves 12-14.

Coconut Macaroons for Pesach (or any time)

Many kinds of pastries made with coconut were brought to Israel by the Sephardi Jews. Tiny coconut cakes adorn the table of every Sephardi simchah. The honey in this recipe moistens the macaroons.

3 egg whites
1 tablespoon lemon juice
1/4 cup sugar
2 packets vanilla sugar
2 tablespoons honey
2 tablespoons potato starch
2 1/2 cups shredded coconut

In an electric mixer, beat egg whites and lemon juice until frothy. Gradually add sugar and vanilla sugar, and beat until stiff. Carefully fold in honey, potato starch, and coconut. Drop from a tablespoon onto a greased baking sheet. Bake in a 325° oven for 20 minutes until edges are light brown. Remove macaroons from baking sheet while still warm. Store in a covered container to keep from drying out. Yields 36 macaroons.

Variation

Chocolate coconut macaroons: Add to mixture 1-2 ounces of grated chocolate, or 2 tablespoons of cocoa.

Pesach Mocha Bars

These bars are good to make throughout the year—not only at Pesach time.

6 eggs
2 cups sugar
1 cup chopped nuts
1 cup oil
3/4 cup Pesach cake meal
1/2 cup potato flour
1/2 teaspoon salt
6 tablespoons cocoa
1 tablespoon instant coffee powder
2 teaspoons vanilla extract, or 2 tablespoons brandy

Beat eggs together with sugar until light and fluffy. Stir in remaining ingredients. Pour into a well-greased, 9x13-inch pan. Bake in a preheated 350° oven for 35 minutes. Ice with Chocolate Glaze Icing (see page 229). Yields 24-28 bars.

Variation

Chocolate chip mocha bars: Stir 1 cup of chocolate chips into mixture, and bake as directed.

Chocolate Flake Potato Flour Sponge Cake

A sponge cake for those who don't eat matzo meal on Pesach.

7-8 large eggs, separated
1 1/2 cups sugar
grated rind and juice of 1 lemon or orange
3/4 cup potato flour
1 packet vanilla sugar
1/4 teaspoon salt
2 ounces semi-sweet chocolate, grated

Beat egg whites until frothy. Gradually add half of the sugar, and beat until they can hold stiff peaks. Set aside. In another bowl, without washing beaters, beat egg yolks and remaining sugar until light and thick. Stir in remaining ingredients except chocolate. Gently fold beaten egg whites into yolk mixture. Fold in grated chocolate. Pour into a greased, 10-inch tube pan. Bake in a preheated 350° oven for 1 hour. Remove from oven and invert over neck of a bottle. When cool, spread with Orange Icing.

Orange Icing
3 tablespoons cornstarch
1/2 cup orange juice
2 tablespoons lemon juice
1/2 cup sugar
1/2 cup water
2 tablespoons margarine
grated rind of 1 orange

Place cornstarch, orange juice, lemon juice, sugar, and water in a saucepan. Cook over low heat while stirring until thickened. Remove from heat, and stir in margarine and orange rind.

Pesach "Candy" Cake

A most unusual recipe. Cake can be frozen.

Cake
12 egg whites (reserve yolks for filling)
2 cups sugar
3 cups ground walnuts
3 tablespoons matzo meal

Filling and Frosting
12 egg yolks, slightly beaten with a fork
2 cups sugar
2½ cups margarine
6 tablespoons cocoa
2 teaspoons vanilla extract

Make cake first: Beat egg whites until frothy. Gradually add sugar, and beat until they hold stiff peaks. Fold in walnuts and matzo meal. Pour onto a 10x15-inch cookie sheet lined with greased aluminum foil. Bake in a preheated 325° oven for 1 hour. While cake is baking, make filling: Place all ingredients in a medium-sized saucepan. Cook over low heat, stirring until mixture is smooth and shiny. Remove from heat and allow to cool slightly. Remove cake from oven, let cool slightly, turn over onto a dry towel, dusted with powdered sugar, and carefully peel off foil. Cut cake in half, horizontally. Place half of cake on platter, and spread with filling mixture. Add top layer, and spread remaining mixture over top and sides. Refrigerate until firm. (To freeze, place unwrapped in freezer until firm, then wrap well with freezer paper. When ready to use, remove from freezer and cut while still frozen.) Yields about 20 small pieces.

Orange Almond Cake with Chocolate Icing

A very moist cake. An unusual recipe using whole, ground oranges and almonds. The tartness of the orange peel adds a special zest. You'll enjoy the contrast in taste between the oranges and the rich chocolate icing.

2 large, whole, unpeeled oranges
6 eggs
1 cup sugar
1 teaspoon baking soda
1½ cups ground almonds

Wash oranges well. Simmer in water to cover for 2 hours (½ hour in pressure cooker). Let cool. Quarter, remove seeds, and cut into 1½-inch chunks (do not peel). Place in a food processor, food mill, or blender, and process until finely ground. Beat eggs, adding sugar gradually until light and thick. Stir in baking soda, almonds, and ground oranges. Pour into a greased, 9-inch springform pan sprinkled lightly with potato flour. Bake in a preheated 400° oven for 1 hour. Cake should still be moist. When cake has cooled slightly, release springform and spread with Chocolate Icing. Yields 12-14 slices.

Chocolate Icing
6-9 ounces semi-sweet chocolate
3 tablespoons margarine
2 tablespoons cognac

Melt chocolate and margarine in a double boiler or in a pan set over boiling water. Remove from heat, stir in cognac, and let cool slightly. Pour over cake while icing is still warm and spread evenly.

Frozen Lemon Pie

Make this pie with either of the pie crusts or, alternatively, line a 9-inch pie pan with 1-inch-thick sponge cake strips.

Pesach Almond Pie Crust

1 egg white
4 tablespoons sugar
1 1/2 cups finely chopped blanched
  almonds
pinch of salt

Beat egg white until stiff, while gradually adding sugar. Gently fold in chopped almonds and salt. Press on bottom and sides of a greased, 9-inch pie pan. Bake in a 375° oven for about 8-10 minutes until light brown. Set aside.

Pesach Pecan Pie Crust

1/3 cup margarine, melted
1/2 - 2/3 cup matzo meal
1/2 cup finely chopped pecans
3 tablespoons sugar
pinch of salt
1/2 teaspoon cinnamon
1 large egg

Mix margarine and matzo meal. Stir in remaining ingredients, and press into a 9-inch pie pan, covering bottom and sides. Bake in a preheated 375° oven for 15-20 minutes until light brown. Set aside.

Filling

2 cups cold water
1 1/4 cups sugar
1/4 cup potato starch
3 eggs, separated
1/2 cup lemon juice
grated rind of 1 lemon
2 tablespoons margarine
1 cup whipped cream or pareve
  whipped topping, optional

Put cold water and 1 cup of sugar into a saucepan. Bring to a boil. Dissolve potato starch in 1/8 cup of water, and pour into simmering mixture. Cook over low heat, stirring constantly until thick. Remove from heat. In a small bowl, beat egg yolks using a fork. Stir in 3 tablespoons of the hot mixture. Add entire yolk mixture to saucepan, and bring to a boil over low heat, cooking for 1-2 minutes. Remove from heat and stir in lemon juice, rind, and margarine. Let cool slightly. Beat whites until stiff, gradually adding remaining sugar. Fold into cooled lemon mixture. Pour filling into baked crust and freeze until firm. Just before serving, top with whipped cream, if desired.

Etc.

FACTS ON FREEZING

Home canning was the popular way of preserving fresh fruits and vegetables when I was growing up. I still recall the full year's supply of home-canned foods that covered our basement shelves. My mother canned almost every type of fresh fruit—there was no such thing as "out of season" in our home.

Today, canning has been largely replaced by freezing foods. Many of us enjoy out-of-season foods that are commercially frozen, but with the increasing availability of large home freezers, homemakers are beginning to appreciate that freezing one's own food has many advantages. Buying fresh fruits and vegetables in season is economical and convenient. If you're planning to be away for awhile, main dishes or complete meals can be frozen in advance and heated and served by the other members of the family. (A microwave makes this particularly easy!) Cakes, cookies, and breads can be baked and frozen. Doughs can be made in large quantities, divided, and frozen until you are ready to fill and bake them. Juices, pancakes, schnitzel and most varieties of fruits and vegetables all freeze well.

What to Freeze and When

When freezing, use only high-quality fish, poultry, meat, or produce. The latter should be chosen at peak season, when it is fully ripe but not too soft. It is important for fresh fruits and vegetables to go from the garden or market to the freezer as quickly as possible to preserve nutritional value and prevent spoilage. Fish and chicken should also be frozen fresh.

Packaging

Proper wrapping is extremely important. Packages must be wrapped tightly and containers sealed securely. Air in a package can spoil or dry out food. Use moisture-proof paper, plastic containers, or glass jars. In containers and jars, leave $1/4$-$1/2$ inch (approximately 1 centimeter) headspace, because liquids expand slightly when frozen. Aluminum foil sheets or containers can also be used. In a pinch, two or three plastic bags will suffice, but expel all air before tying them. A single plastic bag is inadequate. Label packages to be frozen, indicating date, type of food and number of servings. Always freeze food at 0° Fahrenheit or lower to prevent bacterial growth. Packages should be spread on shelves or against walls for faster freezing. Only after frozen solid should they be stacked.

Blanching and Freezing Vegetables

Vegetables should be blanched (scalded) before freezing to prevent the enzyme action that can destroy the vitamins. To blanch, place vegetables in a wire basket or cheesecloth and lower into boiling water. Cover, bring to boil again. Then boil three to five minutes. Remove immediately and cool in very cold water. Drain and freeze immediately.

Freezing Fruits

Do not use over-ripe, under-ripe or bruised fruit. Wash fruit quickly in ice-cold water, drain and dry. Skins of peaches, nectarines, and the like can be removed by scalding for 15 seconds and cooling immediately in ice water. To prevent fruits from discoloring, dip in lemon juice or a solution of 1 tablespoon salt to 1 quart cold water. Pack in meal-sized portions. Serve while a few ice crystals remain. Frozen fruits retain their natural flavor, color and juice if sweetened with sugar or syrup before freezing. Leave $^1/_4$-$^1/_2$ inch headspace in containers.

Freezing Fish

Freeze fish as soon as possible after purchase. For a really fresh flavor use the ice block method: Place fish in a deep container and cover completely with water, allowing a little headspace before sealing. This ultimately freezes into a block, which can be thawed under cold running water. Never refreeze fish.

Freezing Poultry

Never stuff poultry before freezing, as food-poisoning bacteria can develop. Wrap well with waterproof paper and freeze while fresh. Thaw unwrapped in refrigerator or under cold running water. Do not thaw at room temperature. Although one should never refreeze raw meat, poultry or fish, one can bulk-cook and freeze them either whole or in portions, making sure that they are well-wrapped. Never serve thawed food without thoroughly reheating.

What Not to Freeze

The following foods do not freeze well: bananas, raw vegetables (unless blanched first), cooked potatoes, custard, cream fillings, and mayonnaise. Raw egg whites freeze well, but hard boiled eggs do not. Foods vary in the length of time they can be kept frozen.

Following these few simple rules will add to your family's enjoyment as well as their nutrition. Your own kitchen will be transformed into that wondrous place of childhood fantasy. And what's more, Grandma would be proud of you!

FACTS ON MICROWAVING

by Sholom Katz

Defrosting and Reheating

A microwave oven is no substitute for a standard gas or electric range, but it is great for defrosting and reheating, and can save the day when guests suddenly arrive. Take a prepared meal out of the freezer, and serve piping hot in minutes! (Or try Baked Fish with Mushroom Sauce, page 121, cooked on high for 6 minutes.) Make certain to totally defrost raw food before cooking, not only to ensure that it cooks through, but to avoid disease. It is best to separate the pieces before defrosting.

Adapting Recipes

Microwaves come in different sizes, and cooking times will therefore vary. When adapting conventional recipes, reduce cooking time to one-quarter for 700-watt ovens and one-third for 500-watt ovens. Liquid ingredients can also be reduced by one-quarter.

Containers

Always use the appropriate microwaveable dish, without metal components. Containers with restricted openings, such as baby food jars, should be avoided. Plastic bags should be opened.

Vegetables

Vegetables can be microwaved quickly, retaining vitamins, freshness, and color. Frozen vegetables can be cooked without defrosting. Unpeeled vegetables should be pierced to allow steam to escape. (Try microwaving Stuffed Green Peppers, page 137, for 10-12 minutes on high.) Cook vegetables, covered, on high for 4-6 minutes in a few tablespoons of water or oil. Don't salt until serving, as this causes them to dry out. Stir vegetables occasionally while cooking to redistribute heat and moisture.

Sauces

Microwave sauces can enhance your cooking; since no direct heat is applied, you can be sure of a smooth sauce. Cook on high for 3-4 minutes, stirring once each minute, then reheat on medium for 3 minutes. (Try making Creole Sauce, page 119, in this manner.)

Soups

To cook soup, use a covered container 2 or 3 times larger than the quantity of the contents, to prevent boiling over. (Microwave chicken soup in a ceramic pot, with one half-quart less water. Cook on high for 4 minutes, then on medium for 15 minutes.)

Limitations

Remember microwave's limitations: cakes may not rise properly and will be pale; food will not brown; and frozen fried foods will lack crispness.

QUICK AND EASY DECORATIONS

Enliven a buffet dinner, a Shabbat meal, and even lunchtime sandwiches with these fast, easy-to-prepare garnishes and decorations!

Radish Coil

Trim the ends from an oval-shaped red radish. Make several evenly spaced crosswise cuts. Place radish coil in ice water to open.

Carrot Curls

Use thick, long carrots. Remove carrots from refrigerator about two hours before preparation, for easier cutting. With potato peeler or sharp knife, cut each carrot lengthwise, making a long, flat surface. Keep making these long strips until carrot is entirely cut up. Roll these thin strips into coils and fasten with toothpicks. Place in ice water and refrigerate for at least two hours. Remove toothpicks.

Bunches of Carrot Sticks

Place two, three, or four thinly cut carrot sticks through pitted green or black olives.

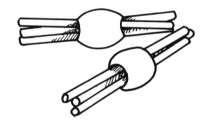

Scored Cucumber Slices

With tines of a fork, score cucumber lengthwise all around. Cut into slices and use in salad or as a garnish.

Pickle Fan

Slice gherkins lengthwise until ½ inch from end, four or five times. Cut rounded ends off so pickle can stand. Place on flat surface and hold the flat end slightly while carefully separating the slices.

CREATING FLORAL DECORATIONS

Decorations carved from fruits and vegetables add a delightful, professional touch to your table. The "flowers" that you make can be placed on a bed of curly parsley, endive, scallions, or lemon and grape leaves, and used to decorate a cold meat platter or a tray of hors d'oeuvres or canapés.

Onion Chrysanthemums

1. Peel off thin skin of a medium, round onion.

2. Cut off part of root extending beyond the onion.

3. Starting at the top of the onion, cut deeply downward to ¹/₂ inch from root. Continue cutting from the top downward until you have cut all around the onion.

4. Soak in hot water to spread the "petals," holding open for several minutes. Then place in ice water to open still more.

5. Place several drops of food coloring in ice water to tint the "chrysanthemum" yellow, blue, orange, or pink.

Cucumber Roses

1. Slice a medium cucumber lengthwise into five or six paper-thin slices.

2. Soak slices in salt water (³/₄ teaspoon salt to 1 cup cold water).

3. Roll smallest slice tightly. Wrap second-smallest slice around it. Continue to wrap each slice in opposite direction, forming the "petals," ending with largest slices for the outside petals.

4. Fasten with toothpicks at bottom. Bend outer pieces, shaping "rose." Tint.

Grapefruit Roses

1. With a sharp paring knife, peel the outer skin of a grapefruit very thinly.

2. Starting again at the navel of the grapefruit, peel the white membrane in a continuous strip, circling round and round the grapefruit until you reach the end.

3. Starting at one end, roll strip tightly for the inside of the "rose." Continue coiling the strip around itself in the shape of a rose and attach end with a toothpick. Turn top of "petals" slightly outward.

4. Dip the rose into colored water or beet juice, until you achieve the desired shade — pink or deep red.

5. If peel breaks in half, two smaller "roses" can be made.

Turnip Daisies

1. Cut round, white turnips into slices ¹/₃ inch thick.

2. Cut slices into circles with a sharp cookie cutter that fits just inside the rim of each slice.

3. Leaving a round space in the center of each circle, make six evenly spaced cuts.

4. Trim around each section to simulate petals.

5. Attach a small, round piece of carrot to the center of each "daisy" with a toothpick.

6. Dip into colored water.

Variation: Make a "zinnia" by using a very large turnip. Cut as directed, smear center with oil, and sprinkle with poppy seeds or black pepper and tiny bits of carrot.

Turnip Daffodils

1. Slice a round disc from the center of a turnip.

2. Make six evenly spaced cuts, leaving center intact. Trim to simulate petals.

3. Form oval-shaped cone out of root end of turnip.

4. Scoop out center of cone and scallop the edges.

5. Attach cone to center of "flower" by placing toothpick through center of both the cone and the "petals."

6. Open part of cone should be exposed.   7. Tint yellow or any other pastel shade.

Turnip Tulips

1. Peel a medium, oval-shaped white turnip.

2. Scoop out center carefully with a melon baller.

3. Cut four "petals" from top edges.

4. Tint desired color with food coloring.

5. Insert three or four green toothpicks (or wooden toothpicks tinted with green food coloring) in center.

6. Stick a raisin on each toothpick end.

CENTERPIECES

Vegetable Vases

Create an interesting base for your floral creations. Use almost any long, thin vegetable or fruit: potato, squash, green pepper, eggplant, or pineapple. Cut top and bottom ends off, making a flat surface on each side. Place in center of platter, on bed of curly parsley or endive. Attach "flowers" with toothpicks. If desired, cover sides of "vase" with greens as well.

Fruit Base

Cut an orange or grapefruit in half. Place cut side down. Attach small "daisies" with toothpick. Top of toothpick can be covered with a raisin or grape.

Bird Centerpiece

Cut off a little less than one-third of a large, fresh apple, making a flat surface on which the apple can rest.

Cut out two V-shaped wedges, each slightly smaller than one-quarter of the apple. The apple will have two cut sections, separated by a dividing section. (See Figure a.)

Cut first wedge into four consecutively smaller "V" shapes. Repeat for second wedge. (See Figure b.)

Dip the "V"s in water mixed with lemon juice.

Place remaining part of apple in center of plate.

Make "wings": Place the largest "V" halfway back on flat section of remaining apple (where the cuts were made). Place second-largest "V" on largest one. Continue until you have placed all the "V"s, ending with the smallest. Repeat for the second "wing."

For the head and neck, slice a rounded strip from another apple, about ¼ inch wide and 1½ inches long. Attach to front of "bird" with a toothpick. (See Figure c.)

Sprinkle lemon juice on entire bird to prevent discoloration.

Figure a

Figure b

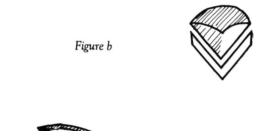

Figure c

MEASUREMENT AND CONVERSION TABLE

American	Metric
1 ounce	.28 grams
1 pound	.450 grams
1 teaspoon	.5 milliliters
1 tablespoon	.15 milliliters
1 cup	.240 cubic centimeters
1 cup butter	.210 grams
1 inch	.2.5 centimeters
3/4 cup less 1 tablespoon flour	.100 grams
1 cup less 2 tablespoons margarine	.200 grams

Standard Measurements

3 teaspoons	.1 tablespoon
2 tablespoons	.1 fluid ounce
4 tablespoons	.1/4 cup
8 tablespoons	.1/2 cup
2 cups	.1 pint
4 cups	.1 quart
16 ounces	.1 pound

Cups used in recipes are standard 8-ounce cups.

All recipe measurements are for level (not heaping) spoonfuls.

Oven Temperature Equivalents

250°F	=	120°C	=	Gas Mark 1/2
300°F	=	150°C	=	Gas Mark 2
350°F	=	180°C	=	Gas Mark 3
375°F	=	190°C	=	Gas Mark 4
400°F	=	205°C	=	Gas Mark 5
450°F	=	235°C	=	Gas Mark 7

Index